SAGE was founded in 1965 by Sara Miller McCune to support the dissemination of usable knowledge by publishing innovative and high-quality research and teaching content. Today, we publish over 900 journals, including those of more than 400 learned societies, more than 800 new books per year, and a growing range of library products including archives, data, case studies, reports, and video. SAGE remains majority-owned by our founder, and after Sara's lifetime will become owned by a charitable trust that secures our continued independence.

Los Angeles | London | New Delhi | Singapore | Washington DC | Melbourne

Advance Praise

Warzone Tourism in Sri Lanka: Tales from Darker Places in Paradise presents an ethnographic account of a specific contemporary politico-cultural practice in Sri Lanka—travel to the North during the ceasefire and after the end of war. The term 'warzone tourism' captures the multiplicity of meanings embedded in the travel to the areas that constituted the geographical, social and ethno-cultural locations of nearly three decades of civil war. The book explores through extensive ethnographic material, questions such as what does travel and tourism into the warzone mean in the context of a civil war tempered by ethnic conflict. What are the political, ideological, cultural and emotional impulses that motivate, define and make sense of such travel? What are the political implications of travelling, viewing and narrating when seen as social and cultural practices given specific meanings during and after war and violence? Is it continuation of war by other means? The book provides a critical and insightful reading of a phenomenon that has been taken for granted and intellectually ignored for far too long.

Jayadeva Uyangoda
Senior Professor, Department of Political Science and Public Policy, University of Colombo

Most anthropologists dwell on the present to write about past practices and focus on the everyday in an effort to make sense of the world as it has been and is known, experienced and understood. Sasanka Perera's book stands out for his extraordinary ability to focus not just on Sri Lanka's turbulent past and the present mobility patterns of people so closely linked to that past, but also to an intricate consideration of why and how people seek to connect to the past. The past is after all what prevails in the present moment, whether or not we acknowledge this past, and Perera makes this smooth association between the civil war that split the country and its people and the present need to connect to that past, as well as to an even earlier imagined past of stability and harmony, through a very visceral, emotional, embodied present…. It is an ingenious portrayal of a new phenomenon and Sasanka Perera has done it with rigorous analysis, thick description, panache and in the process has achieved the impossible in academic writing: told a tale remarkably well.

Meenakshi Thapan
Professor, Department of Sociology, Delhi School of Economics, University of Delhi

As passionately argued and persuasively illustrated by Sasanka Perera in this path-breaking study, 'warzone tourism' in Sri Lanka has a far more complex geography and history to it than often acknowledged. It has evolved in the context of post-colonial nation-building marred by the socio-spatial legacies of a protracted civil war. These legacies have also manifested themselves through highly convoluted and contested discursive battlefields of competing, often colliding, ethnographies, cartographies and iconographies. Mental borders as social constructions have proved to be far more stubborn than walls, fences, barriers, and check posts built during the civil war.... Seen together, the analysis by Perera of the two phases of warzone tourism in Sri Lanka reveals complex assemblages of practices, including state sponsored practices and insightfully unravels several entangled logics and emotions. Against the backdrop of deep-rooted mistrust, large-scale destruction and displacement, they have left behind both intended and non-intended imprints on the mindscapes of both the visitors and the visited.

Sanjay Chaturvedi
Professor, Centre for the Study of Geopolitics, Department of
Political Science, Panjab University, Chandigarh

WARZONE TOURISM
IN SRI LANKA

Thank you for choosing a SAGE product!
If you have any comment, observation or feedback,
I would like to personally hear from you.
Please write to me at **contactceo@sagepub.in**

Vivek Mehra, Managing Director and CEO, SAGE India.

Bulk Sales

SAGE India offers special discounts
for purchase of books in bulk.
We also make available special imprints
and excerpts from our books on demand.

For orders and enquiries, write to us at

Marketing Department
SAGE Publications India Pvt Ltd
B1/I-1, Mohan Cooperative Industrial Area
Mathura Road, Post Bag 7
New Delhi 110044, India

E-mail us at **marketing@sagepub.in**

Get to know more about SAGE

Be invited to SAGE events, get on our mailing list.
Write today to **marketing@sagepub.in**

This book is also available as an e-book.

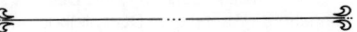

WARZONE TOURISM IN SRI LANKA

Tales from Darker Places in Paradise

Sasanka Perera

Los Angeles | London | New Delhi
Singapore | Washington DC | Melbourne

First published in 2016 by

 SAGE Publications India Pvt Ltd
B1/I-1 Mohan Cooperative Industrial Area
Mathura Road, New Delhi 110 044, India
www.sagepub.in

SAGE Publications Inc
2455 Teller Road
Thousand Oaks, California 91320, USA

SAGE Publications Ltd
1 Oliver's Yard, 55 City Road
London EC1Y 1SP, United Kingdom

SAGE Publications Asia-Pacific Pte Ltd
3 Church Street
#10-04 Samsung Hub
Singapore 049483

Published by Vivek Mehra for SAGE Publications India Pvt Ltd, typeset in Minion Pro 10/12.5pts by Zaza Eunice, Hosur, Tamil Nadu, India and printed at Chaman Enterprises, New Delhi.

Library of Congress Cataloging-in-Publication Data

Name: Perera, Sasanka.
Title: Warzone tourism in Sri Lanka : tales from darker places in paradise / Sasanka Perera.
Description: New Delhi ; Thousand Oaks, California : SAGE, 2016. | Includes bibliographical references and index.
Identifiers: LCCN 2016001972| ISBN 9789351509226 (hardback : alk. paper) | ISBN 9789351509233 (ebook) | ISBN 9789351509219 (epub)
Subjects: LCSH: Tourism–Social aspects–Sri Lanka. | Sinhalese (Sri Lankan) people–Travel–Sri Lanka–Jaffna District. | Ethnic relations–Sri Lanka. | Sri Lanka–History–Civil War, 1983-2009–Influence.
Classification: LCC G155.S65 P47 2016 | DDC 915.49304/32—dc23 LC record available at http://lccn.loc.gov/2016001972

ISBN: 978-93-515-0922-6 (HB)

The SAGE Team: Supriya Das, Guneet Kaur Gulati and Shobana Paul

For Gananath Obeyesekere, Mattison Mines, Donald Brown and David Brokenshaw for early guidance in a transcontinental intellectual journey

Contents

List of Figures

Preface

In this modest volume, I have attempted to achieve a number of interrelated objectives. At its core, it deals with a very specific kind of travel undertaken by Sinhala tourists from the southern parts of Sri Lanka to the country's northern warzones. This became possible as a direct consequence of the conditions created by Sri Lanka's civil war as well as its cessation, and the landscapes of memory along with emotions of politics and nationalism that these situations created. In this context, the book specifically deals with internal travel and tourism in Sri Lanka in two distinct phases: the first phase was between 2002 and 2005 when a ceasefire between the Sri Lankan government and the Liberation Tigers of Tamil Eelam (LTTE) was in operation, and the second phase was after 2010 when the civil war had ended and the major roads to the north were opened to enable civilian travel without restrictions.

In this context, I have attempted to formulate the book as a kind of travel narrative on one hand and as a preliminary ethnography of travel on the other. As a result, it oscillates between a narrative on travel which proceeds to describe where people went and what they saw, and a sociological interest in making initial sense of this travel in the specific contexts in which it took place. For me however, this attempt was not driven by intellectual curiosity alone. It was initially motivated by a distinct discomfort I experienced by the way this kind of travel and the resultant personal narratives were circulating in public and private domains of which I was also a part. More specifically, I was keen to understand the nature and the politics of the gaze that fell upon the warzone. Early on, through casual conversations I could see that warzone travel did not necessarily allow travellers to comprehend in a nuanced manner the calamities and the pain embedded in the places they travelled through and in the lives of people they must have met and seen—albeit marginally. I was keen to understand how these events unfolded; how the silences manifested or were constructed consciously; how certain sites in the warzone trail acquired the incessant attention of travellers and what photography meant in these combined contexts.

I consider this book a prologue to a larger body of potential work and thinking that can emerge from this kind of research, which is not a dominant research interest in Sri Lanka in particular and in South Asia more generally. More extensive research would necessitate a substantial expansion of ethnographic efforts along with longer and more sustained time in the field, which would allow more voices to flow into the overall narrative than I have done in this book. For instance, I did not talk to too many people in the former warzone about their views on the travellers from southern Sri Lanka, as my interest was restricted to follow the trajectory of travels of southern tourists and to see what they saw from their own perspectives. It was also a matter of my unfamiliarity with the Tamil language, my reluctance to employ research assistants in this kind of work and my inability to find the necessary time for long-term research when institution-building responsibilities had become a quotidian reality, and at times a stressful burden and that too, far away from the comfort zones generally afforded by the relative familiarity of one's own country.

Starting from preliminary conversations in 2002, the research was conducted intermittently from 2003 to 2006 and from 2009 to 2013 in the midst of many other activities and responsibilities, which also included long spells of absence from Sri Lanka after 2010. Much of the writing took place in 2013 and 2014. In this overall effort, in addition to the many travellers who quite willingly contributed to my understanding of warzone travel by agreeing to talk with me in different parts of the country, I am particularly thankful to Dushyanthini Kanagasabapathipillai, Harindra Dassanayake and Rudramurthy Cheran for their input in person as well as via email and skype. I also acknowledge the help of T. Shanaathanan and Saminadan Wimal from the University of Jaffna for their help and time in facilitating fieldwork in Jaffna in 2004 while the first phase of warzone travel was well underway. This ensured that I was able to photograph many of the LTTE and other war-related sites which travellers visited in large numbers at the time before they were dismantled by the government after the war was over.

The extensive availability of images from my own research collection as well as the personal narratives of others allowed for the pictorial contextualization of where travellers went, what they saw, why they recorded specific objects and places and the nature of discourse that emerged with respect to these places. For me, a focus on photography was not a matter of simply attempting to understand what people did in the form of a 'thoughtless' technical practice and getting a sense of what they saw in their travels. More importantly, it was also a methodological prerogative in at least partially creating a parallel narrative that would accompany the written text as a necessary subtext of what it was attempting to outline. Though research into the dynamics of travel, reading and some initial writing had been slowly progressing since 2002, the idea of converting these scattered thoughts into a book emerged only in 2013. This was the result of many comments and suggestions offered by colleagues who were present at the Department of Sociology, Delhi School of Economics, University of Delhi, in response to a lecture I delivered on 1 November 2013 as part of the Department of Sociology seminar series on the theme 'Tales of Darker Places in Paradise: Towards Understanding and Theorizing Warzone Tourism in Sri Lanka'. In these serendipitous circumstances, I am indebted to my friend Meenakshi Thapan for inviting me to deliver the lecture which was the catalyst that allowed for the genesis of this book. As more focused writing got underway in 2013, my friend Sanjay Chaturvedi at the University of Panjab in Chandigarh helped considerably by providing me with the much needed literature dealing with dynamics of borders and the politics of cartography, which I was not familiar with at the time. That material compiled by him, as someone formally located in the discipline of International Relations but with a very nuanced understanding of ethnography, was of immense help in deciphering my ethnographic material.

Both Meenakshi Thapan and Sanjay Chaturvedi also contributed to my efforts yet again by writing the Foreword and the Epilogue to this book at a very short notice. I greatly appreciate their friendship and intellectual camaraderie. Finally, I thank Unni Nair for his enthusiasm in ensuring the publication of this book during his tenure at SAGE India as well as the help from Sunanda Ghosh, Elina Mazumdar, Guneet Kaur Gulati, Supriya Das, Neena Ganjoo and Shobana Paul at SAGE India in finally bringing this book into print. I am grateful to Janananda Laksiri in Colombo for creating the maps of warzone travel in phase one and two as well as the map of 'Tamil Eelam' included in this book.

Sasanka Perera
Department of Sociology
South Asian University
New Delhi
1 January 2016

Foreword:
War, Memory and Travel

Most anthropologists dwell on the present to write about past practices and focus on the everyday in an effort to make sense of the world as it has been and is known, experienced and understood. Sasanka Perera's book stands out for his extraordinary ability to focus not just on Sri Lanka's turbulent past and the present mobility patterns of people so closely linked to that past, but also to an intricate consideration of why and how people seek to connect to the past. The past is after all what prevails in the present moment, whether or not we acknowledge this past, and Perera makes this smooth association between the civil war that split the country and its people and the present need to connect to that past, as well as to an even earlier imagined past of stability and harmony through a very visceral, emotional, embodied present.

Sasanka Perera has written a most unusual book. It is about war and memory, and about the people who seek to make sense of their upside-down worlds through the haunting memory and the need to restore connections, make sense of the past, and also restore a remembered, imagined earlier past, so as to make a present socio-cultural identity that is not fragmented. As he tells us, they do this through mobility: travel and 'warzone tourism'. Tourists to warzones visit sites of religious pilgrimage as well as battle-scarred sites and objects with the same sense of awe and attachment and plan both in the same breath, so to speak. Sites of pilgrimage in Sinhala culture are not only religious sites, with myths and legends woven around these places in the collective imagination, but are also infused with an attachment to location, permeated with a religious and ethno-nationalist imagination. War sites attain a similar significance in the imagination of the people, as sites around which myths and legends about war and its aftermath are created, recreated and imagined. This lends to them a quality which we may associate as being integral to the experience of being a tourist: travellers in Perera's book visit war locations that carry a past with them, emanate certain emotions and have connections that are internalized and reproduced in order to make sense of their worlds in the present moment.

Sasanka Perera refers to this process of recreating or reconceptualizing the past, deleting or glossing over the violence associated with war, as 'landscaping', implying a sense of transformation or displacement. In this process, a new or reimagined association is created that suffuses the site with new meanings. In this process, there is also a re-appropriation of religion for the evolution of an identity that is very self-consciously based on a Sinhala Buddhist cultural imagination which has caste its shadow across the landscape of the former warzone. At the same time, the sociopolitical context of war, the 'reality' of conflict, violence and loss of territory all serve as a 'reality check' and offer another kind of landscaping. The book moves seamlessly between emotions and facts, bringing out a richly textured analysis of the strife that engulfed northern Sri Lanka and the reconstruction that followed as well as the aims and dreams through which the past has been reconceptualized and recreated for both display and consumption.

This is only one aspect of this rich and magnificent 'small' book! Perera deftly takes us through a fascinating terrain, unexamined by anthropologists in South Asia: photography and cartography in the field of warzone tourism. Our understanding of photography as the mere capturing of a moment takes on significant meaning when he unpacks the underpinnings of this activity, infused with affect, that reflects particular identities and sensibilities born of these identities. The work of 'mapping' identities and experiences through signposting particular sites worthy of visit is an indication of the effort to establish an overarching all-encompassing identity of being the victors and belonging to a particular religion and nation. Being Buddhist and Sinhala is of essence, the rest merely falls into place.

The importance of this book lies in its consideration of a novel kind of tourism-related travel as an outcome of war and the consequences of war. On the one hand, such travel, with its emphasis on faith in tradition and an ancient and well-remembered past, echoes pilgrimages common to Asian societies; on the other, tourism here is linked to the wars that ravaged the country and the packaging of sites, associated with war, by others who had seen them earlier. In this process, not only is the 'nation' and the ethno-cultural identities imagined anew, but dominant narratives are established and histories rewritten. Through the author's keen portrayal of the motives that drive tourism in warzones, the experience of travellers and, above all, the symbolism that a place, space and territory attains, the book also suggests the tragic outcomes of such travel. Tragedy lies in the loss of a 'paradise' that is reflected now only in its 'darker places'.

Sasanka Perera is a most unusual anthropologist: apart from researching and writing on subjects at the intersection of both sociology and anthropology, he is a poet, an artist, a photographer and he also writes lyrics in Sinhala. He always has an original idea that he follows through with complete dedication and fine research. This book, set in Sri Lanka, in the aftermath of civil war, focuses on the recovery of identity, selfhood and nation through the complex and somewhat curious case of 'warzone' tourism. It is an ingenious portrayal of a new phenomenon and Sasanka Perera has done it with rigorous analysis, thick description and panache, and in the process has achieved the impossible in academic writing: telling a tale remarkably well.

Meenakshi Thapan
Department of Sociology
Delhi School of Economics

1

Approach:
Places, Landscapes, Travels, Discourses

Ideally, travel broadens our perspectives personally, culturally, and politically. Suddenly, the palette with which we paint the story of our lives has more colors.

—Rick Steves in *Travel as a Political Act*[1]

This book is concerned with travel and its implications in cultural and socio-political terms. More specifically, my interest is in the kind of travel that suddenly emerged in Sri Lanka, which took travellers from the southern part of the country to the north which had been closed for a considerable period of time due to war. Collectively, I call these travels and the activities people engage in while travelling as 'warzone tourism', which I will proceed to explain as my reading continues. Why did civilians from the south, many of whom had not hitherto travelled to the north opt to do so while an active war was still ongoing in 2002 and when the war had concluded by 2010 even though its remnants were visible everywhere and not too many comforts were available for travellers in the former warzone? Were these travels motivated purely by considerations of leisure and pleasure? Or, did ideology and emotion play a part in their decisions to travel? What did they intend to do and what did they want to see? What were the implications of that 'seeing'? What was not seen? These are some of the general questions which will inform the progression of this book as I attempt to make sense of warzone tourism in Sri Lanka.

In ethnographic terms and as a point of departure for my exploration, two distinct phases of warzone tourism can be identified:

1. The travels to Jaffna by southern Sinhala travellers between 2002 and 2005 when the ceasefire was in operation;
2. The travels to Jaffna and more extended parts of the former warzones such as Kilinochchi and Mullaitivu by southern Sinhala travellers after the war ended in 2009 and the main road was opened in 2010.

In addition to these two phases of travel and the resultant dynamics, there is another important dimension of tourism that one needs to take note of, which, nevertheless, will not be a focus of this book. The travel to the north in both phases was not the exclusive preserve of Sinhalas even though they consisted of the larger volume of travellers. Tamils resident in southern Sri Lanka as well as from diasporic centres in Europe, North America, Australasia and South India also undertook this kind of travel in so far as the routes and destinations are concerned. However, the emotions involved in these travels were significantly different, marked by notions of nostalgia over homecoming after long periods of absence and intense sorrow and anger at seeing extreme destruction. In the first phase, these emotions also included feelings of triumph over LTTE successes while in the latter phase, the feelings tended to be those of dejection and lack of justice due to the finality of the movement's ultimate defeat. By this categorization, I do not intend to impose a simple and reductionist explanation of travel experience and perception based on ethnicity. However, the fundamental differences of the emotions in these travels to a large extent were in fact based on ethnicity and the resultant differences in political perception. Beyond this, however, there were numerous other factors that affected the emotional structure of Tamils' travels to the north, particularly if they hailed from the warzone itself, which included issues such as a specific family's proximity to the Tamil nationalist struggle, the nature of their personal experiences and grief with regard to the main guerrilla formation, the Liberation Tigers of Tamil Eelam (LTTE), their experiences with regard to agencies of the state in general and the military and police in particular and so on. Notwithstanding this difference in experience and emotion, this reading will not focus on Tamils' travels to the former warzone as it constitutes an entirely different category of travel and experience which requires a very different approach in analysis. As such, my interest is in the warzone travels undertaken by the Sinhalas.

Let me begin by offering a clarification of my deployment of the concept of 'warzone' as a central category in this book. In general usage as well as in social sciences, a warzone is an area in which active combat takes place.[2] In the first phase of tourism that is a major focus of my analysis, combat was officially halted as the result of a ceasefire. Despite this official position, however, combat was unofficially ongoing on a regular basis in different parts of north-eastern Sri Lanka. More specifically, war was barred from the gaze of travellers who ventured along the main road to the north and in the streets and towns they were allowed to enter by the military and the LTTE. It seemed like a performance that had been halted in selected theatres while it continued in more distant venues. Nevertheless, skirmishes and battles took place regularly between the warring parties, and lives were lost and properties destroyed away from the newly established flurry of tourism and the zones where these tourist dynamics were unfolding. In that sense, the kind of touristic journeys that took place in the first phase had to negotiate through territory that was a quasi-warzone though travellers would not have directly witnessed combat during their travels while they would have readily seen its consequences: bullet-scarred buildings and shell-destroyed palms along with destroyed military vehicles literally adorning the main road. In the second phase, the war was over even though the travel paths traversed through the former warzone and most sites of interest were directly related to the war, such as victory monuments set up by the government and numerous former LTTE sites. In this context, I use the term 'warzone' to refer to a place where war was once active in the recent past and has acutely touched, scarred and impacted the landscape and the populace. In this sense, the word does not connote an area identified as a kind of museum entity frozen in the recent past actively maintaining the remnants of war. Rather, it is simply an area in which war once took place. But during the time of war as well as post-war, the area I call a warzone has been constantly undergoing change. Some of these changes will manifest more clearly as my reading continues.

This invites us to ponder over the following questions: Who were the people who travelled to the north when it was an active warzone and who travelled there in its post-war incarnation in conceptual and practical terms? To begin with, it would be useful to recognize certain common denominators among all types of travellers while keeping in mind that significant differences among them in fact do exist. People generally go from their own contexts of living to a specific destination for leisure to essentially caste their gaze on different scenes, landscapes, practices and people which might be considered out of the ordinary or, in the very least, different. In Urry's words, this literally involves moving from place to place 'lumpy, fragile, aged, gendered, racialised bodies' (Urry 2002: 152). As such, 'when we "go away" we look at the environment with interest and curiosity. It speaks to us in ways we appreciate, or at least we anticipate that it will do so. In other words, we gaze at what we encounter' (Urry 2002: 1). Very clearly, travel of this nature has at its epicentre of logic an anticipation of pleasure generated through the conscious consumption of services, goods and specific sites. Such consumption takes place and is the central preoccupation of tourist travel due to the belief that it generates pleasurable experiences quite different from what is possible from routine day-to-day encounters (Urry 2002: 1). In this context, it does not make any difference if travel is undertaken purportedly for religious, educational or any other kind of purpose. Pleasure still remains the main concern, even though the colour and nuances of that pleasure may vary depending on the specificity of travel and the individuals concerned.

In this context, who exactly travelled to northern Sri Lanka during the two phases of warzone tourism? Are they travellers, tourists or sightseers? Is it even necessary or useful to make such distinctions? For Urry, the problem with sightseers, the least nuanced kind of travellers in terms of their sensibly, is literally their excessive focus on sight to the extent of blocking off other senses in capturing the overall experience of travel. As he observes, 'there can be an embarrassment about mere sightseeing' because 'sight may be viewed as the most superficial of the senses getting in the way of real experiences that should involve the other senses and necessitate long periods of time in order for proper immersion' (Urry 2002: 149). In this context, many of the people who flock to the north can be categorized as sightseers, their attention span somewhat limited with an almost choreographed interest in photography of a particular type. That is, the kind of photography that will 'authenticate' their travels rather than provide a nuanced understanding of what these travels could unravel about the calamities brought upon by war, how it has affected the lives of people in the region and so on. However, to me, this overconsumption of sight does not negate its discursive validity. This is not merely a matter of a superficial glance but a recording of that glance and often, in today's contexts, proliferation of that glance as well. In any case, most types of travel undertaken for purposes of pleasure generally embody a 'quest for authenticity' or at least an anticipation of a 'staged authenticity' (Urry 2002: 9–10). In the case of warzone travel in Sri Lanka, much of this authenticity emanates from photographs and these photographs become the source for the multiple discourses which emerge after the travels have been concluded. However superficial their exercise of sight might be in the sense outlined by Urry (2002), the act of capturing moments of that sight in photography ensures that what travellers see goes beyond the moment of actual seeing. The photographically captured sight becomes the basis of discourse in family and kin circles, peer groups and sometimes in much more extended networks such as social media, blogging and so on. In this sense, the discursive significance of sight via photographs cannot be underemphasized in the Sri Lankan context. Within this specific understanding, I will use the more general term 'tourist' to refer to all travellers in this book, while I will revisit more carefully their practice of photography later in this book.

In any case, do the people who visited the north belong to a single category? Can they all be subsumed under the parameters of a single gaze? Urry rightly points out that 'there is no single tourist gaze as such. It varies by society, by social group and by historical period' (Urry 2002: 1). In this sense, one can accept the argument that the gaze of a tourist is not a linear gaze; it is not a simple packaged product. According to Urry, a tourist's 'gaze in any historical period is constructed in relationship to its opposite, to non-tourist forms of social experience and consciousness' (Urry 2002: 1). That is, 'what makes a particular tourist gaze depends upon what it is contrasted with; what forms of non-tourist experience happen to be' (Urry 2002: 1). What is considered 'non-tourist', with which the tourist experience is contrasted with, mostly comes from social practices within the home and workspace (Urry 2002: 1–2). In this sense, at a general level, it is not difficult to accept the variations in the tourist gaze based on temporality linked to historical moments when certain kinds of travel takes place as well as the social backgrounds of travellers.

However, as my ethnographic material is presented in the ensuing chapters, it will become obvious that certain aspects of this gaze can in fact be standardized within limits which supersede personal backgrounds of individuals, varying from education, class and social standing on one hand, to even more subjective considerations such as taste on the other. Under extraordinary circumstances, it is entirely possible that the usually diverse gaze of tourists might look for and see the same kind of things. War and extreme articulations of nationalism are among the many factors that might create such conditions for standardization of both sight and gaze, and finally the resultant discourses as well. As such, while assuming some variations in sight, during the two phases of tourism I deal with in this book, one can also conceive of a Sinhala tourist and Tamil tourist whose sight and gaze were conditioned on the basis of the cultural and political baggage they carried which were differentially tempered by the two dominant nationalisms of the time, namely, Sinhala and Tamil nationalisms which were both mutually exclusive and antagonistic. I will revisit this issue in subsequent chapters when I deal with the actual process of tourism. But for the moment, I should state that the kind of Sinhala travellers who travelled to the north in the first phase of tourism and the ones who journeyed in the second phase are two very distinctly different characters, moulded by their times and circumstances. The same applies to Tamil travellers as well though I will not deal with them in this book.

Sociology of tourism, though a relatively new area of academic interest, has by now added considerably to a growing corpus of knowledge. Much of this has to do with the economics of tourism and the analysis of tourist policy. When studies do involve some elements of political violence, crime and instability, they often tend to focus on the impact these phenomena and resultant instability have on tourism (Enders et al. 1992; Ferreira and Harmse 2000; Hall and O'Sullivan 1996; Mihalic 1996; Pizam 1999). Sally Ness is among the very few writers who have moved some distance away from this kind of linear preoccupations (Ness 2005). She offers a phenomenological explanation of locational violence by focusing on the landscaping of tourist destinations which she suggests leads to embed and signify possible sources of locational violence (Ness 2005). In the Sri Lankan context, what is of interest to me is not if landscaping of specific sites embody or signify possibilities of violence. Rather, the issue is about the transformation of specific places from non-tourist places to tourist places, or once differentially defined tourist places or redefined places that might obscure certain kinds of pre-existing meanings including memories of violence. Nevertheless, the conceptual categories and the theoretical considerations employed by Ness are crucially important to my own work as would be evident as my reading progresses. In general, however, very few studies deal with how war or the after-effects of war become a focus of tourism. Figal's work on Okinawa stands out among the handful of studies that attempt to see how over time, in post-war Okinawa, a preoccupation with Second World War battle sites as the main component of heritage tourism shifted to a more intense focus on a cultivated 'tropical southern island feel', and Ryuku identity within which the emphasis on war heritage tended to be underemphasized, though not completely dismantled (Figal 2008). My interest lies in these general lacunae in the sociology of tourism with a focus on Sri Lanka, both in the midst of war and after.

The process of transforming former battle zones into tourist sites which presents distinct physical, cultural and historical attributes usually bundled together as 'heritage' tends to be fraught with tensions between recreation and respect (Figal 2008: 83–84). After all, these are places where enormous destruction had been once inflicted upon people and property, which has transformed the emotional sensibility of places in the process. Further, in the case of Okinawa described by Figal (2008) as well as the Sri Lankan materials I explore in this book, the tensions between recreation and respect in these kinds of tourist discourses as well as the rearrangement of space are further implicated in differential notions of competing nationalisms. These are places where memories might still linger or might be institutionalized in terms of local and private practice. Yet, people do not visit such places merely for reflection, but also for pleasure. As such, a 'successful' transformation of the residues of a warzone into a tourist attraction should be able to manage the 'sharp juxtapositions between tourist pleasure and pilgrim piety' often within a single site (Figal 2008: 84). This consideration is crucial in understanding how a complex web of meanings might be constructed at these sites, which may vary between these two extremes. It is not a simple matter of what a brochure or dedication plaque might claim of a specific place. It also has to do with how the people in a particular locality might interpret that same place. When the Southern Battle Sites Tours were organized early on at the formal initiation of the heritage tourist industry of Okinawa in the late 1950s, the specifically trained bus guides soon acquired a reputation for their 'poignant narratives of war history that shaped battle site tours' (Figal 2008: 91). As such, in these kinds of travels, the multiple narratives that emerge from these places ultimately give them their overall identity and sense of place. As I venture into my ethnographic material, I will specifically be focusing on the voices that articulate these narratives and the spells of silence that also accompany them.

On the other hand, one needs to understand how these specific sites make contextual sense as 'places'. A place in this context is not a simple fixed geographic location; it is not a simple abstracted cartographic pointer. In the case of my own material, places are given sense by the people who inhabit them, make use of them or have been expelled from them on the basis of their multiple narratives in much the same way as is underscored by Basso when he noted that 'places come to generate their own fields of meaning' (Basso 1996: 56). This is also what Rodman meant when she suggested that it would be possible to fathom how people embody places by attempting to understand how places represent people (Rodman 1992: 652). Ness suggests that place is a reference 'to a lived, event-defined, multilocational happening' that also should ideally be understood as an entity that is 'fully integrated through the senses with the being of the human condition' (Ness 2005: 120). But how would this be possible? Can every place be lived, event-defined and fully integrated with the being of the human condition? The issue that emerges when these conditionalities of place are juxtaposed with the local specificities I will focus on, is not a matter contextual irrelevance. However, local conditions change at different times, making their relationship with these conditionalities to change accordingly. In this scheme of things, places are embedded with a sense of intentionality that is given direction by what Ness suggests are 'thoughtful, even argumentative and emphatically moral characters' (Ness 2005: 120). In this sense, a specific site of warzone curiosity or a ruin is not only about what it is supposed to represent but also about what it has excluded through under emphasis, exclusion or expulsion of people, narratives and memories. In this sense, tourist places or landscapes, particularly in former warzones, cannot be simple domains of innocence without contradictions. By definition, history unwritten or un-narrated will always cast long shadow across these places. And it is unlikely that ordinary tourists will unravel what these shadows mean. In fact, quite literally, they might not even see these shadows in their rather rapid transiting from one place of touristy curiosity to another.

A concentration on the ideas associated with place also suggests that another closely related concept needs to be taken into account. This has to do with 'landscape' which is crucially important in the local contexts within which my ethnographic material is located. The sites on the tourist trails which I shall focus on are not 'natural' locations or relatively 'untampered' localities if one could identify any place anywhere today in this fashion given the manner in which human beings have interacted with and transformed conditions of nature. In this context, I do not consider landscape as a simple natural formation that generates certain aesthetic pleasure, even though this sensibility is a taken-for-granted meaning of the word in general usage. My understanding of landscape within the present work focuses on 'reconstruction, deconstruction, and all other constructions of place' which leads to the 'material transformation and pictorial encoding of a location' (Ness 2005: 120). The word 'landscaping' rather than 'landscape' ushers in this meaning of change and transformation more clearly. Landscaping of a place inherently presupposes a degree of transformation or displacement. In other words, the landscaping of a particular site or place can lead to the dissociation of the pre-existing sense of the place (Ness 2005: 120). This displacement brought about by landscaping is not simply restricted to the transformation of the place itself, but it is also an experience that people linked to a particular place undergo as they experience the material transformations around them and the scenic or differentially defined rendering of a specific place (Ness 2005: 120). In this sense, landscaping entails the rearrangement of geographies and thereby also the rewriting of histories. In this context, what happens in the locality when cemeteries once maintained by the rebel LTTE are destroyed by the government and a military base or a playground is set up in their place? What does it mean when a brand new victory monument emerges in a place where such a monument did not exist before? What kind of sensibility is created when such monuments vocally celebrate heroic military deaths and do not recognize the hundreds of civilians who died in the same areas and the untold stories of pain which are still a part of personal narratives? Do tourists see and experience these transformations as do locals? If so or if not, how are these discourses articulated? These are some of the questions that would emerge and would need to be addressed as the travels of tourists to the north are placed in context.

Literature on tourism often refers to adventure travel or adventure tourism as a specific category (Rogerson 2004; Zurick 1992). Usually, this category of travel refers to activities such as trekking, mountaineering, white water rafting, skydiving and so on which involves the following three parameters: a certain degree of risk, a certain amount of skill and significant physical exertion by participants (Rogerson 2004: 183). Even though the kind of tourism I describe in this book does not fall within these parameters, these travels can also be understood within a certain rendition of 'adventure' despite the fact that the three elements that typically define adventure tourism play no part in this specific context. Many of the southern tourists who ventured to Jaffna between 2002 and 2005, and who continued to go there and to other parts of the former warzone in the north-east from 2010 to 2013, undertook these travels to experience a certain sense of 'adventure' albeit from a safe temporal and physical distance from possibilities of danger. In this case, either the ceasefire was in place or the war had ended offering a degree of physical safety but nevertheless allowing space for a feeling of adventure to manifest through the ability to gaze upon selective destructions and consequences of war and by being in an area that had been inaccessible for a very long period of time. On the other hand, until recent times, travelling and living in these areas were not very comfortable given the nature of infrastructural destruction over a thirty-year period of war. However, a sense of adventure emanated from travelling through former warzones still containing very obvious signs of battle, cooking one's food along the road and sometimes sleeping in the open and being told stories of war and heroism by soldiers and combatants of the LTTE, depending on who one asked.

In the context of the considerations I have briefly outlined above, what I hope to achieve in this book is to explore these two phases of travel, which I have collectively called *warzone tourism* and which have also been referred to by other writers as the 'tiger tail'[3] and 'killing fields tourism',[4] and attempt to understand what these dynamics mean in both political and cultural terms in contemporary Sri Lanka. What kind of stories do the geographies of these travels, the objects of curiosity, places where specific sites are located and travellers themselves narrate about ethnicity, identity, the state, the place, landscapes, borders, development, war, the absence of war and the cruelties and pain of war? How are they narrated and what is made explicit and what is made invisible? How do places and landscapes change according to political circumstances as well as due to tourism of this type? Essentially, my interest is in the discourse that brings together travel, stories, photographs, maps and specific objects that become incessant obsessions for travellers by taking the travellers' journeys as a metaphorical vehicle for exploration. Tourism and the travel associated with it then is the vehicle that will allow me the space to interrogate these interrelated issues.

Notes

1. For more information, visit: https://www.ricksteves.com/about-rick/social-activism-philanthropy/how-to-travel-as-a-political-act/choosing-to-travel-on-purpose (accessed on 25 September 2015).

2. For example, see the definitions offered by the following sources: http://www.thefreedictionary.com/war+zone [The Free Dictionary]; http://www.merriam-webster.com/dictionary/war%20zone [Merriam Webster Dictionary]; http://www.collinsdictionary.com/dictionary/english/warzone [Collins Dictionary] (accessed on 3 November 2013).

3. https://www.colombotelegraph.com/index.php/prabhakarans-bunker-destroyed-in-wanni/ (accessed on 5 November 2013).

4. Frances Harrison specifically refers to the second phase of tourism as 'killing fields tourism', taking her cue from the title of the documentary film produced by England's Channel 4 News, 'Sri Lanka's Killing Fields'. For more information on Harrison's ideas, please visit: http://www.huffingtonpost.co.uk/frances-harrison/sri-lankas-killing-fields-tourism_b_2356247.html (accessed on 1 December 2013).

2

'The Jaffna Photo Album': Sinhala Warzone Tourism in the Time of a Ceasefire[1]

Sumith Ranasinghe was in an adventurous mood. Like most people in the country, since at least January 2002 he had been closely following the unfolding events between the government and the LTTE, which seemed to be leading in the direction of a peace accord. Finally, news reports announced that the LTTE and the government had in fact signed the accord on 20th of February 2002 paving the way towards an era whose characteristics no one knew about at the time. There was some hope that some kind of peace might prevail, but it was clouded by a sense of apprehension that this too might fail as previous attempts had. Just a few days before the local New Year in April, he had heard on the government's television station, Rupawahini, that the A9 road to Jaffna which had been closed for years by the government and the LTTE had just been opened for civilian traffic. That was 8 April 2002. Just to be sure, he also tuned to BBC radio which he had cultivated the habit of listening to over the last four years as the war intensified. For him, it was a matter of checking and double checking 'facts'. To be even surer, he tuned on to 'Voice of America' as well. All of them said the same thing as if it was the chorus of a popular song: the A9 was opened. So he called his child-hood friend and asked him: '[T]he A9 is open. Shall we go to Jaffna at the end of the month?' Like many citizens of Colombo at the time, he had also scanned through global television networks to get a sense of what the road opening meant. In three weeks, the two friends also learnt that many devel-opment workers, Tamils settled down in other parts of the world as well as their own friends and neighbours were now going to Jaffna along the newly accessible road. All the returnees assured the two friends that it was safe even though the road was in bad shape. By mid-May, the two friends were ready to embark on their adventure. They had bought a road map from the Survey Department, Sumith's van was serviced, air pressure in the tyres was checked and, as advised by the family mechanic, two tyres were replaced, diesel was filled to capacity and two additional gallons were loaded into the back of the van as it was known that diesel was difficult to get in the north, and very expensive. Then with their families, the two young men went to the Bellanwila temple and got themselves and the van blessed. Just to be doubly sure, they also made a vow to God Kataragama, known as Kandasamy in the area they were about to visit, and promised him that if they came back safely they would release 20 captive birds so that they can soar into the limitless sky. They had already got a letter from a family elder to the chief incumbent of the Naga Vihara Buddhist temple in Jaffna town requesting the monk to let the young men stay at his temple. Though such a request was not absolutely necessary, the family assumed this would be a foolproof way to ensure that the two friends had a roof over their heads during their sojourn in a city that had no known hotels or guest houses at the time.

Sumith spent the night of 5th May at his friend's home. They watched all the television news channels again that night to be sure that nothing was wrong in the warzone. Early next morning, Sumith worshiped his friends' parents as he had done with his own parents the night before, loaded the rice packets made by his friend's sisters for lunch and their two bags into the van along with large containers of drinking water and a few more snacks and bananas, murmured a Buddhist stanza, asked permission from the gods to embark on a safe trip and turned on the ignition. Very soon, just after 4:00 am they were off to Jaffna, a town they had never visited before and had no friends. They had only heard stories about it from their parents who had visited it in the early 1970s. And on the basis of their memories they had compiled a list of things that should be brought back from the north: palmyra jaggery and roots, nelli wine and a few of the famed Jaffna mangoes, karthakolombam. Their favourite FM radio channel provided music and not much else at that time in the morning. A gentle drizzle tapped on the front windshield as the coconut flower mounted on the front of the van as an offering to gods swayed gently in the morning breeze.

****

If the fictionalized account above adds general colour, mood and movement to the kind of travel that emerged in the first phase of warzone tourism, let me also place in context two specific stories of travel from 2002 which would add ethnographic sense to this phenomenon and provide a point of departure to this discussion. In about the first week of July 2002, I suddenly noticed that some of my neighbours were no longer to be seen. They belonged to a family which made a living from renting a three-wheel auto rickshaw and by offering their services as small-scale contractors in the building construction industry. Usually, they are up early in the morning getting ready to go to work, watering their plants, washing their rickshaw and playing the morning news from at least two television channels very loudly so that the entire neighbourhood knew the state's interpretation of news as well as at least one privately owned channel's rendition of the 'truth'. Due to the sudden cessation of these taken-for-grated morning rituals, their absence was easy to feel and see. Equally as suddenly, they reappeared in about a week with a sense of adventure I had not sensed in them before in my casual conversations. The head of the family told me the next morning after they reappeared, '[W]e went to Jaffna; we met the LTTE; it was quite exciting', and insisted that they shared their story.

Over the next two days, while attending to our mundane morning rituals, he narrated their story to me. It unfolded as follows: Merely a few months after the A9 was initially opened for civilian traffic, this extended family consisting of about 10 individuals had travelled to Jaffna in a van owned by a relative. They had neither friends nor relatives in Jaffna and spoke no Tamil. They did not have any idea where to stay as there was hardly an established hospitality industry at the time in that part of the country. So they stayed in the temple, the Naga Vihara, as many people continue to do once they arrive in Jaffna. They had spoken to many soldiers who were willing to narrate their war stories and, more excitingly, exchanged words with the LTTE sentries at many of the numerous checkpoints they had to go through and with customs and immigration officers of the LTTE at its main checkpoint just after the last government checkpoint in Omanthai and after crossing the no man's land. More importantly, they had posed for pictures with uniformed and sometimes armed LTTE personnel. 'They were very friendly, but strict; some even spoke Sinhala', observed the head of the family. The entire group was quite impressed that many LTTE men and women whom they had met actually spoke a smattering of Sinhala, something they had not expected. For them and many others at the time, this was almost like going to another country. Many young people in general, born in the 1970s and after, had not been to Jaffna before; no one in this group had ever visited the north earlier. Besides, like any foreign trip, they had to go through customs and immigration formalities with the LTTE, fill forms and sometimes pay taxes. Travel permits, which were the LTTE's version of visas, had to be shown to sentries at all subsequent LTTE checkpoints. Moreover, they were also impressed with the organization's sense of discipline that was projected at the time: '[T]heir police are very strict; speed limit is enforced well; and they don't take bribes', observed the wife of the head of the family. A few days later, they showed me nearly 100 colour photographs of their trip containing images of the family posing outside the entrance to Naga Vihara, the Buddhist temple in Jaffna town where they stayed, along with other 'well-known' objects and sites in the emergent tourist trail which I will describe later.

In the second story, at about the same time, a young man I used to know in Colombo similarly disappeared for seven days. People who knew him told me that he had gone to Jaffna to donate some books to the newly refurbished public library that was burnt down by Sinhala thugs on 31 May 1981. Of course, he could have sent the books by post which would have been cost-effective and far more convenient. But travels of this nature have nothing to do with cold logic or economic rationality. That is why they are located in the realm of adventure. The trajectory of places he visited and what he did in each of these places, were strikingly similar to the earlier case. Along with the driver of the vehicle he had hired, he too had visited almost the same places as my neighbours and generally posed at the same places and with similar kinds of people of 'excitement'. He had amassed over 200 images in digital form which documented the annals of his travels. In addition to all this, he had laminated the travel document issued by the LTTE as a special trophy. 'Let me show you my LTTE visa', he said the first time I met him after he had returned, removed it from its plastic folder and presented it to me with both hands, exhibiting the pride of an athlete who had won a major award. It had already become his most cherished warzone trophy, no different from the pieces of the Berlin Wall that travellers brought back who visited Berlin soon after the wall had started to come down in November 1989.

What were the circumstances that made this kind of travel possible consequent to over two decades of war, death, mutual hostility and suspicion accompanied by destruction? The first phase of warzone tourism to Jaffna began almost immediately after the ceasefire agreement brokered by the Norwegian government was signed between the Sri Lankan government and the LTTE on 22 February 2002.[2] Some of the political performances associated with the ceasefire agreement gave it the kind of publicity and seeming credibility and legitimacy that earlier agreements lacked, all of which failed. So, instead of agreements, these earlier examples simply remained 'attempts' and case studies of failure. For one thing, the signatory for the government, Prime Minister Ranil Wickremesinghe, was elected on the basis of a pro-peace mandate merely 10 weeks before the accord was signed. On 22 February 2002, he travelled to Omanthai, the final government checkpoint before the LTTE-held territory began, and handed over a copy of the accord he had signed to Norway's ambassador to Sri Lanka, Jon Westborg, who was to hand over this document to the LTTE chief Velupillai Prabhakaran. The fact that the Prime Minister went to the de facto 'border' beyond which the government's writ had no validity to handover the document was a highly significant symbolic and political act. While for critics it was matter of pandering to the LTTE and giving it undue recognition, to others, it was reflective of the Prime Minister's seriousness in the peace effort. At the same time, Norway's Foreign Minister, Jan Petersen, had confirmed that a similar ceasefire document had also been signed by the leader of the LTTE which would be handed over to the government (Steele 2002). Together, these two documents made up the core of the ceasefire agreement which later came into effect.

Moreover, the signing of the document by the LTTE leader and his publically telecast meetings with visiting Norwegian and Sri Lankan government dignitaries in preparation for the agreement as well as in the context of the two earlier truces that immediately preceded the formal ceasefire and the LTTE's well-known press conference on 10 April 2002 in Kilinochchi ushered in a new kind of political symbolism which offered the organization and its leader a new sense of political credibility as an entity and a person which dealt with government dignitaries and diplomats almost on an equal footing as the Sri Lankan state itself and its representatives. In a performative sense, it almost seemed as if the independent ethnic state that the LTTE was fighting for had been achieved, at least within the confines of these political rituals and performances. For instance, at the April press conference, accompanied by his English-speaking advisors such as Anton Balasingham, Prabhakaran was in civilian clothing as opposed to his usual camouflage fatigues and flanked by two stern looking armed bodyguards in dark glasses and earphones, again smartly clad in civilian dress. The image that was attempted to be created was that of a prominent political leader. But this new image emerged with some accidental nuances of a mafia boss of the Hollywood rendition as the LTTE had not yet completely mastered the art of manipulating the media. Besides, a great deal of space needs to be traversed, literally and metaphorically, in order to arrive in a pictorially convincing manner at the stage of seeming statesman from that of established rebel chieftain. Nevertheless, it was clear such a journey had already commenced consciously in so far as the LTTE in northern Sri Lanka and its diasporic support centres were concerned. Despite unanticipated ruptures of this kind in the process of emergent image-making, the rebel leader seemed to have come out of his military lair into a civilian and more importantly a global public and performative space through the electronic media with international diplomatic recognition. Irrespective of the failures of earlier agreements and anxieties which initially accompanied the 2002 agreement, the semiotics of these images and performances as well as the extent of international involvement in these events gave considerable credibility to the potential of the ceasefire agreement which was further entrenched by the rapidity with which the government of Sri Lanka and the LTTE ensured the opening of the A9 road.

The A9 road which links the city of Kandy with Jaffna is the main road link to the north from the south and had been closed regularly for long periods of time since the mid-1980s by the LTTE as well as the government as the war escalated. The train line was also abandoned by 1990 when the LTTE dismantled long stretches of the rail line and removed the tracks and the sleepers to disrupt travel as well as to use the material for the construction of bunkers and other fortifications. This meant that, since the 1980s, overland travel to Jaffna in particular and the north in general became difficult at first and impossible later on, and very clearly dangerous. As a result, people who needed to leave or visit the Jaffna peninsula for urgent reasons had to use the ferry operated by the International Committee for the Red Cross (ICRC) or the airlines operated by two private companies. When one of these flights, Lion Air 602, disappeared over the northern sea on 29 September 1998 in a suspected LTTE missile attack, it became manifestly evident that even air travel was no longer safe. This state of affair meant that, throughout the war, travel between the north and south was neither easy nor cheap, was very irregular and certainly could not be undertaken for reasons of pleasure. In this context, when travel to and from the north for ordinary people had been difficult for a very long time, the reopening of the road with the agreement of both the government and the LTTE indicated a very significant political moment in recent history.

Soon after the ceasefire agreement was signed, both the government and the LTTE opened sections of the road that were under their control. But this still did not allow uninterrupted travel all the way to Jaffna from the south as some areas remained closed for various reasons. However, the entire road was opened to civilian traffic all the way to Jaffna by April 2002.[3] The Sri Lanka Monitoring Mission which supervised the ceasefire observed on 29 July 2002 that 'the A9 road has been opened for the great benefit of the general public.'[4] The ceasefire agreement allowed access to unarmed combatants to areas controlled by the government or the LTTE under specific conditions. More importantly, the agreement specially allowed for the freedom of movement of civilians as noted in clause 2.10: 'The Parties shall open the Kandy-Jaffna road (A9) to non-military traffic of goods and passengers. Specific modalities shall be worked out by the Parties with the assistance of the Royal Norwegian Government by D-day + 30 at the latest.'[5]

Like the train Yal Devi which travelled between Colombo and Jaffna until 1990, the A9 had considerable military, economic and cultural significance. Like the train line, the road was also strategically important as both could be used to supply the military or the LTTE. Hence the need of both warring factions to control these transport links. These two links were also the main economic lifeline to the area. It was due to the disruption of rail and road traffic that goods and services in the north became exorbitantly expensive during the war years as almost everything that was not produced in the region had affectively become scarce items while the agricultural produce in the region could not be easily brought to southern markets. Whatever agriculture that continued to be operational in the north became part of a very localized subsistence system.

On the other hand, the road and the railway were also seen as the most 'natural' link between the north and the south, a kind of geographic umbilical cord, which had been severed since the escalation of war. In fact, the road, particularly the stretch between Vavuniya and Jaffna which is well within the extended conflict zone, was referred to as the 'The Highway of Blood' at the height of the military confrontations. Poet Rudhramoorthy Cheran has described the wartime transformation of the A9 in the following words in his poem, 'The Story of a Severed Leg':

A road that begins in the mountains
runs through this barren land
to the city,
now lies distraught.

The story of war mixed with blood
in scattered fragments
like restless ghosts,
follow the road in grief.

.... Dismembered by war,
the road survives;
I saw;
where the road forks,
a half broken milestone

(Kanaganayakam 2009: 19–20)

Nevertheless, despite the transformation of the road into an unmistakable metaphor for the war's destruction as well as a symbol of its painful reality, both the road and the railway emerge in many peoples' narratives of the 'good old days' when there was no conflict and how one could travel to Jaffna and visit friends or the Buddhist temple, Naga Vihara, situated in Jaffna Town, the Naga Dipa Temple on Nainativu island or the well-known Kandasamy Hindu Temple in Nallur. In this sense, the enthusiasm with which the opening of the road was received in the south is hardly surprising. For those with pre-war experience in the north, it was a pathway to nostalgia while for others who had no such experience, it was a road of discovery. But in its new incarnation post-2002 the road was not always used for the same purposes it was used before that, at least in the context of Sinhala tourists flocking in large numbers to the north. It was not a simple matter of a pilgrimage to visit temples or friends alone. The more crucial objective was to visit the warzone and gaze upon the consequences of war and to simply be a tourist while pilgrimage factors were also enmeshed within these considerations as many photographs from the period would attest. The idea of pilgrimage emerged in the discussions with many Buddhists. Most visiting families hardly had any friends or kin left in Jaffna, though some had properties which they had to abandon before they fled the region. Almost all Sinhalas and Muslims[6] in the region had been expelled in the 1980s as a direct consequence of the LTTE's own programme of ethnic cleansing. So these travellers were literally venturing into an 'unexplored' area whose construction had only manifested in their consciousness from the narratives of elders, friends and significant others, and in some cases by the fading memories of personal experiences of a bygone era. In this construction intermingled with notions of romanticism, the people of Jaffna were held to be both honest and hardworking, a residue of positive stereotyping from the pre-war period more familiar to people born in the 1930s and 1940s rather than later. Through these narratives, it was also the land of palmyra jaggery, *kottakilangu* or the roots of palmyra, local wine made out of the fruit *nelli* and the famed Jaffna mangoes, *karthakolombam*.

However, this idealized image had been disrupted considerably as a result of Tamil nationalist politics' advent into Sri Lanka's national political landscape since at least the early 1970s. It was more violently ruptured through this nationalism's most virulent form of manifestation in terms of the LTTE since at least the late 1970s. In addition, Sinhala nationalism from the same period onwards steadily constructed a more unfavourable Tamil 'other' far removed from the ideal of the earlier pre-war 'hardworking and honest' stereotype. At the height of war, in most manifestations of Sinhala nationalist discourses, it was not easy to make a conceptual differentiation between an ordinary Tamil and an LTTE 'terrorist'. The image of the LTTE as 'freedom fighters' and as 'boys' that was readily available in the Tamil vocabulary never found any kind of resonance in popular Sinhala parlance. Given this scenario of the deteriorating image of the other and the violent rupture of normal relationships that once existed, it is indeed quite intriguing that the pre-war romanticized ideal of hardworking and honest Tamils and their exoticized landscape as the progenitor of much sought after produce would re-emerge so quickly in the Sinhala consciousness when the first phase of warzone tourism began in 2002 and at least momentarily displace the violent persona of militarized Tamil and the landscape he inhabited which the LTTE had very successfully created during the war years and which was readily consumed by many Sinhalas. This does not mean that the reality of the violence which the LTTE in particular and the war more generally created as well as the fears and anxieties this situation ushered in suddenly disappeared from the Sinhala psyche. On the contrary, many people were glued to local TV and radio as well as to international broadcasts to follow the progress of the ceasefire precisely due to the existence of these fears and anxieties. Many people continued to check for news in this manner prior to each visit to the north and those who had the option also cultivated the practice of calling friends and kin in various institutions that ranged from the military to the police and to the UN and other assorted development agencies prior to northbound travel to ascertain the safety of prevailing conditions.

However, travel to the north would not have been as easily possible if the negative and more generalized image of the 'ordinary' Tamils that was imposed on the Sinhala community via the persona of the LTTE and the war-torn landscape in which they lived was not separated from the LTTE. After all, southern travellers had to assume that ordinary Tamils who inhabit the areas they were about to visit were 'like' themselves from whom they can ask for drinking water and directions while they expected the rules of the ceasefire which seemed to be holding would deal with the LTTE. It is in this context of interrelated anxieties, fears and expectations that Sinhala travellers had the option to rediscover the 'ordinary' Tamil that they had forgotten and which many had demonized as the war escalated. It is this post-2002 preoccupation of southern tourists and their travels that I am initially interested in.[7] Whether the possibility if that rediscovery was actually realized, however, is an issue that needs to be further interrogated. Within these circumstances, which enabled civilian travel to the northern warzone, how exactly did the warzone tourist trail unfold? In what specific locations did people usually stop? What were their motivations to travel? What did they expect to see? What kind of narratives emerge from their interactions in these places? These are some of the questions I hope to answer as I sift through my ethnographic material.

Crossing Borders

Literally and metaphorically, warzone travels to northern Sri Lanka by Sinhalas necessitated the crossing of borders, both political and cultural. While the travels of Sinhala tourists emanated from the southern parts of the country, where the writ of the government prevailed, the actual formal and physical access to the rebel-held north along the A9 was through Omanthai, 264 km north of Colombo (see Figure 2.1 for the general route of warzone travel in phase 1, 2002–2005). Omanthai

Figure 2.1

General route(s) of north-bound warzone travel in phase 1, 2002–2005

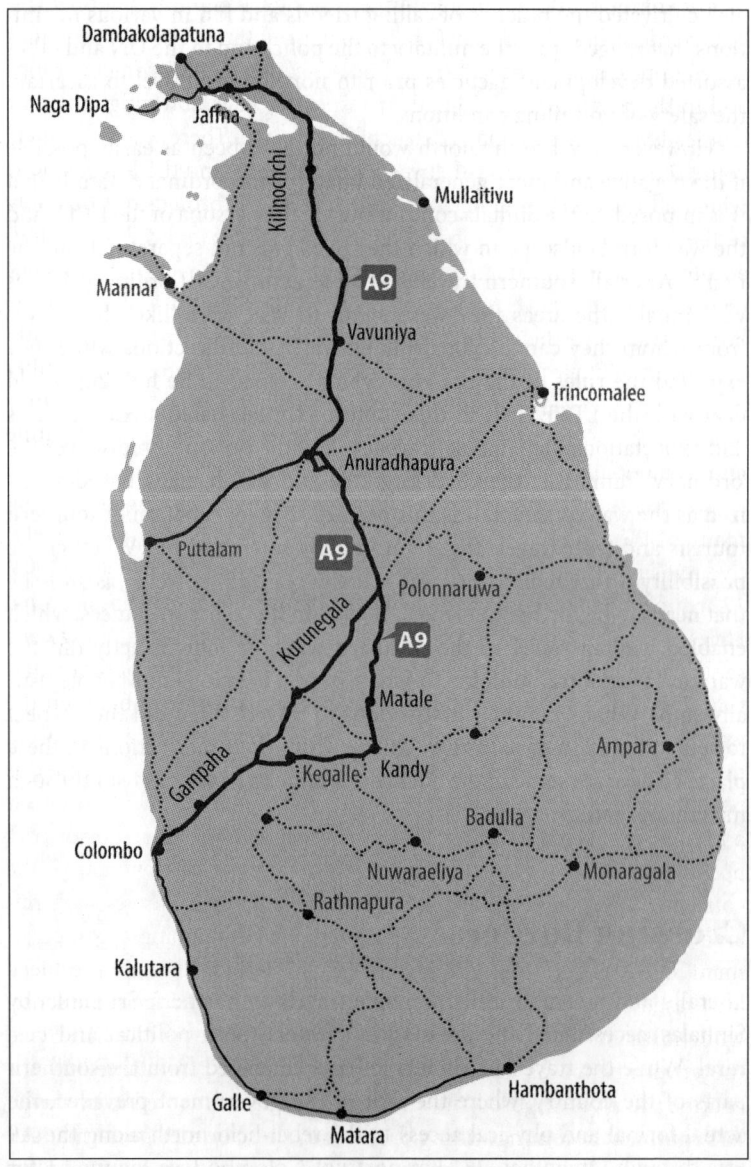

Source: Author. Cartography by Janananda Laksiri, Colombo.

is a town just north of the city of Vavuniya held by the government and it was in affect a de facto border town, irrespective of the de jure validity of the border it enforced in terms of local and international law. This border worked precisely the way major militarized border crossings were supposed to work, controlled in the south by government troops and in the north by the LTTE, their respective flags fluttering in the air iconically indicting the power structures in place. There was a routinely contested 'no man's land' between government and LTTE positions which all travellers in either direction had to go through on their way to the north or the south. The crossing was institutionalized taking into account the A9 as the main artery for transport and travel while no fence or wall separated government and LTTE controlled territories. But the border was nevertheless very much present, often imposed by death. LTTE and military intrusions in either direction were met with hostility and villagers looking for firewood often also met the same fate as they tended to inadvertently cross the invisible border, which in their routine and traditional practices had not historically existed.

Newman's contention that borders 'give order to our lives' and that many of these borders ordering the lives of people, despite their relative invisibility significantly impact their life practices (Newman 2006: 172) applies in this context also, albeit in a somewhat altered meaning. Here, the 'ordering' has extremely restrictive and life threatening consequences which are not necessarily associated with every border situation. Nevertheless, the treacherous regular confrontations between the warring factions in the no man's land ceased considerably as a result of the ceasefire and, more importantly, to enable civilian travel during this period. Since what I refer to here is neither an international border nor a legally recognized local border in the sense of a provincial or district border, it seems relevant that I discuss briefly my deployment of the concept of border in this specific context. As Pratt observes with reference to international borders, 'the border is an ongoing accomplishment' even though 'the processes by which it is continually produced are erased by its apparent self-evidence' (2005: 185). In the same sense, while it lasted, the border between the power centres of the LTTE and the government was an accomplishment that was maintained by the routine practices imposed and enacted by both sides as well as by travellers routinely becoming willing partners in these border performances. However, unlike suggested by Pratt (2005), rather than the Omanthai border's self-evidence or its obvious presence erasing the processes which produce it, these practices tended to emphasize its presence repeatedly despite the government's insistence that there was no border. The government's own procedures ensured this non-acknowledged border to manifest itself in practice.

Wonders has suggested that contemporary borders can be perceived as an amalgamation of complex performances of state power exhibited at specific locations and utilizing technologies and practices of detection, selection, deterrence, expulsion and pre-emption directed at specific people (Wonders 2006: 63–86). In other words, rather than simple lines on the ground, borders are, in the words of Newman, 'institutions' with internal rules specific to them which govern their behaviour and practices and are self-perpetuating in terms of governing the extent of inclusion and exclusion (Newman 2003: 14). Though both Wonders and Newman were writing with reference to international borders controlled by states, much of what they suggest are applicable in the context of the internal border that I am exploring here. Clearly, all the practices that Wonders has identified were in operation on both sides of the Omanthai border and were aimed precisely to deter the entry of certain kinds of pre-identified people and groups. The only difference was that the performance of power was not the exclusive preserve of the state. Instead, on the south of the border the state was performing these powers while in the north, the LTTE was performing them for the precise reason to be seen and to be considered a 'state'. Taken in this sense, what existed in Omantahi was a functioning border crossing with practices characterized by regular militarized borders well in place. Though not an international border in any strict sense of the word, it nevertheless functioned very much similar to a border crossing from one country to another rather than the often taken for granted borders between provinces or other local entities which people often cross and re-cross as they will without going through any kind of border control. This formal separation of the north from the south and the institutionalization of elaborate entry and exit practices ensured that the separate state that the LTTE was aspiring for, was at least partly and forcefully enacted on the ground. These rituals indicated that the state of Eelam, however contested, had already arrived. This also formally enacted the political rupture of Sri Lanka's territorial integrity despite the rhetoric to the contrary by the state.

The legal system, political attitude and structure of power beyond the border in the north were very clearly different from the south, as was the language itself. It was essential for the LTTE to emphasize this difference, which they performed through border control while all travellers had to take part in these deliberate performances and practices in order to ritually enhance the differences that were maintained beyond. On the other hand, as I have already noted, while the military and the government officially did not recognize the idea of an 'internal' border that was militarily enforced, it was a fact of life. Words such as *mayim gammana* which literally means 'border villages' and *awasan hamuda murapola* which means 'the final military checkpoint' in reference to the Sri Lanka Army-controlled checkpoint at Omanthai had already entered the popular discourse even though they are often scoffed by Sinhala nationalists in their own discourses. Sinhala columnist Nalin de Silva had suggested that the words 'mayim gammana' should not be used as they connote the recognition of an internal border and suggested instead the use of words such as *tharjitha gammana* and *tharajanayata lak wu gammana* both of which mean 'threatened villages'.[8] Here, the 'threat' was a reference to the constant dangers posed to Sinhala villages by the LTTE in a situation where armed and unarmed villagers had been often targeted by the LTTE simply due to their ethnic identity as Sinhalas and their perceived and real support of military forces operating nearby. These constantly threatened and attacked villages and similar Tamil villages threatened by military forces effectively became the de facto border between the government controlled Sinhala south and the LTTE-controlled Tamil north. Many of these villages were abandoned while the war lasted. These villages, in their threatened and abandoned incarnations, were the walls and fences that marked the border. As such, despite the semantics of the debate, a clear border did exist and the reality it articulated was not something mythological but concrete, with severe politico-military as well as life-threatening consequences. On the other hand, the military's own practices at the border that they did not legally recognize affectively enforced the practical existence of the border itself in real terms and, in that process, made available to the LTTE certain essential practices typically attributed to states which the organization greatly coveted. In this sense, for the LTTE, the Omanathai border crossing and other checkpoints beyond were affectively theatres where it performed its drama of statecraft for the consumption of civilians who were obliged to be a captive audience. This was also a drama of self-gratification as it allowed the LTTE to repeatedly relive its position as an almost independent state despite obvious limitations well before it could militarily achieve this much aspired final goal. And that too, amidst a large transient audience. It was through this practice that the LTTE communicated first hand to civilian travellers from the south its own sense of power and control.

In practical terms, all travellers to the north first had to disembark at the military checkpoint at Omanthai and undergo a security check that included a thorough physical check of the vehicles they were travelling in, personal baggage as well as commercial material and finally a body search of each individual and the establishment of their identity mostly on the basis of the National Identity Card issued by the Government of Sri Lanka, and in some cases passports. Consequent to the completion of this time-consuming performance, individuals slowly enter the no man's land and proceed towards the LTTE checkpoint located within a kilometre. For Sinhalas, this is literally a matter of leaving behind what is familiar and entering a space and experience that is unfamiliar and embedded with anxieties, which not too long ago might also have been quite possibly an encounter with death.

Once a person enters the LTTE border crossing, he or she had to undergo the same kind of procedure they had already experienced further south at the final military checkpoint. This is a simple matter of establishing who was in control. Instead of being questioned in Sinhala and broken Tamil at the military checkpoint, now the questioning was in Tamil and accented Sinhala and sometimes in perfect Sinhala. Some LTTE officials were known to inform Sinhala travellers of their previous positions in the government hierarchy as if to explain their fluency in language. LTTE customs routinely taxed items such as CDs, cameras and other such items if they considered them to be in commercial quantities or not necessary for private consumption. The definition of what is commercial was not self-evident. Each entering vehicle was also taxed depending on its size and type unless some kind of waiver was granted by the officer in charge. If anyone was deemed to physically resemble a military person, he or she was incessantly questioned by LTTE intelligence officers before being allowed to proceed. Sometimes, such individuals are not simply allowed to proceed. If all these phases of the screening process were successful, a travel permit was issued to each traveller or group which had to be presented at all subsequent checkpoints northwards as well as when coming back. This was affectively the LTTE's version of a visa. In this sense, this was not a simple inconsequential crossing of a provincial border but, in terms of the performative political rituals in place at the time, almost the crossing of a 'national' border marking the exit from one country (Sri Lanka) and the entrance to another (Eelam). In fact, the primary purpose of all LTTE performances at the border was geared towards establishing this fact. For travellers, the LTTE border crossing was the portal through which they actually entered the warzone.

The radical change of the political landscape beyond the crossing was self-evident to anyone who crossed the border while the change of the general cultural landscape from Sinhala to Tamil and from Buddhist to Hindu was already evident as far south as Vavuniya itself with the demographic transformation from a Sinhala majority area to a Tamil majority area. Even so, as one left Vavuniya behind, even the Sinhala language signage that was evident in Vavuniya with regard to street signs, identification of government offices, place names and so on suddenly ceased as the LTTE's Tamil only policy in public space manifested itself. In a more telling manner, other indicators of state presence suddenly vanished and LTTE equivalents of these manifested themselves: one could only see smartly clad LTTE police strictly enforcing the speed limit on deteriorated roads instead of government police; armed LTTE sentries in their 'tiger' striped uniforms and civilian clothing instead of government soldiers and home guards at checkpoints; LTTE courts and police stations instead of government courts and police stations. The national flag with its iconic figure of an armed lion, which was visible up to Vavuniya was nowhere to be seen. In its place was the LTTE flag prominently fluttering in the air with the unmistakable image of a ferocious growling tiger as its central motif.

After crossing the border and travelling northwards on the neglected and war-damaged A9 road for five hours, the next prominent place to arrive was Kilinochchi, the 'capital' of the LTTE-held territory. Tamil and English language signage on the side of the road announced the presence of the town ahead and travellers would invariably know they have arrived at a place of significance given the presence of larger and more visible LTTE armed presence as well as more and better-maintained buildings. However, the sense is not that one has arrived at the 'national' capital of Eelam, as the LTTE preferred to refer to Kilinochchi and was attempted through the rituals and statecraft at the Omanthai border crossing and afterwards, but more like the arrival in a frontier town. Nevertheless, it was still a town with a certain politico-cultural personality, which was hard to miss. It is after all the only place along the A9 controlled by the LTTE that had a seeming commercial presence. As such, it is not surprising that Kilinochchi was the only obvious place where the LTTE had put in place facilities specifically to cater to the post-ceasefire tourist traffic, such as the series of restaurants it established in the town soon after the road was opened. While the traffic lasted and the ceasefire held, these were popular stopovers for many tourists and became institutionalized aspects of the war tourist trade and its dynamics. People ate, drank tea and took a respite at these places if they had not brought their own food or provisions to cook on the way.

In 2005, a Sri Lankan journalist noted that the initial phase of 'economic development' in Kilinochchi, after the ceasefire was signed was 'heavily funded by the LTTE, which invested on the restaurants, guest houses and communication centres, all of which generally bring a good return for the investment' (Jayasuriya 2005). He further notes that all three guest houses and restaurants operating in Kilinochchi at the time were owned by the LTTE, maintaining a clear monopoly in the emerging hospitality industry in the region (Jayasuriya 2005). The most popular of the LTTE-run restaurants were Cheran Suvaiakam and Pandian Unavakam.[9] The 'A9' was the only inn with lodging as well as restaurant facilities and, more importantly, also boasted of the only bar along the A9 road within the LTTE-controlled territory, which also catered to the tourist trade but with an emphasis on foreign development workers.[10] It has been referred to as the 'paradise in the warzone' (Rutnam 2005). It was easy to see how uncontaminated alcohol with recognizable labels created an image of paradise in the warzone in the minds of development workers.

Places, Stories and Photographs: 'Stops' in the Warzone Tourist Trail, 2002–2005

After this almost inevitable respite in Kilinochchi, the next place most travellers specifically stopped for purposes of tourism was at Elephant Pass, the official entry into the Jaffna Peninsula. The LTTE held territory south of Elephant Pass while the government held territory north of it including the Jaffna town and the peninsula itself along with the islands off the western coast. Many people invariably got off near the damaged and defaced Elephant Pass road sign with its Sinhala writing almost completely erased but Tamil and English not-so-elegantly highlighted in black paint. Most got themselves photographed with this sign as their backdrop to document their official and corporeal entry into the peninsula. Not too far from the sign, on the right side of the road, with the ravages of time, war and politics inscribed upon its surface, was yet another popular and constantly photographed site that had captured the imagination of almost everyone who embarked on the warzone tourist trail. This is the disabled bulldozer that had been used as a modified battle tank by the LTTE in one of the many battles against the Sri Lanka Army in 1991 (see Figure 2.2).

It is supposed to have been stopped in the midst of its destructive path by a Sri Lankan soldier called Gamini Kularatana[11] who had already entered the popular annals of Sinhala heroism in the south through the

Figure 2.2

LTTE Bulldozer Monument commemorating a 1991 battle with the Sri Lanka Army, Elephant Pass

Source: Author.

electronic and print media. Almost every Sinhala who travelled to the north during this period would have known his name, the action he was credited with and the reference this action had to this disabled tank. However, soon after the battle in which the Sri Lanka Army triumphed, and for a considerable period of time afterwards, it simply remained as yet another remnant of war which only local residents could identify with any degree of accuracy. For others, it was merely yet another metal carcass created by the progression of war. However, soon after the road was opened, it quickly became a major attraction and a forum for Tamil and English language graffiti. As it was well within LTTE-held territory, the political wing of the LTTE placed an official sign on it in Tamil in 2003 declaring it a monument in memory of the 1991 battle and decreed its protection and that no handbills should be pasted on it. With this act, the LTTE converted what was effectively an impromptu monument into a more formal one.

However from the moment travel to the north became possible in 2002, this monument narrated two distinctly different narratives depending on the nature of the gaze. The more dominant, formal and institutionalized presence at the site during this period was that of the LTTE. As such, for most Tamil travellers who could both read the graffiti and the LTTE's formal notification, the silent hulk of the bulldozer narrated a story of Tamil nationalism, heroism and selfless sacrifice for the cause of Tamil Eelam. That is also the story told to them by the LTTE representatives in plain clothes at the site who were nevertheless not available on a routine basis. Interestingly enough, however, the LTTE never specifically dedicated it to the man who died driving it into battle, unlike the latter Sinhala metamorphosis of the monument which was almost obsessively focused on one person. It was simply an abstract monument to the cause of political separation that the LTTE militarily pursued and the kind of heroism it entailed. By 2013, the name of the man who drove the vehicle, known informally as Sara,[12] was forgotten by many writers who have written about Tamil nationalism and its various manifestations and by many others who live in the region with whom I had discussed the matter. His memory had slipped through the annals of a defeated insurrection.

For Sinhala travellers, most of whom would not have been able to read the writing on the mental remnant or speak with the LTTE representatives who were sometimes on site, the story was one of Sinhala resistance, national pride and selfless sacrifice for the motherland by their own hero, Corporal Gamini Kularatna, the man credited for disabling the modified battle vehicle and stopping the LTTE advance in the 1991 battle. Their collective consciousness was simply not receptive to the story of Sara or what he represented. Instead, Kularatna's story had already become popular lore in the Sinhala south through the heroic narratives constructed by the print and electronic media. Besides, in 2001, 10 years after his death, the government issued a postal stamp worth LKR 3.50 carrying both his image and that of the disabled vehicle, affectively resurrecting his memory one year prior to the opening of the road. Thousands of ordinary letters crisscrossing the country often carried this stamp, making its presence quite omnipresent well into the time the road was reopened. In this context, Sinhala tourists already came equipped with a widely circulating heroic narrative with which they could easily associate the bulldozer irrespective of the official LTTE story which was more audible and visible on site. So for my neighbours and the young friend who made their adventure trip northwards in 2002 and very self-consciously posed in front of the battle tank to generate their own collections of print and digital images, the LTTE and Tamil nationalist interpretation was irrelevant. It seemingly had not even entered their consciousness. As my neighbour's wife said pointing to the photographs of the bulldozer, '[T]his is where "elder brother"[13] Kularatna sacrificed his life. Can't believe he could stop something this big.'

At this stage of tourism, if the bulldozer monument was the first 'formal' stop in the trail, the second stop for logistical and logical reasons for most Sinhala tourists, once they arrived in Jaffna town, was the Naga Vihara Temple. Most looked for accommodation in the temple for the time they were going to be in town as well as for advice on where to go, where to buy things and also where to stay if the temple could not accommodate them. Located in Stanley Road in the heart of Jaffna town, the temple did offer basic and very reasonably priced community-type accommodation. While most people who went to the temple seeking accommodation were Sinhalas and Buddhists, it was not necessary to be either to be accommodated in the temple. The temple was initiated in the 1960s to cater to the spiritual needs of the handful of Buddhist civil servants posted to the north as well as the religious needs of the small but prominent Sinhala Buddhist business community settled in Jaffna since at least the 1950s. From the beginning, for Sinhala travellers to Jaffna, the temple was a place of Sinhala and Buddhist cultural familiarity located within a landscape of Hindu and Tamil cultural unfamiliarity. Its facilities and the practice of accommodation was nothing unusual given the fact that all Buddhist temples would ideally not turn back a traveller looking for accommodation and would put him up in a sermon hall or other such building that was not in use all the time. But, ideally, such accommodation was not open to women. However, larger and more affluent temples which were also regular pilgrim sites had constructed special dormitory-like facilities called *vishrama shala* (halls for resting) with cooking facilities to accommodate relatively large groups of people. This is the kind of public facility that the Naga Vihara provided, in a very small scale in the pre-war period, which expanded into a fairly large operation when the ceasefire came into effect, which remain in place up to now. Heavily damaged in the war, the temple was abandoned for about a decade from 1986 to 1995. This was during the LTTE occupation of Jaffna in 1986 and the Indian Peace Keeping Force's (IPKF) occupation of the city in 1987, as well as from 1989 to 1995 when the LTTE ruled the city again. After the military's recapture of Jaffna in 1995, significant reconstruction of the temple took place under both military and state sponsorship. This was mostly because the temple was seen as an extension of the state's and the military's Sinhala-Buddhist identity.

Officially known as the 'Nagavihara International Buddhist Centre', the temple is clearly a relatively recent structure in Jaffna and is more a cultural centre than a spiritual site. It served as the most important routing, guidance and accommodation centre for Sinhala tourists during the first phase of warzone tourism. Nevertheless, despite this history of recent origins, the temple seems to have embarked upon an informal process of acquiring a longer and hazier historical trajectory for its existence. This reinvention has to be located and understood in the specific context of the temple's revived post-2002 importance in political and cultural terms. In the Sri Lankan context, and particularly beyond the craft of formal historiography which itself is now a politically motivated dying art, the lines of separation between historical fact, mythological assumption and pure fantasy of recent origin are not always too clear. A Buddhist monk who stayed at the temple in 2003 as part of a group of pilgrims told me the following story in a conversation:

[E]ven though the present buildings in the temple are not very old, it is actually a very ancient site. The war has destroyed the ancient evidence. As we know, when the Jaya Sree Maha Bodhi was brought to Sri Lanka by Theri Sangamitta, King Devanampiyatissa went to Jaffna from Anuradhapura to bring it back to the capital. She landed in Dambakola Patuna where there is a temple now to mark her landing. On his way back to Anuradhapura with the *bo* sapling accompanied by the Theri and her company who had come from India on the instructions of Emperor Asoka, the leaders of a local Naga tribe had requested the king to keep the *bo* sapling in their locality for one week for veneration. The king readily agreed. The place where the *bo* sapling had been kept for one week at that time is where the present Naga Vihara now stands.[14]

This story has been constructed with reference to the historical fact that a *bo* sapling (*ficus religiosa*) was brought to Sri Lanka for veneration by an emissary of Emperor Asoka soon after Buddhism was introduced to the country. The emissary has been identified in the *Mahawamsa*, the historical chronicle of Sri Lanka written in the Pali language, as Theri Sangamitta, the daughter of the emperor. In one strike of mythical imagination, a temple of recent origin had been transported deep into the hazy beginnings of Buddhist history in the island. It is not important if the story is believed by visitors or if it is widespread. What is important is that the story did emerge at this time, which is often narrated now by many visitors while it also has at least limited internet circulation.[15] So on ground, the story is in the process of becoming fact by virtue of public consumption.

One of the most sought after and revered destinations in this phase of warzone tourism for Sinhalas was the island off the western coast of the Jaffna peninsula known in Sinhala as Naga Dipa, which laterally means the 'island of nagas or snakes' (see Figures 2.3 and 2.4). Locally, the island is known as Nainativu in Tamil. Often, after a rest at Naga Vihara in Jaffna town, the trip to Naga Dipa was the next destination in the warzone tourist trail even though the significance of the island had nothing to do with Sri Lanka's civil war. Interestingly, however, in terms of mythological references, the importance of Naga Dipa to Sinhala Buddhists comes partially from a war that almost happened but did not, due to the intervention of the Buddha in an interesting and ancient narrative of what one might call 'conflict resolution' in today's context. Naga Dipa hosts a local population of about 3,000 Tamil-speaking people, most of whom are ethnic Tamils, along with a few hundred Muslims. Most locals are fishermen. The island's most important buildings historically have been the Naga Dipa Buddhist temple which is the focus of my attention here and the Naga Pooshani Amman Hindu Kovil. The island is

Figure 2.3

Boat ride to Naga Dipa Island

Source: Author.

approximately 30 km from the mainland coast of the Jaffna peninsula. The main access point to Naga Dipa is from Kurikattuwan, located in the island Punkudutivu. Depending on ocean conditions, one could reach Naga Dipa by boat in about 20 to 40 minutes from Kurikattuwan. Punkudutivu itself is connected via a causeway to the island Kayts, known in Tamil as Urkavarrurai, which is the largest island in this group of islands while Kayts needs to be reached via a longer causeway from the mainland. This combination of motor transport via low lying causeways and by boat adds to the sense of adventure that people experience in travelling to Naga Dipa, while the relative difficulty of access and the time spent on travel despite the small distance from the mainland also reiterates its identity as a pilgrim site and not as a simple destination of leisure. During the first phase of tourism, travel was more difficult as the war was still ongoing though mostly away from the sight of travellers. At the time, local fishermen were not allowed to venture into the sea and the sea itself was a contested space. This meant that travellers had to travel in overcrowded navy boats and had to wait for long hours to find a boat.

Figure 2.4

Buddhist temple, Naga Dipa

Source: Author.

Nevertheless, it does not seem that these difficulties hindered the interest of travellers in visiting the island. In fact, it remained one of the most visited sites in the first phase of warzone tourism, mostly emanating from its religious significance.

The importance of Naga Dipa had nothing to do with the war, as already noted. However, access to it had been denied to local travellers and pilgrims for well over a decade due to the expansion of the civil war. The only outsiders who could visit the island and the temple with its unusual silver coloured *stupa* for a long time were the naval personnel based on the island. Prior to the outbreak of war, the island was a well-known pilgrim destination for Buddhists as one of the '16 great places of worship'.[16] As such, it was part of the Buddhist imagination of the geographic space of the country itself. Its significance in the trajectory of Buddhist worship comes from the belief that the Buddha himself visited Naga Dipa in his second purported visit to Sri Lanka. The Pali historical chronicle of the country, the *Mahawamsa* (Pali Text Society 1912), in its first chapter titled 'The Visit of the Thathagatha', narrates all the stories of the Buddha's visits to the country including the visit to Naga Dipa. Verses 44 to 70 specifically present the details of his visit to Naga Dipa as well as its wider political context in considerable detail.

Mahawamsa notes that the Buddha in his fifth year of buddhahood foresaw 'that a war, caused by a gem-set throne, was like[ly] to come to pass between the Nagas Mahodara and Culodara, uncle and nephew, and their followers' (Pali Text Society 1912: verses 45–46). In order to avoid a destructive war, the Buddha 'took his sacred alms-bowl and his robes, and, from compassion for the Nagas, sought the Naga Dipa' (Pali Text Society 1912: verse 47). So according to this story, the Buddha's visit to Naga Dipa was for the explicit purpose of halting an impending war between two closely related individuals, not unlike the civil war that consumed closely culturally related Sinhala and Tamil communities since the late 1970s. As narrated in the chronicle, the inhabitants in the island were Nagas, which in the Sinhala imagination varies between two meanings: a group of tribal people called Nagas who worshiped *nagas* or snakes or simply a personification of snakes. What is clear is that the current Sinhala term of the island, Naga Dipa, emanates at least from the time of the *Mahawamsa* and is a direct reference to its perceived original inhabitants of the place.

According to the *Mahawmsa*, one of the warriors preparing for war, Mahodara, was a king 'in a naga-kingdom in the ocean, that covered half a thousand yojanas' and was 'gifted with miraculous power' (Pali Text Society 1912: verses 48–49). So clearly, the main protagonist was not just any regional king, but someone with enormous supernatural power. Mahodara's challenger was his younger sister's son (his nephew), Culodara (Pali Text Society 1912: verse 49–50). According to the *Mahawamsa* story, Culodara's grandfather had given to his daughter 'a splendid throne of jewels' (Pali Text Society 1912: verses 50–51) and its ownership was not clearly decided prior to the death of the elder Naga king. The impending war between uncle and nephew over this throne was to settle this issue. On the other hand, Mahodara was not the only character with access to supernatural power in this scenario. As the *Mahawamsa* observed, Culodara's followers, 'the Nagas of the mountains were armed with miraculous power' (Pali Text Society 1912: verse 51), and as a result, the consequences of the war were likely to be catastrophic. It is to avert this catastrophe that the Buddha is believed to have intervened in coming to Naga Dipa.

In order to avert the crisis, the Buddha decided to hover 'in mid-air above the battlefield' (Pali Text Society 1912: verses 58–59). Even though he usually 'drives away (spiritual) darkness', on this occasion, from his position in mid-air, he instead 'called forth dread darkness over the Nagas' (Pali Text Society 1912: verses 58–59). This spectacle terrified them and led to the halting of the war that was about to begin. Making use of this respite, the Buddha comforted 'those who were distressed by terror' and 'once again spread light abroad' (Pali Text Society 1912: verse 59). When the Nagas saw the 'Blessed One they joyfully did reverence to the Master's feet' (Pali Text Society 1912: verse 59). In this context of the Buddha's victory, he is supposed to have preached the *dhamma* to the Naga kings and their followers who accepted the moral positions of Buddhism contained in the dhamma (Pali Text Society 1912: verse 62). As an outcome of this encounter, the two Naga leaders who nearly went to war 'gladly gave up the throne to the Sage' (Pali Text Society 1912: verse 61). The story on the genesis of Naga Dipa as a Buddhist place of worship is woven within these mythological references and suggests that the original shrine had entombed this throne as an artefact blessed by the Buddha himself during his presence in the location. This story elaborated in the *Mahawamsa* is widely known in Sinhala Buddhist society and is often narrated to children as a story, though many of its details might be dropped in these numerous re-narrations.

Nevertheless, Naga Dipa's importance to Buddhist travellers comes from their belief in this long established and widely known story. It is quite literally a place steeped in mythology, and the stories of this mythological cluster has survived the passage of time and in the present context have become an integral part of the island's formal historiography. So, the entire story is no longer myth; it is a historical fact which is popularly seen, perceived and narrated as such. On the other hand, as a story with its own internal structure of logic, it is not merely a story of the Buddha's visit to the island. It is also a story of exhibiting his enormous miraculous power, the defeat of a non-Buddhist tribe by the Buddha himself, the victory of Buddhism in this encounter and, more importantly, the conversion of the Nagas to Buddhism, which was also symbolically the arrival of light or civilization in a place of darkness. Seen in this sense, Naga Dipa is seen as a place where Buddhism had arrived and made its presence felt among the people and within the place in the life time of the Buddha himself, which is long before Buddhism had formally and historically arrived in Sri Lanka.

It was then a hallowed place of worship that was lost to Sinhala Buddhists as a result of the expansion of war and the threat posed by the LTTE. In this context, the newly found ability to visit the location on one hand was a matter of re-establishing a practice of faith that had long been un-practiced while on the other hand it was a matter of revisiting, albeit momentarily and amidst considerable challenges, an important spatial entity in the Buddhist imagination of the country itself which had been inaccessible. In this manner, visiting Naga Dipa at this time was both the fulfilment of a religious obligation as well as a political obligation in at least monetarily reasserting the territorial integrity of the land in terms of collective Sinhala Buddhist political consciousness.

After the visit to Naga Dipa was concluded, many people undertook yet another activity that is presented as a pilgrimage in contemporary times. This is a visit to a location known locally as Madagal, on the north-western edge of the Jaffna peninsula. About 20 km from Jaffna town by road, this seaside location literally faces the south-eastern coast line of the Indian subcontinent located approximately 35 km across the Palk Bay further north-west. Known to Sinhala Buddhist travellers as Dambakola Patuna, its location has considerable politico-cultural significance which has become more emphasized in the post-war era. In fact, Dambakola Patuna does not constitute an established pilgrim centre in the conventional sense. As such, it has never been part of formalized pilgrimage trajectories such as the worship of 'eight great places' or the 'sixteen great places'. However, there are many pilgrim sites in the country that do not fall within these two trajectories but are nevertheless important pilgrim sites on their own right. Their status as pilgrim sites has evolved historically as a result of continuous practice. As importantly, their claims for veneration usually stem from historical factors associated with the site or mythological assumptions associated with these sites. Compared to these general possibilities, there is no tangible historical evidence from the recent or the more distant past to suggest what is presently identified as Dambakola Patuna has been a pilgrim site at any time. It also offers no archaeological evidence on the ground for the mytho-historical claims of the new Buddhist temple and the accompanying structures that have recently come up at the site.

The temple that has become the site of recent attention is officially known as the Dambakola Patuna Sangamitta Viharaya (see Figure 2.5) and is named after the Buddhist nun who is believed to have brought the original plant of the *bodhi*[17] tree to Sri Lanka during the reign of

Figure 2.5

Stupa at Dambakola Patuna temple, Madagal

Source: Author.

King Devanam Piyatissa (307 BC to 267 BC). The arrival of the nun and the sapling being ultimately planted in the capital city of Anuradhapura which survives up to now are historical facts. Two chapters in the *Mahawamsa*, Chapter XVIII titled, 'Receiving of the Great Bodhi Tree' and Chapter XIV titled, 'The Coming of the Bodhi Tree', offer considerable details enmeshed in miraculous embellishments: the story of the Sri Lankan king's desire for the bodhi tree as an object of veneration, his dispatching of an emissary to the court of Emperor Asoka in India with the request, the Emperor's attempts at securing the sapling and, finally, its arrival in Sri Lanka and it being planted in Anuradhapura amidst much fanfare and royal patronage. These stories are also as importantly an integral part of the very strong collective consciousness of Sinhala Buddhists that informs the genesis of their religious identity as a specific moral community and are an active part of their imagination of the past.

Beyond the essential historical facts, the narrative of Sangamitta's arrival as well as the sacred bodhi tree's final location in Anuradhapura have given rise to numerous sub-narratives which often change their details and add extraordinary elements to the narratives that take them beyond formal understandings of history into the realm of myth. In fact, what the *Mahawamsa* offers in great detail constitutes an amalgamation of both of these elements. It is in this active discursive space where the reasons for the location of the present temple in this place and the structure of recent mythologies that have arisen around it could be understood. *Mahawamsa*, it its Chapter XIV notes that 'on that same day, the great Bodhi-tree arrived here in Jambukola' (Pali Text Society 1912: verse 23). The place name Jambukola (sometimes also known as Jambukola Pattana) has been rendered into Sinhala as Dambakola (or Dambakola Patuna). The Pali word *pattana* and the Sinhala word *patuna* literally mean harbour. In this context, it is quite clear that historical references as well as popular belief have a strong tradition is asserting that the bodhi tree and Sangamitta arrived in Sri Lanka via a harbour called Dambakola Patuna. Beyond this, however, its exact location has never been historically and archaeologically established. Equally as importantly, the local village of Madagal where the temple is now placed and is being called Dambakola Patuna by Sinhalas by popular practice was never referred to as such in any formal governmental documents including maps of the Survey Department until the relatively recent temple-building project began. Equally as importantly, there is no evidence of any local narratives in the area which refers to Sangamitta's purported arrival in Madagal with such a crucial cultural artefact such as the sapling of the bodhi tree. Given this liminality in historical and archaeological facts as well as the absence of mythological significations to specifically mark the place, it is not clear why the present location around Madagal has been popularly and specifically identified as the ancient Dambakola Patuna by many Sinhalas. But in the emotional landscape of interpreting Sri Lanka's past, this has never been questioned or been of any consequence to most people once the assertion had become part of a tradition of belief which has now merged into fact. As such, for travellers and pilgrims who began visiting the site in the first phase of warzone tourism in relatively small numbers which steadily increased once the second phase began after the end of war, the temple simply marks the place where Sangamitta landed with the bodhi tree.

However, according to available information, the temple's present incarnation stems from the 1997 action of the Sri Lanka Navy to plant a sapling of the famed bodhi tree in Anuradhapura, which itself is one of the holiest Buddhist pilgrim sites in the country. So instead of the bodhi tree travelling from the court of Emperor Asoka via historic Dambakola Patuna to Anuradhapura over 2000 years ago, what is clearer is that a sapling of the ancient tree in Anuradhapura travelled to Madagal in 1997. And with that event, the temple's legitimacy was popularly and publically established as the site of ancient Dambakola Patuna irrespective of the absence of tangible evidence. It seems that its importance as a pilgrim site initially came about mostly as a result of the influx of Buddhist tourists in the first phase of warzone tourism, which has significantly expanded in the second phase of tourism due to construction activities in the place that are facilitated by the absence of war and the 'adoption' of the site by the Sri Lanka Navy since the late 1990s. Since 1997, the navy has actively built infrastructure at the temple while also simultaneously promoting pilgrimage to the site. By now, the temple specifically identifies itself as a pilgrim centre and offers instructions to potential pilgrims on how to be dressed, what not to do and what not to bring to the site.[18]

The temple's official website operated by the Sri Lanka Navy makes the following observation about its history:

> Arhat Mahinda's historic visit was soon followed by the arrival of Arhat Sangamitta on an Unduwap Full Moon Poya Day with a sapling of the Southern bough of India's Jaya Sri Maha Bodhi under which the Buddha attained Enlightenment. It was Arhat Sangamitta who pioneered the Order of Bhikkhuni (Bhikkhuni Sasana) in Sri Lanka.[19]

The website further notes,

> [A]s the mission was a success Arhat Sangamitta and retinue arrived in Dambakola Patuna Port with the Bo Sapling placed in a golden bowl. The king Devanampiyatissa got into sea up to a neck-deep depth and received the Sri Maha Bodhiya. After performing the necessary rituals, the Bo Sapling was ceremoniously carried to Mahamevuna Uyana in Anuradhapura and was planted at an auspicious time.[20]

So the temple's claim to fame and historical legitimacy which establishes its logic as a site worthy of pilgrimage is not based on a simple assertion. As noted above, one of the two most important historical events associated with Buddhism in Sri Lanka is supposed to have happened at this site: the bringing of the bodhi tree by Sangamitta. With that event, the country underwent what can only be described as a cultural revolution. That is, the establishment of a specific type of Buddhist worship based on the veneration of this specific tree as a practice which at present is prevalent throughout the country and the establishment of the order of nuns in Sri Lanka by Sangamitta, which the website itself refers to. Moreover, as Sangamitta is strongly believed to be the daughter of Emperor Asoka, the temple's location is also associated with the perceived landing of such an important emissary that directly links the Indian and Sri Lankan histories of the ancient period. So the temple is not only presenting itself as a historical site, but also as a seminal gateway to Buddhist culture and religious practice in Sri Lanka and a point that links two great histories.

The temple's perceived historical demise and its recent reinvention has been explained as follows:

> It was ruined from the times of invasions of Cholas, Portuguese, Dutch and English and due to LTTE terrorist activities. It was safeguarded by the Sri Lanka Navy, they renovated it and now it is opened for the local and foreign devotees for their religious observances.[21]

So, the temple, which according to the website 'has been one of the sacred places of Sri Lanka Buddhists from the times of King Devanampiyathissa' went into decay as a result of South Indian and European invasions and finally due to the activities of the LTTE. So affectively, what the Sri Lanka Navy claims is that the temple whose presence was erased as a result of the activities of historical foes has finally been overcome by making visible its presence again. This also conveniently explains the post-1997 temple with its active expansion since 2011 in a situation where no historical evidence for long-term historical continuity can be seen on ground. By 2012, a statue of Sangamitta (see Figure 2.6) and another depicting king Devanampiyathissa receiving the bodhi sapling had been built at the site by the Sri Lanka Navy, introducing a sculptural rendition of the temple's narratives of historicity and authenticity while also addressing contemporaneously the absence of archaeological evidence on the ground to substantiate these claims. Moreover, by now the temple undertakes regular religious activities as well as a special ceremony to mark the arrival of the bodhi sapling, which has made it a functioning fully fledged temple even though its regular devotees still happen to be members of the Sri Lanka Navy stationed in the peninsula.

What does all this mean in terms of travel and its politics? The Sri Lanka Navy's adoption of the temple and building its infrastructure, particularly after the war ended, has clearly established the navy's self-identity as an entity that is very Buddhist without contradictions. More importantly,

Figure 2.6

Statue of Teri Sangamitta at Dambakola Patuna temple, Madagal

Source: Author.

given the close correlation that religion has with ethnicity in Sri Lanka
and Buddhism's close association with Sinhalas in this scheme of things,
the temple is a self-consciously Sinhala Buddhist cultural enclave in an
expansive Hindu Tamil emotional and socio-cultural landscape. In a way,
it is not too different from the cultural role of familiarity that the Naga

Vihara in Jaffna town plays, as described earlier in this chapter. However, from the beginning the Sangamitta Viharaya has been promoting itself as a historically identified site which has played a crucial role in the evolution of Sinhala and Buddhist cultural practices. On the other hand, though in small numbers in the first phase of tourism and in significantly large numbers in the second phase of tourism, people's attraction to the place also means that the politico-historical identity that the temple has created for itself is widely accepted by many Sinhalas. The more they visit the temple, the more the historical contradictions and gaps will cease to be seen and the seamless history that the temple narrates would become part of a larger popular discourse. This has already happened to a significant extent. At the same time, pilgrimage to Sangamitta Viharaya in the first phase of warzone tourism was a matter of piety in terms of touching base with a place that most visitors believed was the location through which the sacred bodhi tree entered the country. At that time, it was also a place that was relatively difficult to access due to prevailing war conditions. However, when pilgrim numbers dramatically increased in the second phase, it was not simply a matter of piety but also a political act of reclaiming what was perceived as land lost, not too long ago, to the LTTE. On the other hand, the establishment, expansion and increasing popularity of the temple was well in line with addressing a major concern that has been long articulated by Sinhala nationalists. That is, Buddhist sites in the Tamil-dominated north-east had been steadily Tamilized, Hinduized or simply erased due to the relative absence of a Sinhala Buddhist presence in the area. In this specific situation, if the Sri Lanka Navy addressed this concern by establishing a new temple in a location that 'tradition' (if not history) and convenience had vested with religio-historical and nationalist importance, this effort was legitimized by the larger Sinhala population through the rapid popularization of the site as a major pilgrim destination within the travels of warzone tourism.

A somewhat 'unusual' but popular destination in the warzone tourist trail after 2002 until the ceasefire ended was the Jaffna Public Library (see Figure 2.7) located in close proximity to the remnants of the Dutch Fort in Jaffna. That popularity remained even after the war ended in 2009 and the second phase of warzone tourism began. I refer to the library as 'unusual' as it is neither a religious site nor a structure set up by or associated with the LTTE. However, rather prominent statues of Saraswati, the goddess of knowledge and Reverend T.M.F. Long, a former rector of St. Patrick's College in Jaffna and a highly respected educationist in the

Figure 2.7

The Jaffna Public Library with a statue of goddess Saraswati at its front entrance

Source: Author.

area, creates a sense of curiosity in the minds of tourists about the iconic building which stands in the background. Beyond this curiosity, the history of the library and its location in the civil war has some relevance with regard to why it became a tourist destination when no other library or non-LTTE structure in the country had ever achieved such status.

The library began as a personal initiative of K.M. Chellappah in 1933 in his own home. In 1934, a number of Jaffna citizens came together to take this personal initiative to a more formal phase by establishing a full-fledged library. On 1 August 1934, this group succeeded in setting up a formal library in a rented room at Hospital Road in Jaffna. Two years later, the library was moved to a building near the municipal offices and town hall. The construction of the library in the present location began on 29 March 1953 and was opened to the public on 11 October 1959 (Thurairajah 2002). From the very beginning, rather than being a government venture, the Jaffna Library was a collective venture of enlightened citizens of Jaffna, even though it later became an entity under the Jaffna Municipality. Over a considerable period of time, the library became a well-known repository of priceless manuscripts that had much to do with the social and cultural life of the people in Jaffna and the northern region of Sri Lanka. According to Thurairajah (2002), there were more than one hundred thousand rare books and documents and manuscripts and those written on palm leaves and stored in sandalwood boxes'.

The library also hosted a collection of 'newspapers and journals published hundred years ago in Jaffna' and 'about 10,000 hand-written documents' and 'Roman Catholic books published in 1586' (Thurairajah 2002). Thurairajah further notes that that the library contained an extremely rare copy of the well-known book, *A Historical Relation of the Island of Ceylon*, written by Robert Knox, based on his experience as a prisoner in the Kingdom of Kandy in the 1600s as well as a copy of *Ceylon During the Dutch Rule* by Philips Baiudius written in 1672 and numerous other texts pertaining to the history of the region and written by local scholars of local significance (Thurairajah 2002).

The library was designed in the Indo-Saracenic style, in this specific case informed clearly by Tamil architecture from South India, and was designed by the Madras-based architect, S. Narasimhan while S.R. Ranganathan, a Delhi-based expert, was appointed as the advisor to set up the logistics of the library according to international standards available at the time (Thurairajah 2002). Since its establishment in the present location in 1959, the library has been a visible and dominant presence in Jaffna befitting the pride and reverence with which the people in the region perceived the institution. It is also quite clear that the library evolved over a long period of time in different stages as a collective community effort and the final edifice that came into being was a central component of Tamil cultural and nationalist pride in northern Sri Lanka.

This library, in addition to being a source of significant knowledge, was very closely associated with the Tamil ethno-cultural identity in northern Sri Lanka and was also an important reference to the region's past. Irrespective of this context, or perhaps because of it, the library was burned down between 31 May and 2 June 1981 by Sinhala thugs belonging to the United National Party (UNP) which formed the national government at the time (Kanagasabapathipillai 2014). The culprits were transported to the site for that specific purpose while the entire incident was carried out as police and security forces looked on. The immediate catalyst for the violence and the destruction was the District Development Council elections which was won by the Tamil United Liberation Front just before the incident and a rally held by the party in the context of which three Sinhala police officers were killed. In a single incident and within two nights, such a crucial aspect of Tamil self-identity was violently erased, which has since been referred to by many Tamils as an act of 'cultural genocide'. It remains a significant emotional blow to the collective Tamil psyche. Kanthaswamy Karunakaran, a citizen of Jaffna, recollected the incident in the following words:

I saw the popular Jaffna Public Library was in flames in 1981, from my home.... It was heartbreaking for me to witness the library in flames, but I had no way to go anywhere near the library during the attack, in order to safeguard the books. (Kanagasabapathipillai 2014)

Rohini Pararajasingam, former chief librarian of the University of Jaffna, shares her own memories of the incident:

I think that, when libraries are targeted, the idea is to destroy entire culture, and to deny learning. There is a famous Tamil saying, that to look at one's own reading is to know one's mind and culture. It extremely hurts us. We love our books, and we lost most precious ones. (Kanagasabapathipillai 2014)

In 2004, a 70-year old resident and a regular user of the library who also saw it go up in flames articulated his own thoughts of the incident in the following words:

When the library was burnt that day, what was destroyed was not simply a building and a collection of books, but a reference to our existence in the history of this land. With that act, a part of me died and a part of everyone in the north was also taken away by force. How can one forget that?[22]

The trauma of the destruction of the library was not merely a matter of the past. It was an emotion that continued well into the present.

In 1982, though an attempt was made by concerned citizens of Jaffna to collect books as well as funds to renovate the library, and in fact work on repairs was begun, by 1983 the continuing militarization of the inter-ethnic conflict caught up with the library yet again. After the ambush of 13 Sinhala soldiers in Jaffna in July 1983 and the resultant anti-Tamil violence in many parts of Sinhala-dominated areas in the country, the partially repaired structure was damaged by bullets and bombing. Subsequently, in 1985, consequent to a Tamil rebel attack on a nearby police station, soldiers reportedly entered the partially constructed building and detonated explosives, destroying much of the building. After this, no other community efforts were undertaken to rebuild the library, mostly as a result of deteriorating security conditions.

In 1998, the government of President Chandrika Kumaratunga began the process of rebuilding the library, both as part of the president's reconciliatory approach to ethnic politics as well as a point of departure to blame the UNP for the destruction of the library as a long-term political slogan. The renovation work attempted to ensure that its iconic outer façade resembled its pre-1981 stature and personality. A request by some citizens to keep a section of the library in its destroyed form as a constant reminder of the tragedy which consumed it was turned down by the government. Though the government was critical of the previous UNP government under whose watch the library was destroyed, the Kumaratunga regime was also interested in an exercise of complete erasure of the library's demise within the physical reconstruction of the building. It was fearful that any attempt to preserve a section of the building as a monument to the tragedy might make it a shrine to nationalist elements among the population as well as for the LTTE. By 2001, much of the reconstruction was complete while the public was given access to the library largely devoid of books in 2003. However, due to pressure from the LTTE, the library was never officially opened, though it was something that President Kumaratunga was very keen to do. Nevertheless, local people came to the library in reasonable numbers to read newspapers and young people used it as a place to study. But by and large, when the first phase of warzone tourism began, the library mostly offered visitors a large number of empty bookcases while the scars of its destruction had been physically erased as a necessary part of the reconstruction effort. This is the sight that greeted the Sinhala tourists when they began pouring into the library since about late 2002.

Their visit however was not of intellectual or academic interest, in the sense that no one came to use the library in search of knowledge. Busses, cars and vans simply parked outside the premises in the street and people trouped across the library chatting as if they were visiting any other tourist site, sometimes clicking photographs of the empty book-shelves. Kanti Amarasinghe, a housewife who had come to Jaffna with her family in 2004, pointing to six photographs of the Jaffna library out of her collection of 73 colour prints neatly collected in a plastic pho-tograph album said: 'See, almost all the bookshelves are empty. What damage the war has done. This is what the LTTE and the Indian army has done'.[23] Interestingly, while she immediately knew that the library was destroyed and the present incarnation was its reconstructed former self, she assumed this was a direct result of the war itself in which the LTTE and the Indian Army (known as the IPKF) were responsible. She did not realize that the damage was caused by Sinhala elements quite some time before the interethnic mistrust between the Sinhalas and the Tamils had lapsed into a full-blown civil war. My neighbours who visited Jaffna in 2002, with whose story I began this discussion, also visited the library accompanied by a soldier who was a friend of the family. As the head of the family told me,

> [I]t was a beautiful building. Like a Hindu temple. There was a statue of Goddess Saraswati at the entrance. She is the goddess of knowledge. But the library was quite empty. The books were not there. I saw some Tamil newspapers. But they need more books. The younger brother from the army who took us there said that the library was burnt by the LTTE in 1980s. What a waste.[24]

In this case also, while my neighbour was saddened by the absence of books in the library, the information he was given by their soldier-friend as to who was responsible was incorrect. As indicated by these narratives, it appears that with the lapse of over 20 years since the destruction of the library, at least in some instances, attempts have been made to shift the blame from Sinhala thugs and military and police personnel who were clearly responsible for the act to the LTTE and the Indian Army who had nothing to do with the incident. Interestingly, at the time of the incident in 1981, almost no newspapers in the south reported it in any significant details and no attempts were made to bring the culprits to book even though oppositional elements have on and off blamed the UNP for the incident. One clear exception to this state of relative silence in the Sinhala public sphere was that of H.A.I Goonetileke, a well-known librarian and bibliographer. Writing to the *Tamil Times* in October 1981, he observed,

> [T]he gutted building is a grim testimonial to savage and bestial tendencies of communal hate.... Complete destruction by an act of calculated and cold-blooded vandalism of the Jaffna Public Library is the most wounding to the sensibility of our brethren in the North and must outrage the humane feelings of every person in the land, whatever his political, racial or religious persuasion. (Kanagasabapathipillai 2014)

However, this does not mean that Sinhala society is unaware of what happened. But distancing the incident from their collective conscience and, in at least some instances, shifting the blame allows visiting Sinhala tourists to go through this iconic building as 'tourists' without openly expressing any feelings of societal guilt. It was simply an interesting building that was damaged by war, which is now repaired by the government, a sign of 'development' and 'reconciliation'.

Beyond what has been described previously, much of what remained in warzone travel had to do with locations that were directly linked to the war itself. In this context, one of the first sites most people visited after their obligatory stops at Naga Vihara, Naga Dipa, Kandarodai Temple and often at Sagamiththa Viharaya and the Jaffna Public Library was the Kittu Memorial Park simply because it is conveniently located within Jaffna city. The LTTE referred to the park as the Kittu Children's Park. It was established in memory of Sathasivam Krishnakumar, who was better known locally as Colonel Kittu. The park also memorialized nine other LTTE members who died in an action of collective suicide in January 1993 in an encounter with the Indian Navy. The Indian Navy captured the ship the LTTE group was travelling in and attempted to arrest the group. To avoid capture the entire group committed suicide and the incident has since entered the annals of LTTE heroism. This version of the story has been collectively accepted without contradictions by many local people as well. The monument complex was established by reorienting the pre-existing park managed by the Jaffna Municipality by the LTTE as a site of remembrance when Jaffna was under its rule.

In the immediate local context, no significant transformation took place in the manner in which the park was utilized by local people. They came to the park in the evenings, quite often with their children as they had been doing for a considerable period. The difference after the park's reinvention was that the people were obliged to relax, spend their leisure and play with their children under the unavoidable gaze of the larger than life image of Kittu that was prominently installed in the middle of the park (see Figure 2.8). However, there was significant difference in the pictorial rendition of Kittu compared to most LTTE public imagery of its fighters, which are usually shown in military fatigues and often carrying automatic weapons. In this specific instance, Kittu was depicted wearing civilian clothes. Even so, he also wore a highly visible belt of bullets and a pistol in a hip holster, as if to indicate his military role despite the civilianization of his public personality. As a backdrop for this central image, and emanating from it, one could see a painting representing the midsea incident in which Kittu and his colleagues perished. This background painting consists of four interrelated elements: the sea, a moving boat, an explosion and small images of four of the others who died in the incident in LTTE military uniform. At the time the LTTE was in charge of Jaffna, this reincarnated park functioned as a space for annual memorial activities in memory of Kittu and special commemorations of other

Figure 2.8

Kittu Memorial (main artwork), Jaffna

Source: Author.

LTTE-related events on selected days while it continued to be a place of leisure on almost all other days when memorial activities were not taking place. Also, since the signing of the ceasefire agreement which enabled the LTTE to renovate this and other monuments destroyed by the Sri Lanka Army until the complete disruption of the ceasefire agreement, annual memorial events in the park resumed under LTTE sponsorship[25] with the participation of supporters, kin of the dead and local civic leaders.

The earliest accompaniments of the memorial, which included a number of cement sculptures constituting a larger monument complex, were destroyed by the Sri Lanka Army when it recaptured Jaffna from the LTTE in 1995. Nevertheless, making use of the brief moment provided by the ceasefire[26] agreement signed in 2002, the LTTE initiated a rapid process of refurbishing the monumental aspects of the park as a matter of priority. Interestingly, the Sri Lanka Army which had completely destroyed the original monument in 1995 did not interfere in this resurrection. The accompaniments that attracted tourists in the 2002–2005 phase of warzone tourism dates from this period. However, the resurrected monument did not have any of the original sculptures and was in fact an amalgamation of simple pictorial accompaniments mounted on an iron frame, covered on top by a crude tin roof and protected by a low blue-coloured wall. This specific combination gave the monument a somewhat temporary appearance despite its crucial importance in the LTTE's calendar rituals of memory.

In a manner similar to that of the Bulldozer Monument, Kittu Children's Park also offered vastly divergent meanings to different people. Kittu was a popular and well respected leader of the area. So the monument in the park made much sense to many locals except for those who had been specifically victimized by the LTTE. For many, it was a public reference to one of its own. Similar sentiments were shared by many Tamil diasporic tourists because by this time different versions of his story had percolated into a larger discourse with active diasporic participation often through the internet, popular magazines published in diasporic centres and LTTE literature. In this way, his story of heroism had become part of the Tamil popular imagination both locally and diasporically in a manner quite similar to the way Kularatna's story had become part of the Sinhala imagination. On the other hand, LTTE activists and workers who were assigned the task of resurrecting and maintaining the monumental structures in the park were always willing to narrate the story of

Kittu to Tamil-speaking visitors. At the same time, as a result of lapses in language coupled with a pronounced lack of interest, these narratives did not reach the consciousness of most Sinhala tourists. As Nimal Kumara, a 31-year old Sinhala tourist from Kandy observed while resting in the park and enjoying a few snacks with his group, '[H]e is a terrorist after all. The monument is here only because the ceasefire has allowed it'.[27] Yet, he and his group had the desire and found the time to pose in front of the monument for a series of photographs. While Kittu's heroism was lost to them, his association with 'terrorism' in the Sinhala nationalist discourse nevertheless made his monument a viable place for photo opportunities. This is because, through these images, tourists could pictorially trace their travels through the warzone to eager listeners in their kin and peer groups. To put it more simply, the contextual and political associations which the park and its monumental attributes easily narrated to locals and visiting Tamils were lost to the Sinhalas. For them, it served two purposes. At one level, it was simply a place to rest like any picnic area while touring the north. On the other hand, and more importantly, it was place that offered photo opportunities. Like my neighbours with whose story I began this discussion and the example of Nimal Kumara and his group of friends referred to above, many Sinhalas were keen to be photographed with the colourful image of Kittu as an interesting background which pictorially referred to an episode in the war. These sessions were not too different from studio-based photo shoots using painted screens which many of them would have been familiar with. Nevertheless, the specificity of the narratives of his heroism that the monument was designed to articulate seems not to have entered their collective consciousness at any point.

Many tourists also made a brief stop at the Thileepan Memorial (see Figure 2.9), not as part of a specific visit to the monument itself but as a residual act while visiting the well-known Kandasamy Temple in Nallur. The monument is a simple structure consisting of a central blue pillar surrounded by a metal fence supported by a set of standing lights designed to look like candles. It is situated very close to the Kandasamy Temple. Its proximity to the temple is crucial in understanding its attraction as a regular stop in the tourist trail. Many people who visit Jaffna, irrespective of their religious or ethnic backgrounds, invariably visit the temple for different reasons. For Tamil Hindus, it is a key religious site with a long historical tradition. For foreigners and Christians, it is an iconic cultural location in the area, which should not be missed even though it might

Figure 2.9

Thileepan Monument, Nallur

Source: Author.

not have any religious significance for them. Many Sinhalas Buddhists, who might not have visited Jaffna in the previous two decades before the road was reopened, would quite possibly have heard of the temple as one of Jaffna's main cultural and religious landmarks. In most cases, this information comes to them from their elders who had visited the temple before the 1980s when travel to the north was not an issue. Besides, the main god venerated at the temple, God Kandasamy, is also well-known to Buddhists. He is known in the Sinhala Buddhist pantheon as God Kataragama and is an extremely popular god among the Sinhalas whose main shrine in the Sinhala south is located in Kataragama, which in itself is a major pilgrim destination for both Buddhists and Hindus. So for the Sinhalas visiting the Kandasamy temple, it is simply a matter of visiting the temple of a god they are not only familiar with but also hold in high reverence. Interestingly however, the visit to the temple in Nallur is not understood by Sinhalas in simple pilgrimage terms as the visit to the temple of the same god in Kataragama. It appears that the god's location deep in the Tamil Hindu cultural landscape of the north has diminished some aspects of the usual pilgrim discourse of piety from the Sinhala consciousness. Even so, Sinhalas follow the same basic practices as local Tamil Hindus when they visit the interior of the temple.

In any case, despite the liminal space within which the temple is visited by Sinhala tourists which does not allow it to be located in a simple discourse of piety and pilgrimage, it is nevertheless a consistent destination for them. This visit means that the Thileepan Memorial simply cannot be missed. On the other hand, when situated in the practice of photography, which is a crucial recurrent aspect in the war tourist trail, the monument becomes as important a location for people to be photographed at as it is to be pictured within the outer premises of the temple. As Kumari Weerasinghe observed,

> I don't know who Thileepan is. I heard the name mentioned by people near the temple. Only the name registered in my mind as they were speaking in Tamil and I did not understand the language. But it is something that is difficult to miss if you are near the temple. It is worth seeing.[28]

Soon after, she took out her wad of colour photographs from her trip to Jaffna in 2004 and said pointing to a number of images, '[L]ook, this is my brother making a funny face and this is my sister. Can you see the monument? It is quite tall.'[29] For her and the other tourists who went to the north with her, the Thileepan Monument was one of the places to be photographed at due to its iconic recognizability as a place from the warzone.

Beyond the fleeting attention of tourists, the monument narrates a very specific story. It memorializes Rasaiah Parthipan, popularly known as Lt Colonel Thileepan, who died in 1987. He was a popular early leader of the LTTE and was its Political Wing leader for Jaffna at the time he died. His demise came about as the result of a hunger strike he had embarked upon to demand that the 'Indian government honour the security undertakings it gave to the Tamil people alongside its Accord with Sri Lanka'.[30] As this suggests, his agitation unfolded when contingents of the Indian army, the IPKF, were operating in Jaffna. As such, his fast was against IPKF operations more than Sri Lankan military operations as Sri Lankan security forces were restricted to barracks at the time under the terms of the Indo-Sri Lankan agreement which brought the IPKF to north-eastern Sri Lanka. In this context, the monument was as much a tribute to a fallen LTTE leader as it was a symbolic gesture against the Indian state and its military presence in Jaffna. Within a compartment reminiscent of a small shrine embedded within the central pillar of the monument, a small colour photograph of Thileepan was situated. A similar but larger image of him was also located immediately outside the monument premises. This functioned as a formal sign announcing the presence and the purpose of the monument. Even though it visually competed to establish its presence amidst the clutter of Nallur town, the monument was one of its most visible structures and was certainly one of the town's best known locations. In 1995, the Sri Lanka Army dismantled the original monument after its capture of Jaffna that year. What was present when the first phase of warzone tourism began was a resurrection of the original monument by the LTTE. Between the initial establishment of the monument and the LTTE's expulsion from Jaffna in 1995 by the Sri Lanka Army and from the beginning of the ceasefire until about 2004, the site functioned as a crucial space for the LTTE's public performance of rituals of memory and sometimes also for public practices of memory by ordinary citizens given the fact that Thileepan was an extremely popular leader at the time he died.[31] But the political history of the person, the place and the LTTE as a an organization that the monument is expected to narrate was lost to Sinhala tourists like Kumari Weerasinghe due to lapses in language and decisive differences in ideology and political sensibility of tourists.

The monument was again destroyed by the Sri Lanka Army after its final defeat of the LTTE in 2009.

A number of Sinhalas who came to Jaffna at the time also visited the Sea Tiger Monument in Tiruvil, Jaffna (see Figures 2.10 and 2.11). However, this was not a pre-identified destination in the trail as it was not too well-known beyond the region. As such, many people who visited it did so if they were specifically informed about it by local people or military personnel that visitors might have been in contact with. As in the case of Kittu Children's Park, the Sea Tiger Monument was initially constructed by the LTTE in a pre-existing park adjacent to a body of water. It was made up of a cluster of concrete statues depicting members of the naval wing of the LTTE, generally known as Sea Tigers, in the pose of performing what appeared to be a maritime operation. In fact, the location of the monument so close to a body of water was not an accident but a calculated decision to give more contextual poignancy to an LTTE unit whose duties were directly related to the sea and therefore water. This initial monument was dismantled by the Sri Lanka Army after its capture of Jaffna peninsula in 1995. Since then, the remnants of the statues remained un-cleared as a pile of recognizable rubble up to

Figure 2.10

Destroyed Sea Tiger Monument (detail), Tiruvil

Source: Author.

Figure 2.11

Reconstructed Sea Tiger Monument, Tiruvil

Source: Author.

2004, symbolically indicating the falling and rising fortunes of the LTTE. However, as in many other similar cases, utilizing the respite and relative freedom of movement offered by the ceasefire agreement, the LTTE re-established the Sea Tiger Monument complex. However, this was not done by rebuilding the destroyed statues. Instead, the LTTE established a more abstract monument nearby, in the same park and closer to the water. Many visitors who came to the site initially went to the rubble and thereafter made their way to the newer construction. This overall context became a moment for many to ponder over and discuss what seemed at the time as the 'resilience' of the LTTE to reinvent itself from the calamities and reversals of fortune it had faced as an organization.

One of the most sought-after sites in the war tourist trail in the first phase was the ancestral home of the LTTE leader Velupillai Prabhakaran in Velvetiturai. Situated very close to the beach, it was a small nondescript house owned by the rebel leader's parents where Prabhakaran and his siblings grew up. Covered in Tamil, Sinhala and English language graffiti, the house continued to stand even after it suffered considerable damage during military operations in 1987, though the family had abandoned it about four years earlier. Even after the LTTE fled and the military took control of the area, the house remained a well-known location in the locality given its associations with the town's best known son. Soon after the ceasefire operation came into effect in 2002, a hand-painted English language sign mysteriously appeared on its boundary wall near the front gate announcing that this was 'Honoured Veluppilai Prabakaran's House— The President of Tamileelam,' which remained well into 2005 without being removed by the Sri Lanka Army which was in control of that area at the time. With the advent of the war tourist trail, the house became one of the most photographed places in the north. My neighbours had also specifically visited the house during their trip to Jaffna. While pointing to some of the photographs of the place they had taken, the head of the family noted, '[I]t's a very small house, like my mother's house. I can't believe such a man came from this kind of humble place. His family seems like ordinary people'. I remember hearing similar comments during my own visit to the house in 2004 when the place was crowded with Sinhala as well as Tamil tourists and the town's tea shops were experiencing a tourism-led boom and the house was its only attraction. While serving *vada* and tea, at his tea shop in Velvetiturai town, not too far from the house, the owner noted in accented and basic Sinhala, 'It's a good thing the house is there. That is why people come here, to see it. And then they bring business too. That is good for us'.[32] While he was saying this, through the shop window I saw a lorry with Sinhala writing on its sides, slowly drive up and make a stop close by. It was carrying chairs from the south. Very soon, two people got out and started crying aloud '*nākālika*' (chairs in Tamil) while carry- ing two sample chairs at a time to the interior lanes trying to sell them as if they were selling fruits, vegetables or fish, going from house to house. So tourism was not the only thing that the ceasefire had allowed to come into the north from the Sinhala south. Business was also percolating in different forms, paying taxes at the main LTTE checkpoint at Omanthai and bringing in essential items long deprived to the people in the north while the prices were becoming more affordable. In this sense, tourism was only the most obvious of the numerous activities which emerged at the time, opening up a number of economic opportunities along with multiple politico-cultural scenarios.

> You must visit the LTTE cemetery in Jaffna. It is quite a place. They know how to look after their heroes when they die even though they are terror- ists. For that matter, our fellows haven't even begun to think about a war centenary. You must visit it. In a way, it also shows the scale of war.[33]

This was an observation made by a 28-year old Sinhala tourist two weeks after he had returned from Jaffna while flipping through the photographs he had taken of the LTTE War Cemetery in Koppay (see Figures 2.12 and 2.13). In the official language of the LTTE, these cemeteries, including the one at Koppay are known as 'Heroes' Resting Homes of Liberation Tigers'. He had been to the cemetery and a number of other sites in the war tourist trail with 11 people from his extended family in July 2004. 'Look how carefully they have maintained the place'[34] he said pointing to one of the photographs showing rows upon rows of standardized tombstones set amidst manicured lawns. 'And can you see their flag right at the entrance,'[35] he observed again pointing to yet another photograph showing the LTTE flag fluttering high above the entrance to the cemetery. The 42 pictures of the cemetery in his collection showed not only members of his own group but many other Sinhalas, going by what some of them wore. Some photographs were taken at the entrance to the cemetery with its large steel gate and the LTTE flag clearly visible in the background. Many others depicted curious people posing in front of tombstones, their inscriptions and the stories of those interred or commemorated there

Figure 2.12

LTTE War Cemetery, Koppay

Source: Author.

Figure 2.13

Tombs (detail) at LTTE War Cemetery, Koppay

Source: Author.

completely lost to them. However, the photographs established beyond any doubt that they had visited the Koppay cemetery, an important stop in the warzone tourist trail at the time. Even when I visited the cemetery in October 2004, it remained a popular pre-identified destination for Sinhala tourists. For Sinhalas, the Koppay cemetery was not a place one stumbled upon by accident. Just like the Naga Dipa Buddhist temple, it was a place one visited by design, even though obviously not for religious purposes or for sombre reflection. It was a place that beckoned the curious. For many Sinhala visitors, the carefully laid out and landscaped cemetery with workers diligently working regularly on maintaining it was a place which indicated some of the inner workings of the LTTE as they played out in the public domain. It was part of the LTTE's public performance of glorified death and exalted heroism. Of course for many Tamils, the emotions involved in visiting this place extended much beyond mere curiosity.

Koppay was not the only LTTE cemetery in the north. There were cemeteries in Uduppidi, Kodikaamam and Vealani among others. But as the first phase of warzone tourism began, the Koppay cemetery was the only cemetery that was well within the tourist trail that was carefully renovated by the LTTE after the ceasefire. The cemetery was destroyed by the Sri Lanka Army after it captured Jaffna from the LTTE in 1995. As part of the resurrection, the LTTE placed some of the rubble from the original cemetery in a glass box set upon an elevated pedestal, literally indicating the organization's established ability to rise from the ashes, at least up to that time. While the cemeteries lasted, they became central platforms where individual grief and the memory of those lost in battle serving the LTTE's goals could be performed in public space. At the same time, the LTTE itself used the cemeteries to formally narrativize and perform its own institutionalized rituals of memory and heroism. Even the renovated Koppay cemetery re-initiated some of these public LTTE-sponsored ceremonies under the watchful eyes of the Sri Lanka Army making use of the relative safety of operation offered by the ceasefire.

While most Sinhalas who visited the cemetery could not read the tombstone inscriptions written only in Tamil or could not understand the conversations of visiting Tamils or the rhetoric of LTTE ceremonies that were organized at times, they knew quite well that these were clearly the graves of the 'others' or the 'enemies' who had killed their own loved ones who were formally memorialized in military monuments in southern parts of the country. That realization itself created considerable distance between them and the basic tenants of respect that are generally anticipated and observed in a cemetery as a plain of the dead. That is why one October in 2004, while I was in the cemetery, the LTTE workers on site requested a group of visiting Sinhala tourists not to laugh or talk too loudly as they walked across the cemetery, clicking photographs, and engaging in casual conversation and merry laughter. On the same day, it did not seem such advice was necessary for the large number of Tamil diasporic and local visitors who were also at the site. Some left flowers while a few lit candles. Many others simply looked in silence or touched the tombstones with both hands while some wiped off the tears that they could not hold back. These highly differentiated forms of interacting within the space were a necessary condition of the kind of tourism that evolved in the area. The multiple rows of standardized tiled tombs reminiscent of many military cemeteries in the world did not always contain the remains of dead combatants of the LTTE. Often, when bodies of those missing in action could not be found, but were deemed dead by the LTTE, they were allocated tombs in one of the cemeteries. Irrespective of the presence or absence of remains in tombs, they functioned as clear references to the commemorated individuals' existence, heroism and the supreme sacrifice they had made for their cause. As a principle, the inscriptions on tombs never indicted the date of birth of an individual as was common practice in any other cemetery in the country. Instead, they only indicated the name of the individual, his or her place of birth and finally the date of death or disappearance. The reason for withholding the date of birth could be understood when juxtaposed with the LTTE's keenness to ensure that the existence of child soldiers should not become apparent. This could not have been fulfilled if both birth and death references were publically presented. The intricacies of the LTTE's public politics through their cemeteries were, however, not always clear to visiting Sinhala tourists simply because they did not contribute to the wider discourses of emotion and nationalism among Tamils that would have made such nuances self-evident. For the most part, they were simply curious sightseers.

In their role as sightseers, there was an important local consideration that many Sinhala tourists visiting the Koppay cemetery missed, given the ethno-nationalistically tempered frame of mind within which they perceived the site. As noted already, despite the curiosity that attracted them to Koppay, for most of them, it was nevertheless a place where 'enemy' combatants were laid to rest. However, this was a sentiment that was not as unilaterally shared by the local community and visitors from the Tamil diaspora. Though there were always exceptions in the Tamil perceptions of the LTTE, for locals and diasporic Tamils who opted to visit the cemetery, those who were commemorated within the space were not simply combatants or abstracted and depersonalized individuals. They were people they knew as sons, husbands, wives, daughters, kin, neighbours and friends. For them, they were the same as the soldiers commemorated in various military and police monuments were for the Sinhalas. Nevertheless, despite their disconnect from the discourse of respect that was expected from the interactions in the site by the LTTE as well as locals as a site of death, many Sinhalas also admired the care that was taken to maintain the place and often wondered aloud why institutionalization of memory in this manner, in the form of dedicated military cemeteries, had not taken root in their part of the country.

What does all this mean when contextualized as a single trajectory of travel? If there was a lose sense of triviality, casualness and non-serious leisure intermingled with a clear sense of curiosity in the visitations to war-related sites, the visits to religious sites provided the overall experience with a sense of appreciable piety. However, this was not a simple religious affair despite what was overtly apparent and what people said. Particularly, visiting Buddhist sites amidst a Tamil Hindu cultural landscape militarily dominated by the LTTE, which was affectively closed to Sinhala Buddhists for over a decade, was also an acute political act in this specific context when the war had not yet ended. After all, to fulfil their curiosity and piety, southern tourists had to travel through militarily contested swaths of land where they saw with their own eyes not only the destruction caused by war, but also the power of the LTTE and the loss of territorial integrity of their country as a result of this power. Travelling through the reality of this loss of land, ruptured territory of a once integrated country, dealing with the power of a non-state actor such as the LTTE almost in possession of a state was also a reality check that superseded and dismantled the political rhetoric of Sinhala nationalism that many of the travellers would have been discursive partners of. Warzone travels were the first time Sinhalas would have seen the reality of the Tamil political demand for the separate state of Eelam. This is an issue I will revisit in the next chapter and in the final chapter of the book in more detail.

In any event, once the visits to religious and war-related sites were concluded often within two or three days, travellers were ready to head back home with their memories, stories, photographs and the blessings of the gods. The length of stay was limited at this time, mostly due to limitations on places one could visit, lack of lodging facilities and perceptions of safety despite the ceasefire. No one had illusions about its ruptures not too far from the routes they were allowed to travel in. At the time, it was not uncommon to hear some people somewhat flippantly attempting to explain and justify the kind of unrestricted and unmonitored tourism that took place in this phase of travel as a possible way to build bridges between two distrustful ethnic communities separated by decades of war (Perera 2005). While this possibility existed in a theoretical sense, it is quite evident in hindsight that this was not an objective that was achieved. It was also not an objective in the minds of many people who actually made the trip. That assumption was immediately lost in the rhetoric of the populist conflict-resolution discourse propagated by some development actors active at the time as well as within the commonsensical nostalgia of some of the elder tourists. On the other hand, such an assumption hardly had a significant presence within the vagaries of warzone tourism that actually took place. Clearly, the kind of tourism that unfolded was not an activity of 'innocence' within which the theme park amusement atmosphere which often emerged 'helped trivialize the pain, destruction and havoc of war in these areas' in the minds of many visitors (Perera 2005). As some of the narratives presented in this chapter would indicate, tourists hardly met local people in their travels or had any interest in doing so. If there were interactions, that was often in the context of fleeting market negotiations. In the minds of many tourists, locals were merely a marginal presence in the distant and not so clearly visible landscape. As such, what was heard from many returning tourists were not narratives of understanding the consequences of war but stories that narrated a 'sense of adventure articulated in a manner similar to the orientalist discourse that defined the essence of the east in the colonial period' (Perera 2005).

The travel narratives of the north-east coming from these tourists reminded one of Edward Said's analyses of how the notion of the Orient was constructed in the European imagination. In the local context, an exotic, mysterious and deprived sense of Jaffna and the north was created as something that should be explored as a matter of leisure, pleasure and curiosity, and that too from the safety of the disengaged distance offered by tourism. As such, it was not surprising when antiques such as the horse images of ritual vehicles from Hindu temples that had survived the war very quickly found their way to Colombo's upmarket antique stores, negotiating through both LTTE and military checkpoints with surprising ease. They were not cultural treasures worthy of protection but market objects that should be brought quickly to the newly opened markets in the south. It is in this general context that the chief incumbent of the Naga Vihara in Jaffna warned on national television at the peak of post-ceasefire war tourism in 2002 that 'people who visit the north should be sensitive to the cultural and social aspirations of the people in the north', and his advice came in the context of specific insensitive activities that had already emerged as a result of southern war tourism (Perera 2005).

Notes

1. The title of this chapter, 'The Jaffna Photo Album' is borrowed from my essay of the same title published in *The Island* (Colombo) on 4 September 2002. Some of the ideas and information in this section are reproduced from that essay. To read the complete essay, please visit: http://www.island.lk/2002/09/04/ midwee01.html (accessed on 15 January 2016).

2. For more information on the modalities and contents of the ceasefire agreement, please read, 'Sri Lankan Government and LTTE Sign a Tentative Cease-fire Agreement:' http://www.wsws.org/en/articles/2002/02/sri-f27. html (last accessed on 28 September 2013) and 'Text of Sri Lanka Truce Deal:' http://news.bbc.co.uk/2/hi/south_asia/1836198.stm (accessed on 28 September 2013). A more detailed version of the peace agreement inclusive of the annexures can be accessed via the United States Institute of Peace at: http://www.usip.org/sites/default/files/file/resources/collections/peace_ agreements/pa_sri_lanka_02222002.pdf (accessed on 28 September 2013).

3. http://www.tamilnet.com/art.html?catid=13&artid=6833 (accessed on 28 September 2013).

4. http://www.slmm-istory.info/SLMM_Archive/Operational_statements/2002/2 9%2F07%2F02++The+Government+of+Sri+Lanka+and+LTTE+are+preparin g+for+a+Lasting+Peace.9UFRnI1U.ips (accessed on 28 September 2013).

5. http://www.usip.org/sites/default/files/file/resources/collections/peace_ agreements/pa_sri_lanka_02222002.pdf (accessed on 21 December 2013).

6. The film *Ira Mediyama* (*August Sun*) by Prasanna Vitanage paints a very poignant picture of the expelling of Muslims, among other facets of war.

7. As already noted in the previous chapter, Tamil diasporic tourism is a distinctly different kind of travel within overall warzone tourism. While in many cases they involve a certain sense of adventure, they also often involve a sense of nostalgia, homecoming and an eagerness to meet relatives whom them have not seen in a long time. Within the focus of this book, I will not address this important type of travel.

8. I would like to thank Harindra Dassanayake for this information via skype on 28 December 2013.

9. Information provided by R. Cheran, Department of Sociology, University of Windsor, Canada via Facebook on 20 October 2013. T. Shanaathanan from University of Jaffna has identified the two most popular restaurants as Pandiyan and Suvai Aruvi (personal communication, 24 October 2013).

10. For brief descriptions on the 'A9', known formally as the A9 Inn or A9 Lodge consisting of a bar, restaurant and 10 rooms, please read Shashikumar (2005) and Rutnam (2005).

11. The story of Gamini Kularatana will be described in more detail in the next chapter when his story remerges with a reincarnation of the monument itself.

12. I would like to thank Dushyanthini Kanagasabapathipillai for providing me the name of this almost forgotten LTTE fighter during an interview in Colombo on 24 December 2013.

13. Many Sinhala speakers often refer to an unrelated male older than oneself as '*aiya*' in routine conversation which literally means 'elder brother'. It is a mark of respect based on age and has no formal kinship connotations.

14. Interviews conducted in Kandy on 25 May 2005.

15. A very similar rendition of the same story exists on the following website and has been presented as historical fact. The website itself is exclusively

maintained as an information portal for global travellers: http://www.tri-padvisor.in/Travel-g304135-c138404/Jaffna:Sri-Lanka:Naga.Vihara.Temple. html (accessed on 29 December 2013).

16. I will be discussing the importance of the 'sixteen great places of worship' in the overall context of tourist travel later in this book.

17. The bodhi tree is known in Sinhala as the bo tree.

18. For more information, please visit: http://www.dambakolapatuna.info/pil-grims.html (accessed on 15 January 2016)

19. Information from the official website of the Dambakola Patuna Sangamitta Viharaya: http://www.dambakolapatuna.info/history.html (accessed on 26 February 2014).

20. Information from the official website of the Dambakola Patuna Sangamitta Viharaya: http://www.dambakolapatuna.info/history.html (accessed on 26 February 2014).

21. Information from the official website of the Dambakola Patuna Sangamitta Viharaya: http://www.dambakolapatuna.info/history.html (accessed on 26 February 2014).

22. Excerpts from interview conducted in Jaffna in October 2004.

23. Interview conducted in Jaffna, September 2004.

24. Interview conducted in Colombo in July 2002.

25. For a description of the 2005 Kittu Memorial Celebrations in the park (while the ceasefire was holding) and to see some images of the event, please read *Tamil Net* (2005).

26. The Norway-brokered ceasefire between the LTTE and the Sri Lanka government officially lasted from 2002 to 2008 amidst numerous violations. Since about late 2005, limited military operations had already been initiated by both parties.

27. Interviews conducted in Jaffna, September 2004.

28. Excerpt from interview conducted in Colombo in July 2006.

29. Excerpt from interview conducted in Colombo in July 2006.

30. For more information, read *Eelam View* (2012).

31. For an extensive pictorial narrative of the Thileepan Memorial as a site of memory, visit https://www.facebook.com/media/set/?set=a.33556181653017 9.75509.335090929910601&type=3 (accessed on 25 September 2013).

32. Excerpt from interview conducted in Velvetiturai in October 2004.

33. Excerpt from interview conducted in Colombo on 24 August 2004 with a Sinhala tourist who visited Jaffna in July 2004.

34. Excerpt from interview conducted in Colombo on 24 August 2004 with a Sinhala tourist who visited Jaffna in July 2004.

35. Excerpt from interview conducted in Colombo on 24 August 2004 with a Sinhala tourist who visited Jaffna in July 2004.

3

Travels with the Lion Flag: Sinhala Warzone Tourism in an Era of Post-war Triumphalism

Nalaka Weerasinghe and his extended family had been watching the progression of the Sri Lanka Army in its march and final assault against the LTTE since at least the end of 2008. They watched the news on BBC and Al Jazeera English and complained to each other when the military was accused of human rights violations. 'What about the LTTE? This is Tamil diasporic propaganda', was the most common collective family response to each other in such situations. More enthusiastically, they watched local television and in particular the government-owned Rupawahini and ITN news and current affairs programmes which had 'embedded' journalists travelling with the advancing troops. These journalists brought to them news of the war as it was preferred to be received in the south: clean, professional, no civilian causalities and the end of the terrorists. And all this, in the comfort of their living rooms. From that comfort zone, they saw the collapse of LTTE bastions, one after another, along with numerous war trophies which seemed to provide a kind of unmistakable emphasis to what was transpiring in the distant battlefields.

When Kilinochchi, the erstwhile capital of the LTTE fell to the Sri Lanka Army in early 2009, they saw the entry of victorious troops into what appeared to be a ghost town: a blasted massive water tank lying sprawled in the middle of town, blown up and bullet-scarred buildings, blackened palms with their tops blown off, skinny stray dogs in the streets looking for food and their vanished masters, and almost no people. They were aghast at seeing what appeared to be a functioning wartime airport at Iranamadu maintained by the LTTE. When Mullaitivu fell in May 2009, they watched and enthusiastically discussed the details of the intricate bunker of the LTTE leader where he and his family had spent considerable time in much luxury. 'We have to go and see that', said Nalaka at one point. 'That must be some sight to see.' They were intrigued to know about the life of luxury Prabhakaran had lead in the midst of surrounding poverty and deprivations which the electronic narratives also always emphasized. For them, the LTTE facilities which came to their attention, thanks to the work of the embedded journalists, were things they had simply never seen or heard before. They debated on the authenticity of the images of dead Prabhakaran. But at one point of time after the president had declared that the war was over, they all agreed that he was in fact dead. Nalaka's father declared after hearing the president's announcement, '[W]e must go and see these things. After all, we can now travel anywhere in our own country'.

And travel they did to the north to fulfil their sense of adventure soon after the A9 was opened again in early 2010. Nalaka hired a 60-seat Tata bus. The back windshield was covered with a colour photograph of three camouflaged and bandana-clad Sri Lankan soldiers in jungle fatigues carrying heavy machine guns and garlanded with what appeared to be necklaces of bullets. The image had already become extremely popular in the internet and was endlessly reproduced in posters, bus adornments, greeting cards, magazine and newspaper articles, and so on. No one really knew the identity of the sol- diers; but then, that really did not matter. A large national flag was affixed to the front of the bus as was the prominent coconut flower for good fortune. A sticker inside the bus claimed that this was 'the land of Gautama, the Buddha' while a small national flag fluttered in the air on the driver's side of the bus.

Friends, relatives and neighbours of the Weerasinghe family were packed into the bus with their clothes, pillows, bed linen, sleeping mats, cooking utensils and food provisions for six days. Though the A9 was open, some of the sites they wanted to see were not yet open to the public. But Nalaka had some classmates in the army and they had assured him that they would take them to the sites, including Prabhakaran's bunker.

So, long before the sun came up that morning, they left on their adventure of the north, the first such trip for the family after the war had come to an end.

****

In his interesting analysis, *The Gulf War did not Take Place* (1995) written at the time the 1990–1991 US-led and UN-mandated military intervention in Kuwait against the initial Iraqi invasion of that country was unfolding, Baudrillard's central argument was that this war, known as the 'Gulf War', did not take place (Baudrillard 1995). Deploying his ideas on simulation and the hyperreal, he argued that this war was a carefully scripted media event or a virtual war (Baudrillard 1995). Of course, Baudrillard's thesis was not the simplistic argument that the war did not take place, but that it was crafted, sanitized and played out as a media product which was readily consumed by thousands of people in its edited form. In other words, the sanitized and politically packaged war which came to living rooms across the world via television did not take place while at the same time, what did take place with horrendous consequences was something that was not readily experienced beyond the places and individuals intimately touched and scarred by unfolding events. Similarly, and as most things in the present time when communication technologies have evolved significantly, the final stages of the civil war in Sri Lanka came to the living rooms of most Sri Lankans courtesy of the government-owned television station Rupawahini as well as other private channels since at least 2008. Taking a cue from the US military-controlled media coverage at the time of the Gulf War, the Sri Lanka Army had 'embedded' television and print media journalists to regularly report on the war from the vantage point allowed by the army and the Ministry of Defence. People saw LTTE bastions such as Kilinochchi falling as if they were watching great battle movies and became familiar with the progression of specific military thrusts to the extent that the names of some military units such as the 57th and 58th as well as the 53th and 55th Divisions of the Sri Lanka Army became part of the popular discourse. They were often used in regular conversations like casual technical terms in video-based war games. Certain events came to people live from the battle zones courtesy of these 'embedded' reporters. Some military leaders and their well-wishers had already created Facebook pages to promote specific military leaders as heroes of epic proportions.[1] However, what came to Sri Lankan living rooms was not the war itself, but an edited version of it, which in government terminology was called the 'Humanitarian Operation' undertaken to rescue Tamil civilians from the 'clutches of LTTE terrorists'. In that virtual rendition, soldiers were heroes and the LTTE were evil with no room for any other interpretation while no civilian casualties were reported due to government action though the LTTE consistently used them as human shields. It was a clinical, black and white representation of a messy situation that could only be projected in this manner in the virtual space afforded by television as an edited and carefully crafted media product. It was literally an electronic text with no contradictions.

Interestingly, however, this media product was consumed very differently by different sections of society. While most Tamil citizens in the country and the diaspora did not consume this as it was presented and went on to create their own versions of the truth in the internet, most Sinhalas opted to consume this linear narrative and steadfastly opted not to recognize the contradictions beyond the mass-produced electronic representation of the war itself. Along with this electronic media onslaught also came the kind of triumphalism that later came to typify post-war Sri Lankan politics both of the government as well as many people from the south, which continues to date in different degrees. The fall of Kilinochchi in early 2009 was greeted in the south with bursting firecrackers in people's gardens and in the streets, and was a harbinger of the colour and direction of the celebratory mood that was to emerge in a more pronounced fashion in the coming months. On 16 May, the president informed the citizens via national TV that the rebels have been defeated and the war was over. Again, there was more pronounced jubilation in the streets and homes in the Sinhala south. Three days later, on 19 May 2009, addressing Parliament, the president formally declared to the country and the world that the war had ended and observed, '[W]e have liberated the whole country from LTTE terrorism' (Weaver and Chamberlain 2009). The next day, 20 of May was declared a national holiday to savour this victory. In a communication emailed to *Associated Press* on behalf of the LTTE, Selvarasa Pathmanathan acknowledged defeat and said,

> [T]his battle has reached its bitter end.... It is our people who are dying now from bombs, shells, illness and hunger. We cannot permit any more harm to befall them. We remain with one last choice to remove the last weak excuse of the enemy for killing our people. We have decided to silence our guns. (Weaver and Chamberlain 2009)

Formally, informally, legally, locally and internationally, the war that reached its brutal climax over a period of 30 years was finally over, even though the crises that the militarization of the interethnic conflict between Sinhala and Tamil communities introduced to national politics were far from over.

The initial declaration of the end of war on 16 May and the more formal declaration in Parliament on 19 May as well as the LTTE's own acceptance of defeat led to wild day-and-night parties in the streets of Colombo and beyond accompanied by firecrackers, street music, fluttering national flags as an omnipresent phenomenon, and the cooking of milk rice[2] in the streets and in people's homes to usher in what was perceived as a new era. On the night of 16 May in the Colombo suburb of Nugegoda, a group of partying men and women stopped my car and insisted that I eat some *kiri bath* or milk rice they had cooked in the street. A number of auto-rickshaws were parked nearby with smaller versions of the national flag mounted on each one, and loud music emanated from one of them accompanied by songs about the war and the heroism of soldiers. This was a genre of music that became popular among the Sinhalas during the war, some of them sung by soldiers but many others by regular singers. Some young people were waving the national flag while others were wearing it on their backs like the cape of Superman. Some were clearly intoxicated with alcohol, as indicated by their demeanour and the hovering smell of cheap spirits in the air. One of them was beating a bongo drum with all his might in no particular rhythm and invited me: 'Have a piece of *kiri bath*. Now that this cursed war is over, we can be free. Here, have a piece. I am waiting for my brother to come back from the north'.[3] As this young man's soldier-brother had survived the war, he and his family were particularly joyful. Some others in the crowd also had relatives serving in the military. This particular street party was therefore a public display of private joy, not only because the war had ended but also because of the realization that their loved ones will no longer die or be maimed in battle.

The phenomenon of offering food to strangers in the streets is not unknown in Sri Lanka. During festivals to mark the birth, the enlightenment and the death of the Buddha as well as the bringing of Buddhism and the sacred bodhi tree to Sri Lanka, many people organize large offerings of food and non-alcoholic drinks in makeshift halls known in Sinhala as *dan sel* (halls for alms). People who eat and drink at these places are not necessarily poor, but are simply accepting a gift during a celebratory moment and thereby becoming a part of a larger community of faithful. What was happening in the streets on 16 May 2009 and few days thereafter was a creative and spontaneous refashioning of a traditional practice to celebrate a very new situation. By sharing food and venting out their emotions in these places, most people were simply engaging in an exercise of the catharsis of coming out of a war. What I accidently witnessed and took part in was not an isolated celebration. It was merely one example out of numerous micro events of this nature that took place in many parts of the Sinhala south often as community or individual efforts. These were not events sponsored by the state. But these festivities also drowned the sighing of the people in the battle zone and surviving under the most difficult of conditions, and affectively made invisible their collective pain.

In the formal declaration of the end of war in Parliament, the president assured the Tamil people, speaking in their own language that '[O]ur intention was to save the Tamil people from the cruel grip of the LTTE. We all must now live as equals in this free country' (Weaver and Chamberlain 2009). He also noted, 'We must find a homegrown solution to this conflict' and 'that solution should be acceptable to all the communities' while it must be 'based on the philosophy of Buddhism' (Weaver and Chamberlain 2009). However, in the celebratory mood that ensued and was promoted by the government itself over the next few years for its own political gain, the relatively reconciliatory and sober tone in the president's address to Tamils in their own language was lost, and its meaning did not extend beyond what appeared to be populist conflict-resolution rhetoric. What emerged in its place in government attitude and actions as well as people's perception was a widespread and long lasting sense of triumphalism. The people's own sense of celebration was not difficult to understand. For many Sinhalas and others in the south touched and scarred by the violence of the previous three decades, the end of war meant a pronounced and immediate cessation of the death of their loved ones in battle. It also meant the end of the unannounced sudden death of civilians in the streets far away from the battle zones as a result of regular bombings. On the night of 16 May in another small street celebration in the Colombo suburb of Ratmalana, a woman having tea in the midst of firecrackers, music and general revelry noted,

> [B]ecause of this war, our entire lives had to change. Because of bombings, we never took our children to school as a family as our parents used to. My husband took my daughter and I took my two sons. And we went at different times in different buses. This way if something happened, not all of us would die. One of us might survive to take care of others.[4]

Many civilians were moved to take such calculated, cold and practical decisions on how to engage in even the most mundane and routine activities in their lives as a result of the war. Irrespective of the controversy on how the war ended and the nature of deaths and destructions it caused, its end signalled the end of a destructive chapter of Sri Lankan politics marked by large scale sudden death and destruction. In the south of the country, there was no divergent opinion on this matter.

In practical terms, this also meant a radical drop in deaths and destruction in the war-weary north. However, the post-war life in refugee camps, the extent of death and destruction seen and experienced by people and the extensive emotional toll this had infused into the collective memory of survivors while continuing to live amidst this destruction meant that most survivors of war in the north did not find much to celebrate despite the fact that the war had come to an end. Besides, selected disappearances continued after the war for a considerable period of time as did the anxiety of uncertainty, which was not the case in the south. On the other hand, for many local people in the warzone, even the LTTE could not simply be dismissed as an 'enemy' as was quite legitimately perceived in the south. In many cases, the organization simply represented their own kith and kin, even if they had differences at the level of ideology and politics. This state of mind which had become part of the collective experience of the Tamils was not something that was readily understood by most Sinhalas.

The inability to comprehend the extent of this emotional landscape was one of the clearest pitfalls that the post-war celebratory mood clearly indicated. This inability and the resultant invisibility of the extensive emotional toll of the north has to be understood at least in part as a matter of contextual convenience as very eloquently sketched in a somewhat different fictional setting by Salman Rushdie in his novel, *The Enchantress of Florence*. After his inability to win the heart of Alessandra Fiorentina, Marco Vespuchi hung himself and his dangling body was visible to Alessandra Fiorentina even though she never saw it (Rushdie 2009: 190). That is because, in the words of Rushdie, she 'had long ago perfected the art of seeing only what she wanted to see, which was an essential accomplishment if you wanted to be one of the world's masters and not its victim' (Rushdie 2009: 190). In this fictional narrative, 'if she did not see you then you did not exist' (Rushdie 2009: 190) and simply became a casualty of her erasing gaze. In a similar manner, most Sinhalas did not see the pain, death and destruction of the north-east as they had willed not to see it mainly because it was not convenient and would have gone counter to the state's mega narrative of a just war that was clinical with no or few civilian casualties. But this was not because they wanted to be masters of the world, as suggested by Rushdie in his fictional narrative. Instead, this erasing gaze was necessitated by a sense of guilt over the massive destruction that the war had caused which ideally the

Buddhist collective conscience could not reconcile with. But if the deaths were perceived to be those of 'terrorists' and the level of destruction was thought of as the result of an unavoidable war initiated by these terrorists, which had to be won in order bring in peace, then, it became possible to pragmatically deal with the burden of guilt. Dealing with this situation however did not allow for the emergence of contradictions, particularly in terms of Buddhist sensibilities, into the general stream of consciousness which were nevertheless evident all around. This state of affairs has much to do with how the second phase of warzone tourism emerged and blossomed as well as in understanding its mood.

By 2010, the A9 was reopened yet again (see Figure 3.1 for the general routes of warzone travel in phase 2, post-2010). It remains open to easy civilian traffic at the moment, facilitated by its complete refurbishment. The contemporary incarnation of the road itself is seen by many tourists as an example of post-war developmental and economic benefits, while the government presents it as a sign of reconciliation mostly within a discourse of development within which the pains and the negative fallout of the war are expected to be forgotten. The post-2010 warzone tourism has to be understood in the context outlined above which was very different from the conditions that ushered in the tourist trail after 2002. Even though it generally covered the same area as the earlier phase, it also extended much further into areas beyond the Jaffna peninsula which remained under the control of the LTTE until the war ended. More importantly, the geography of the terrain of memory and artefacts also changed substantially along with the attitudes and the emotional atmosphere of the new phase of war tourism compared to the earlier phase. If the earlier phase had a certain degree of 'innocent' curiosity as exhibited by most Sinhalas, in the second phase, that curiosity was tempered by the prevalent triumphalism stemming from a very obvious preoccupation with Sinhala nationalism. The new trail was not laid out through territory controlled by an enemy that was held in some awe mixed with hate and fear as in the first phase but literally through a land that was vanquished, conquered and defeated. There were no LTTE sentries to pose with though there were plenty of soldiers to do the same thing. But in post-war tourism soon after the tourist onslaught started, the 'exotic' fascination to pose with soldiers waned quickly as they became a kind of common commodity, bringing to mind Pierre Bourdieu's observation that 'popularization devalues' in a context where objects and situations 'tend to lose

Figure 3.1

General route(s) of North-bound warzone travel in phase 2, post-2010

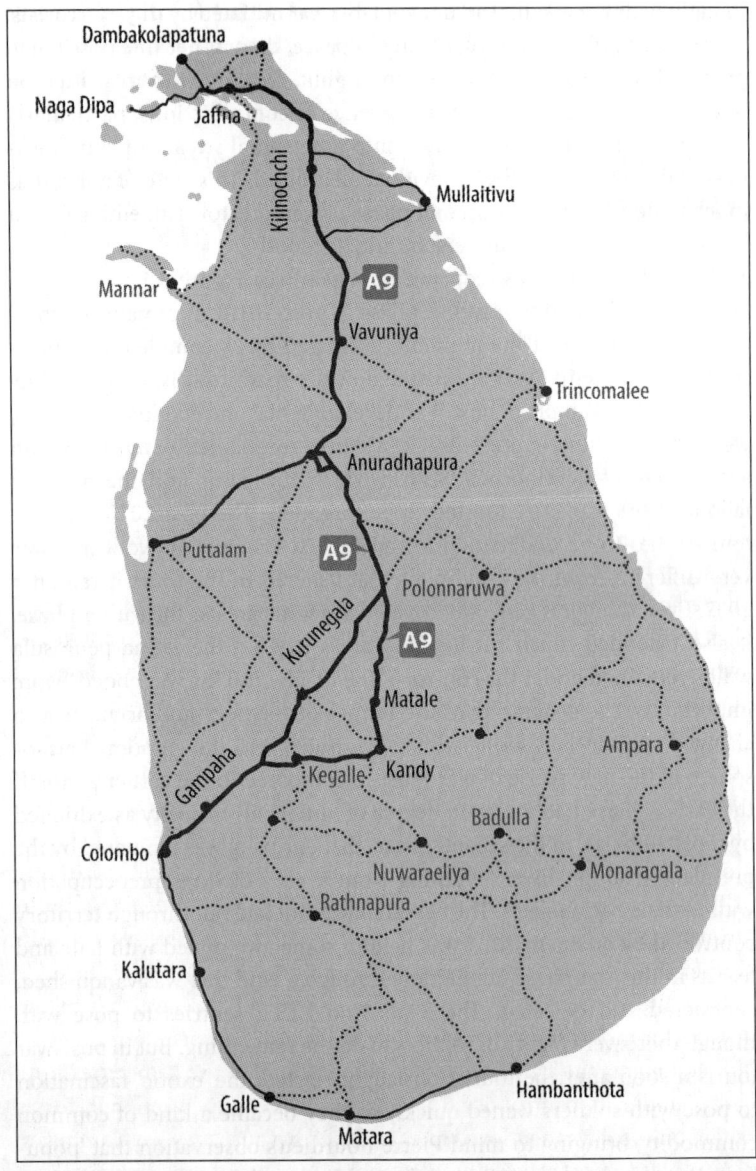

Source: Author. Cartography by Janananda Laksiri, Colombo.

some of their relative scarcity and their distinctive value as the number of consumers grows' (Bourdieu 1995: 114). On the other hand, many of the locations that made up the warzone tourist trail in the earlier phase were no longer available and continued to diminish rapidly as time passed by.

Rearranging Geographies; Rewriting Histories

Almost from the beginning of the government's victory over the LTTE, the rebels' structures of memory became deliberate casualties of the post-war regime's interest in both rewriting history as well as reorganizing the landscape. In the context of this preoccupation, what emerges is a single narrative, a mega narrative of triumphalist victory with no self-evident spaces for sombre recollection. As such, LTTE cemeteries in places such as Koppay, Uduppidi, Kodikaamam, Vealani and many others have been systematically demolished. The Koppay Cemetery in particular, as described in the previous chapter, was a very popular destination for warzone tourists in the first phase of tourism during the ceasefire. One estimate has suggested that the post-war process of dismantling LTTE sites has so far claimed 25 LTTE war cemeteries consisting of 20,400 tombs[5] while the most recent demolition was in October 2013 in the Kilinochchi District.[6] The issue here is not the accuracy of numbers but the reality of the act, and what it means. In reality, as already noted, many tombs in these cemeteries did not contain the remains of those who had died in combat but were affectively markers for combatants who were believed to have died and whose bodies were never recovered. Nevertheless, other tombs did contain human remains. The cemeteries were built more for the LTTE's own projection of its public self and power as well as a forum to narrate and perform its obsession with a relentless sense of heroism rather than as spaces of mourning for ordinary people. Nevertheless, as I have already noted in Chapter 2, even in the earlier phase, they became spaces for mourning and remembrance for ordinary people at times.

As long as the LTTE survived and maintained the cemeteries in the areas under its control, local people did feel confident enough to visit them on the days their loved ones had died because they were among the few places where such deaths were publically remembered, acknowledged and recognized. In addition, people did take part in LTTE-sponsored ceremonies in these places as well, either willingly or due to political compulsion. In cemeteries such as the one in Koppay which had been under military control since 1995, people were not as comfortable in visiting the place for fear of being watched by the army as possible LTTE sympathizers. And yet, in the ceasefire period when Koppay was refurbished by the LTTE and the movement of people became less stressful and less infused with anxieties over safety, large numbers of individuals did visit it for purposes of tourism as well as memory. At that time, it was not uncommon to see a few flowers or burnt candles on some of the tombstones. Even in the period prior to the ceasefire, the Koppay Cemetery as well as similar sites in areas under military control were destroyed. But that destruction was never as complete and final as in the post-war period. It was precisely due to that lack of finality that the LTTE was able to refurbish sites like Koppay which quickly became major attractions in the war tourist trail of the first phase.

In the post-war period however, it is clear that the government and the army did not intend to leave space for such resurrections, particularly with reference to sites which commemorated and articulated notions of LTTE heroism. It is in this context that one can understand that the newly built Jaffna Security Forces Headquarters emerged on the land which previously held the Koppay Cemetery. Noting the specific context of the demolishing of LTTE cemeteries and the building of post-war victory structures by the government, a recent report by the UN High Commissioner for Human Rights brings out its implications for memory:

> Following the end of armed conflict, memorialization, an integral component of reparations, has been non-inclusive, a fact that risks further disaffecting the minority population. While memorials to soldiers and war museums have been built by the Government, it has to date made no efforts to commemorate the civilians who lost their lives in the war.... Furthermore, since the end of armed conflict in May 2009, the military has reportedly prevented civilians in the north from holding private and religious ceremonies to commemorate family members, both civilians and combatants, killed in war. (Office of the United Nations High Commissioner for Human Rights 2013: 15)

While it is unlikely that the military would have prevented family members commemorating their loved ones in the privacy of their own homes, the indications are that such private ceremonies were discouraged in public spaces, which included temples. However, more often than not, people refrained from engaging in such ceremonies in public space due to fear of possible retribution rather than as a result of a clearly imposed ban. On the other hand, given the reality of the extensive post-war military intelligence network which evolved in the former warzone, even private commemoration of LTTE activists in the privacy of the domestic sphere was not tolerated and was filled with anxieties. They were simply seen as the enemy and not as someone's son, daughter, father, relative or friend. This is an indication of the nature of post-war erasure mandated by the state, which ranged from the extensive rearrangement and dismantling of public structures of memory to the policing and control of the emotions in the intimate private sphere of the home.

In addition to cemeteries, all formal LTTE monuments scattered in and around Jaffna and beyond had been demolished by 2013 as a necessary part of the government's post-war reconstruction effort. For instance, the Thileepan Memorial which many people visiting the Nallur Kandasamy Kovil had also visited in the first phase of warzone tourism was destroyed by the military in March 2010.[7] The fallen tower and the base which languished for some time were completely reduced to rubble in December 2012.[8] The post-war fate of the Koppay Cemetery and the Thlieepan Memorial indicated a pattern of planned demolition that all formal sites of LTTE memory faced. From the perspective of the government, the reminders of the LTTE in the form of monuments and cemeteries were simply not conducive for the promotion of what it conceived as 'reconciliation' and more importantly as 'tourism' even though these were central attractions in the earlier phase of warzone tourism.

In the imagination of the government, reconciliation had to be achieved through 'development' accompanied by a complete erasure of the past. In fact, the word 'development' with reference to post-war northern Sri Lanka is a euphemism for erasure of social and political memory of the region and rewriting of history. In this understanding, the past refers to the LTTE and the destruction it caused and the politics it represented, which should be erased. However, in another plain of thinking, that same past does not preclude the government from celebrating in a very obvious fashion the resounding military victory over the LTTE and its triumphalist manifestations. In the same context, development means the rebuilding of damaged infrastructure, the building of new edifices and essentially the wiping out all signs of damage that the war had created unless in some manner remnants of this destructive past suited the mega narrative the regime was in the process of constructing. In this scheme of things, there is no room for the local people to publically express emotions over incidents linked to the violence of the immediate past. It is within the context of the dominant discourses of development promoted by the state that one can also see the nature of tourism that the regime has intended for the north-east. The government's own rationale was outlined in 2010 by the Secretary to the Ministry of Tourism:

> The official government policy is not to highlight former LTTE land-marks for tourism purposes. The government has already begun to clear some LTTE landmarks in line with the government's view that terrorism, the LTTE and violence which affected the public during the war should be forgotten. (*Tamil Guardian* 2010; see also *Daily Mirror* 2010)

What then affectively constitutes the second phase of warzone tourism?

In the first week of December 2012, on my way to Jaffna I was briefly stopped at the first permanent Sri Lanka Army checkpoint at Omanthai which used to be the main military checkpoint during the war where everything and everyone grounded to a halt with long delays before it was possible to venture into the LTTE-held territory beyond, after cross-ing a narrow stretch of 'no man's land'. In the previous chapter, I explained in detail the politics, the polemics and the performative logistics of this border crossing while the war lasted, and its political importance in maintaining the public personality and the identity of the LTTE. Now, it is almost a ritual stop, structurally not unlike the routine and habitual stops at wayside shrines for various local and 'national' gods setup along main roads. People quickly emerged from their vehicles at these sites, murmured a few stanzas, tossed a few low denomination coins into the nearby till as a gift to the gods and paid them the ritualized homage that was expected in exchange for their blessings and protection, and were on their way again. Now, the structure and the pace of activity at that check-point have completely changed. Guns are still visible but are not at the ready; soldiers and travellers are visibly far more relaxed than they used to be prior to the end of war. As if completely uninterested in what they are doing, the men and women on duty note down in a large book the registration number of every vehicle, the National Identity Card number, and the name and other details of the driver and lazily look through the

National Identity Card or passport details of the other passengers. They almost never search the vehicles or the baggage as they once used to, unless there is an intelligence alert. While undergoing this ritual, in the midst of some unpalatable music coming from a small transistor radio hung precariously on a rafter of the main guardroom, one soldier in a conversational mood asked me where I was going, suggested that I could have tea from the nearby kiosk run by the army and passed on to me a brochure printed by the Sri Lanka Army Headquarters in Kilinochchi. It was a tourist promotional brochure called 'Travel Guide Kilinochchi', containing maps of Sri Lanka and Kilinochchi District identifying the roads to travel as well as 12 places of interest along with photographs of these places which included a number of recently built war memorials, the water tank in Kilinochchi destroyed by the LTTE during its retreat from the town, an LTTE prison complex and the four-storeyed bunker in Mullaitivu used by the LTTE leader Prabhakaran. It also advised potential tourists to be civil in their interactions with people in the areas they are to visit. I will revisit the politics of this brochure in Chapter 4 when I explore the dynamics of cartography and photography in the context of these travels in more detail. So despite the government's declared goal in 2010 to wipe out all traces of LTTE's presence, part of which had been carried out by the army as indicated in the complete destruction of LTTE structures of memory, as late as 2012, the army itself was promoting some remnants of LTTE wartime structures as potential tourist destinations. Nevertheless, the main intention of the brochure was to point travellers in the direction of its own newly unveiled monuments. There is also an interesting and not too evident tension between the army's promotion of warzone tourism, which includes LTTE sites, and the government's promotion of tourism in the same region which does not include these sites, which I will address later in this chapter.

'Stops' in the Post-2010 Warzone Tourist Trail

The regular 'stops' in the post-war trail of warzone tourism promoted by the Sri Lankan government and the army have by now become an accepted and taken-for-granted routine by many travellers with a somewhat predictable degree of consistency. Stewart has noted that 'domestic tourists are the main clients of the tourist industry of the North' at present, and that to cater to them the Sri Lankan government has 'set up a number of rather morbid tourist spots that act both as spaces of leisure and as monuments to the glories of the Sri Lankan military' (Stewart 2013). He calls these sites 'exciting tourist destinations' (Stewart 2013). For most people, the first stop is either the water tower in Kilinochchi that was blown up by the LTTE in 2009 when it withdrew from the town or the nearby war memorial constructed by the army in 2010. Usually, the buses and cars carrying southern tourists stop at one of these places while the individuals walk from one place to the next. Both are impossible to miss given their rather visible location along the A9 road.

The water tank is a crumpled mass of concrete enmeshed in metal which nevertheless retains obvious signs of its former vertical self which has been resurrected by the military as a museum of sorts along with a souvenir shop (see Figures 3.2 and 3.3). The shop sells ice cream, soft drinks and an assortment of biscuits and, more importantly, copies of a postcard carrying the image of the water tank in its collapsed form which also informs the public that the idea to convert the remnant into a museum came from

Figure 3.2

Water Tank Monument Complex, Kilinochchi

Source: Author.

Figure 3.3

Water Tank Monument Complex (detail), Kilinochchi

Source: Author.

President Rajapaksa's eldest son. One could walk along the footpaths laid out and gaze into the destroyed structure lying in the midst an extensive and well-maintained lawn. As a museum, it only hosts one artefact, which is the water tank itself. Its presence in the present form is significant given the fact that the government actually wants to erase all traces of violent conflict from the surrounding landscape. Most of the damaged buildings, bullet-riddled walls, shell-destroyed palm trees and defaced signposts that one could see abundantly as late as 2011, can no longer be seen as easily when travelling on the A9. That destruction has been erased almost as a damaged image has been airbrushed to what appears to be photoshopped perfection. So this single-artefact museum is a reference to a war and an era while most other evidence of its tangible destruction is fast disappearing. The soldiers who maintain the place are generally very conversational. As they told me in December 2012, the LTTE blew up the tank because they wanted the civilians to suffer as it was the main source of piped water to the town. Of course there were more nuanced strategic reasons for this action though the lack of pipe-borne water is a source of significant inconvenience. When the LTTE withdrew, it wanted the civilians in the town to come with the organization to use them as a civilian shield in its rapidly approaching final battle. The lack of water was one important condition in addition to the fear of the advancing army and the fear of the LTTE itself that forced civilians to follow the LTTE further east towards Mullaitivu where the battle finally ended. Second, the LTTE also wanted to ensure that life for the pursuing army was not going to be easy in the town given the difficulty in securing water.

In any event, the narrative that emerges from the soldiers around the water tank focuses on the LTTE's cruelty. In this context, the destroyed water tank is a symbol of that cruelty as well as symptomatic of an era of deprivation. In fact, the information plaques in Sinhala, English and Tamil articulates these associations with no room for confusion:

> [T]his fallen tower was once the source of water, the fountain of life for the people of Kilinochchi, destroyed by LTTE terrorists in the face of valiant troops converging on Kilinochchi in January 2009. This tower is a silent witness to the brutality of terrorism.... This is a monument to the futility of terror and to the resilience of the human spirit.

The soldiers also do not fail to inform visitors that the government, with the army's help, has now restored the water supply to the town and are engaged in 'numerous development activities'. This image of itself as the LTTE's other, that the government wants to promote is based on juxtaposing a number of binary opposites between itself and the LTTE: harbinger of development and prosperity versus conveyor of destruction; promoter of life and peace versus death and chaos and, finally, legitimate governance versus illegitimate terrorism. This binary campaign was initiated by the government well before the war ended when its last stage was officially called the 'humanitarian operation'. A tourist from the southern town of Matara noted in a conversation with reference to the Water Tank Monument,

> [M]ore than anything else, this shows the brutality of the LTTE. It was depriving water, the source of life to its own people. I am eternally thankful for the armed forces for ensuring that this war was won and that we can move about freely.... People here [in Kilinochchi] should be equally thankful though I am not sure if they will ever acknowledge it. That is what is called politics.[9]

At one level, what this person was saying made sense. It was a very reasonable and often-heard narrative about the diminishing of anxieties after the end of war. At another level however, in that plain of thinking, it was also a matter of wishing away and distancing of the extreme difficulties that the war had impacted upon this area and its people. But what was quite clear in these observations was the very clear amalgamation of the representation of reality offered by the state and the kind of reality often narrated and shared by many north-bound Sinhala tourists.

In May 2010, about one year after the cessation of the war, the government set up a monument in close proximity to the Water Tank Monument that is officially known as the Kilinochchi War Hero Memorial (see Figure 3.4).[10] Most people who go through the town for purposes of tourism would invariably visit both the water tank and this monument as a matter of routine. If the water tank reminds visitors of a specific dispensation that has been dismantled, the new monument points to the arrival and continuing presence of a new dispensation led by the military. This is not just any monument in the former warzone. Kilinochchi was the long-term capital of the LTTE after its withdrawal from Jaffna in 1995 until its retreat in 2009. The capture of Kilinochchi was an important stage in the final war against the LTTE and indicated conclusively that

Figure 3.4

War Hero Memorial, Kilinochchi

Source: Author.

the future of the organization was limited, and its final end was quite near. As such, this monument set up by the government is an important marker in the post-war rearrangement of the landscapes of memory and the geographies of contestation.

The Kilinochchi War Hero Memorial is situated in the midst of a carefully manicured park with lush green grass accompanied by a row of trees which not only provide shade but also the semblance of a natural guard of honour. When travelling from the south, the monument is on the right side of the A9 road. It is a very visible structure which at the same time is quite simple in its aesthetic rendition. According to the narratives that officers and soldiers milling around the area often narrate, before the establishment of the monument and the landscaped space in which it is situated, the area was a public park situated in close proximity to an LTTE base and its prison. Many locals still refer to the space as Seelan Park in their relatively inaudible discourses which almost never reach the rapidly transiting visitors or the official forums of the government and the military. This was the name used by the LTTE in memory of one of its own members. The monument consists of a number of interrelated structures which narrates a simple story without lapses in communication: a large concrete block representing the formidable LTTE defences in wartime Kilinochchi is depicted as being hit and ruptured by an incoming missile or large bullet. The projectile symbolizes the power of the Sri Lankan military and its ability to destroy the might of the LTTE. From the crack in the concrete where the projectile had hit, one can see a large bronze flower emerging. This blossoming flower indicates the future and hope. The symbolic structure of the monument is self-evident to most visitors despite its simple and abstract rendition, which enables the monument to speak to visitors without the aid of interpreters. Nevertheless, there are often soldiers and military police personnel within the premises who are quite willing and ready to play the role of tourist guides with vested authority and explain its symbolism. Without being prompted, they also narrate the official history of the war and the capture of Kilinochchi as an integral part of the military-mandated historiography of the locality. According to the Ministry of Defence, the monument 'symbolizes the gallantry of warriors whose unparalleled warfare skills torpedoed all terror tactics and rescued the entire district, sending shock waves across the world'.[11]

Most local as well as many visiting Tamils do not seem to visit the site unless it is necessitated as part of work which may vary from journalism to research. For many such individuals, even if they were not closely associated with the LTTE, the defeat of the LTTE and collapse of the town was an emotional defeat; it was the victory of one form of nationalism over another form of nationalism, both of which were tempered by an obvious sense of ethnic pride. For them, it is a rearranged emotional landscape of sorrow. As such, for many such people, the moment is both 'offensive' and 'bombastic'.[12]

Yet large numbers of Sinhala tourists invariably get down from their vehicles to see the place, talk to soldiers briefly and more importantly pose for photographs with the monument as their backdrop, and move on. As a school teacher who had brought his Grade 10 and 11 students from the town of Kurunegala told his students in December 2012: 'This marks a great moment in our history. The people who made this possible came from villages like ours. We should always remember them.'[13] This teacher's words to his students suggest that the monument had been able to communicate its key ideals to him. It is also clear that his basic ideas and that of the Ministry of Defence as quoted above tend to be similar in their fundamental assumptions which indicates a certain affinity between the ideas of the state and the perceptions of Sinhala tourists in essential details. In any case, the information plaques on site ensure that all the monument's meanings are clearly articulated to anyone who pauses to read. Its explanations in Sinhala and English take these meanings much beyond collectively shared assumptions when it makes the following observation:

[T]his memorial is a tribute to the glorious forces and to the state leadership by His Excellency the President and Commander in Chief of the Armed Forces, Mahinda Rajapaksa who was born for the grace of the nation with the guidance and coordination of the Secretary of Defense, Hon. Gotabhaya Rajapaksa for the greatest victory achieved by capturing the town of Killinochci on 2nd January 2009 through a humanitarian operation which paved the way to eradicate terrorism entirely from our motherland and restoring her territorial integrity and noble peace.

In this sense, this is not simply a monument in memory of fallen soldiers or a significant battle that was won not too long ago. More specifically, it is also a monument for two contemporary political leaders of the country. In the final analysis, if this monument might more fully be understood as a monument for a specific battle victory, soldiers who had died in action making this victory possible, notions of Sinhala nationalism, the president who was born for the grace of the nation and his brother's ability to guide and coordinate military activities at the height of war, it is also a monument that marks by default the decimation of the LTTE and the ideological death of a virulent manifestation of Tamil nationalism in the public sphere. In this context, it is hardly surprising that it is not a stop for most Tamil tourists who made it to the north after 2010. Besides, the significant absence of Tamil language explanation plaques on site as late as 2012 seems to suggest that the monument's formal narratives are meant primarily for Sinhala tourists.

Despite the clear moorings to Sinhala nationalism and a sense of adulation of military heroism which attracted Sinhala tourists to this place, these feelings were not the only dynamics at play among tourists who opted to stop by. For instance, while the teacher referred to earlier explained the nature of the monument to his students within the prevalent discourse of Sinhala nationalism and their attention to his words also explained their own affinity and familiarity with the crucial tenants of that discourse, their actual activities on site seemed to be more distracted from these lofty ideals of heroism and memory. They were much more interested in taking and posing for photographs. Not too many were keen on reading the explanatory plaques on site even though they were available in Sinhala. It appears that the monument had already become a routinized tourist stop, which had shorn off some of its politico-military and ideological significance. As one student told me in response to my question on what they would do with all these images: '[O]h, it's great for Facebook. When our friends see them, they will also want to come.'[14]

After travellers pass Kilinochchi, the next main monument on the war tourist trail is the Corporal Gamini Kularatna Monument (see Figure 3.5) which essentially consists of a modified LTTE bulldozer that was used as a battle vehicle for an attack on the army at Elephant Pass in 1991. In addition to the water tower in Kilinochchi, this is one of the few actual war remnants that have been converted into a monument by the government and the army as opposed to the more typical specifically constructed post-war monuments. Interestingly, this is the same remnant that had attracted much attention as a formal LTTE monument in the previous phase of warzone tourism as referred to in the previous chapter. I noted in Chapter 2 that even in the earlier phase, despite the LTTE's adoption of this same bulldozer as a monument for

Figure 3.5

Gamini Kularatana Memorial, Elephant Pass

Source: Author.

its own military history, ethnicity and differential notions of nationalism decided how people perceived the monument. In the present phase of warzone tourism, instead of the LTTE, the government and the Sri Lanka Army have claimed the monument for one of its own, this time the young Sinhala corporal from the Sri Lanka Army who is credited with stopping the incoming modified LTTE combat vehicle in 1991 in an altruistic act of suicide. In his act, he saved his camp and his colleagues though he died in the explosion he created when he jumped into the advancing vehicle carrying two live grenades. Kularatna is the only known suicide bomber among the Sinhalas as opposed to the many produced by the LTTE. What remains of this modified vehicle has been the centre of attraction in both incarnations of this monument.

Huge billboards in Sinhala and English set up on the opposite side of the monument announces the existence of the monument, carrying poorly photoshopped images of the monument itself and Kularatna in uniform against a backdrop consisting of fragments of the national flag (see Figure 3.6). Those fragments depict the lion and the sword, the central image of the flag which refers to the warrior spirit of the

Figure 3.6

Roadside billboard announcing the presence of the Gamini Kularatana Memorial, Elephant Pass

Source: Author.

Sinhalas. It narrates briefly the details of his heroic act and the fact that for the first time in Sri Lankan history, he was presented with the highest medal for gallantry in the country. The repainted bulldozer is now devoid of the Tamil and English language graffiti as well as the LTTE announcement which it once contained in its previous incarnation. It is placed upon a low concrete pedestal but open to the sky amidst a large park with shady trees at its further end on the side of the A9. A granite slab embedded in concrete erected close to the monument gives yet again the same details of Kularatna's heroism already presented in the billboards but, in addition, it also offers a heroic verse in free style written in Sinhala, which most Sinhala speakers will not find difficult to read and understand:

> In the name of the motherland,
> To sacrifice their lives,
> Many great men
> Were born in this land.

When such great men,
Numbering in hundreds and thousands
Were on the ready
To sacrifice their lives
For the land of their birth,

To protect such great heroes
By sacrificing your own self
For the motherland's freedom,
You are that great hero
Oh son, born in this land.[15]

In a sense, Kularatna has been transformed into a heroes' hero in death, close to the place where he actually died. But the sombreness that one might have expected from a site of death and memory does not emanate from the site despite the explanations on what the monument means on either side of the road. This partly comes from the park-like atmosphere the overall monument complex has created. On the other hand, a children's playground and rest area are part of the design of the complex while the playground is sponsored by a multinational milk powder company and its local agent (see Figure 3.7). Local and global capital has found it convenient and profitable to advertise at and sponsor numerous warzone tourist sites. When children are at play, one cannot expect conditions of meditative sombreness to emerge from such places. Their joyous crying, laughter and demands from parents drown any tangible voices of elders' conversations on nationalism and heroism the place might have conjured. It is clear that the government and the army not only got a cue from the LTTE on how to turn this mass of metal into a monument from the LTTE's previous attempt but also on how to incorporate ideals of nationalism and heroism within a space frequented by children as the LTTE had done with Kittu Children's Park in Jaffna. The space offered to children for play and also for elders for relaxation is the single most important dynamic that has converted the monument complex into a park for relaxation and a site of curiosity and relentless photo opportunities. Almost no one on the tourist trail passes this place without taking at least a few photographs.

At present, the monument is the most popular attraction on the warzone tourist trail as it is also perhaps the most often photographed

Figure 3.7

Children's park sponsored by Anchor and Newdale milk products within the Gamini Kularatana Memorial Complex, Elephant Pass

Source: Author.

site. This is mostly because the disabled bulldozer, the central attraction in the park, already has a dynamic discourse among the Sinhala public which precedes both phases of tourism and ensures that there is a steady stream of people coming to see it on a routine basis.

After they pass Kilinochchi, most travellers stop their buses or cars near the café run by the army opposite the monument, read the large description of the site and what it means on the billboards set up near the café and might opt for a few refreshments in the dimly lit café with its inelegant but reasonably comfortable plastic chairs. From the interior one can look upon the A9 stretching into the distance towards the south. Even though a very non-elegant place, like most other military-run cafés in this part of the country, it serves a specific purpose: basic refreshments and shade from the sun and rain. Besides, if anyone cares to ask the cashier what the uneven floor is made out of, he would say the floor boards are made out of discarded ammunition boxes, which links the café directly with the reality of war. Some visitors, after crossing the road, have some refreshments in the park where the monument is located, in the shade of the trees further away from the road. After some time, many would walk to the next monument, the Elephant Pass Monument, situated within walking distance from both the café and the Kularatna Monument.

In the second phase of warzone tourism, the entry into Elephant Pass became an altogether different experience for tourists. The war-damaged and defaced signboard which greeted tourists in the earlier phase was gone. Now, as part of the newly emergent on-the-road traffic discourse in the country, tourists are greeted with new green luminous signboards carrying the name of the location in all three languages; no defacement and no bullet holes. But still, as in the earlier phase, many people pose for photographs near the sign to document their entry into a land that is no longer contested. In a way, the almost omnipresent white-on-green luminous town-and-direction signs which now appear along most major roads as with the A9 suggest symbolically that a single dispensation has now exerted authority in all parts of the land. All around one could see large billboards in Tamil and English selling everything from mobile telephone services to wall paint to insurance (see Figure 3.8). This was clearly a sign of global and local capital's relentless influx into an area

Figure 3.8

Influx of post-war capital to the warzone: Billboard for selling mobile telephone services, Elephant Pass

Source: Author.

which was closed to investment for a considerable period of time. Unlike formal war monuments, the languages in these commercial billboards are Tamil and English; there is no Sinhala. Purveyors of local and global capital have understood a very simple truth: despite the relative lack of audibility of Tamil nationalism in these parts of the country after the defeat of the LTTE, if one has to sell anything it has to be presented in Tamil and to some extent in English, but not in Sinhala. In this sense, this is the new post-war frontier not only for local tourism but also for capital. Most war-damaged buildings and trees too close to the main road have been removed while the road itself runs smoothly from the south all the way to Jaffna via Elephant Pass. These are the hallmarks of post-war development, reconciliation and peace that the government points to, an image which many Sinhala tourists quite readily consume almost as if it is something that should be self-evident. But for locals, this is simply the cover of a book which camouflages the damaged pages of recent chaos. It is through this newly emergent landscape of visible 'development' and its contradictory narratives of pain and the continuing erasure of the outcomes of war that one would arrive at Elephant Pass, the official gateway to Jaffna over which many battles had been fought and hundreds of people had been killed not so long ago. There is still a checkpoint, but nothing like the busy, tense checkpoint that greeted travellers during the ceasefire. This is almost a rest stop, a routine stop where drivers have to note down their Driving License details and the vehicle registration and insurance information in a book maintained by the army. Soldiers are conversational and in no tangible mood of tension while they lazily browse through the identity papers of other travellers and wave them across. Some would also engage in casual conversation as one did with me in December 2014 particularly if they might assume the travellers understood Sinhala: 'Sir, the Elephant Pass monument is over there, to the right. Go and have a look. You can come here today because so many of our people died, and the monument is for them'.[16]

He was right; I could visit Jaffna in this manner only because a historical process has been concluded through extremities of death and destruction. But the monument across the road, rising atop a small hillock is only a memorial for the victory and the heroes of the victors. The dead and the injured among the locals and the 'enemies' in the war are not part of its narrative or part of any overt official discourse. Their presence had disappeared from the landscape and the dominant and officially sanctioned public memory in much the same way the bullet-riddled buildings and the shell-destroyed and blackened palms that once sorrowfully swayed in the gentle breeze are no longer to be seen from the main road. All these are affectively edited out of the post-war master narrative of victory.

The Elephant Pass Monument is officially identified as the 'Elephant Pass War Hero Memorial' (see Figures 3.9 and 3.10).[17] It was opened to the public on 30 April 2010, approximately 11 months after the war came to an end. As a causeway, Elephant Pass links the Jaffna peninsula to the rest of the island. In addition to this geographic and symbolic link binding Tamil-dominated Jaffna with the Sinhala dominated south, Elephant Pass had considerable military and strategic importance as well as emotional considerations for the Sri Lankan military as well as the LTTE. To begin with, it was the location of one of the largest and most significant and fortified bases of the Sri Lanka Army which was attacked and captured by the LTTE in April 2000. This debacle remains the Sri Lanka Army's most devastating defeat culminating in the death and disappearance of hundreds of soldiers in addition to the loss of weapons, munitions and military vehicles, all of which were used by the LTTE in future battles against the army itself.[18] This victory was a significant military success for

Figure 3.9

War Hero Memorial, Elephant Pass

Source: Author.

Figure 3.10

Relief depicting a phase in the civil war (detail), War Hero Memorial, Elephant Pass

Source: Author.

the LTTE. Partly, this comes from the military and strategic advantages in controlling Elephant Pass. On the other hand, the symbolic and emotional value in literally controlling the gateway to Jaffna cannot be underestimated. Within this cluster of meaning, retaking Elephant Pass was important to the Sri Lanka Army for strategic as well as emotional reasons. As such, locating one of the army's most important and visible public monuments in Elephant Pass is not difficult to understand. It is not just a mark of victory but also a symbol of regaining lost pride. Due to the deaths and destruction the debacle caused, the wide press coverage it received locally, and its emotional toll in the south, most Sinhalas who visit the monument are acutely aware of what the monument means in emotional terms.

The government has officially claimed that the monument is 'a tribute in memory of the fallen heroes in the struggle in trying to free the nation of the menace of LTTE terrorism' and that it 'also stands out as a token of living memory for soldiers since it was the point where northbound 57 and 58 Divisions met up with their fellow soldiers from 53 and 55 Divisions who were moving southward from Jaffna'.[19] So according to this narrative, the importance of the monument comes from the fact that a number of Sri Lanka Army units coming from different directions on their final assault on LTTE units met up in the area; by the same token, it is also a payment of gratitude for what they made possible. Interestingly, however, the on-site information notes that the monument 'was erected to mark the event of opening the way for the free movement of North and South citizens in this land of victory which bridges North and South'. In this sense, it is a monument for freedom of movement and a monument for bridging divided entities, which nevertheless was made possible only by a military victory on the ground, with devastating emotional consequences. As in the Kilinochchi monument, it also notes that the former president who gave political (state) leadership for the war effort was born for the 'grace of the nation' and thanks his brother, the Secretary of Defence for his 'guidance' and 'coordination'. They are the only individuals specially named in the monument as worthy of specific gratitude. Many others who have died in the war effort are interestingly remembered only by association and not as individuals.

Perched atop a hillock along the A9 road and designed by the government's National Design Centre, the monument is a visible structure consisting of an array of accompaniments that convey a cluster of symbolic references which are elaborated on site, most of which cannot be grasped immediately without the help of on-site interpretations. Stewart describes the main sculptural components of the monument as 'four hands holding up the island of Sri Lanka, a lotus flower blooming from the top. It is meant to illustrate the solidarity of the Sinhala people, uniting to stop the terrorist threat' (Stewart 2013). This main structure is protected by four lions symbolic of the Sinhala people. Beyond these main sculptures, the monument consists of a number of other interconnected structural elements which includes the hillock upon which the main monument stands, specific plants selected for their symbolic value, flights of stairs and a series of sculpted murals depicting in a very representational style different stages of the war and the contributions of various branches of the armed forces to the war effort. Together, these interrelated elements attempt to narrate a cluster of symbolic and political messages. However, beyond the obvious notions of heroism and victory over war, much of the details of these meanings are lost in the clutter of the monument's symbolic vocabulary unless visitors pay attention to the on-site explanations:

This monument rising to the sky from the centre of a circle consisting of two similar shapes situated opposite to each other depicts the relationship existing in and out. The vegetation peculiar to the North is seen in the northern semi-circle. Vegetation peculiar to the South is seen in the Southern semi-circle. This grove of trees festooning one another depicts the power of exuberant Sri Lanka which is rising itself out of the unity of all religious and ethnic communities. This giant hill looming from the centre of this forest depicts the horrendous era which till then caused suffering to Sri Lanka. The flight of steps rising from the base of this hill signifies the members of the dignified three forces and the steadfast political leadership unshaken as a mountain which brought an end to the era of terror. The circular path originating from the flight of steps and treading up the hill signify the difficulty and tediousness of the humanitarian effort aimed at saving the mother country. The flight of steps at the end of the path further signifies courageous political commandership which defeated the coups and impediments that propped up within and out of the country and the unshaken resoluteness and determination of heroic soldiers which they maintained till the last hour of victory. The next step from this flight is towards the final victory. The imposing figure of lion mounted on the four corners mould the great power in which majesty, strength and leadership are embodied. The lion is a typical figure to Sri Lanka. The square seen above the lions means independent and unitary strength of motherland and the four brimful pots (pun kalasa) placed around the square symbolize the prosperity of all the communities. The other square rising from the centre depicts the unity of the nation. The four giant hands, strong, heroic and powerful, rising from this square towards the sky depicts the supreme victory achieved after surmounting all impediments. The blossomed water lily, our national flower on the floor of Sri Lanka depicts the supremacy and pride while its bud symbolizes the strength, unity, prospect of peace, confidence and purpose for hopeful tomorrow.

It is interesting to note that on numerous occasions, in its explanatory plaques and a number of symbolic references in the sculptures, the monument specifically stresses issues of national unity. In this sense, it traverses beyond the limitations of ethno-cultural pride and cultural nationalism which are the main features of many other monuments. It is not an accident in this context that the extensive description above is offered in all three national languages. Nevertheless, the Sinhala ethno-cultural presence is unmistakable over all other cultural references.

It does not appear that all these symbolic references necessarily enter the minds of the large flock of tourists who invariably visit this place every day in their northbound warzone tourist trail. They are interested in the place as it has become a 'must see' location in the already well-established tourist trail, which is also considered an important photograph location by practice. Naturally, as already noted, many of them also have at least a general sense of what happened in Elephant Pass and what it means. Writing about the Elephant Pass Monument, Stewart notes that 'none of the sites were more crowded than the giant sculpture at Elephant Pass' (Stewart 2013). He also notes the interest of tourists at the time of his visit to listen to 'a military officer explaining the victories at Elephant Pass' (Stewart 2013). For many of them, given the complexity in the symbolic structure of the monument beyond basic sensibilities, it is the military that speaks of the monument and what it means rather than the monument itself.

Once people moved beyond Elephant Pass and arrived in the Jaffna peninsula, in most cases, the religiously oriented aspects of tourism that was evident in the first phase of tourism manifested again. That is, people visited both Naga Dipa and Dambakola Patuna temples. In this period, the Dambakola Patuna temple underwent considerable physical transformations through a concerted building programme facilitated and funded by the Sri Lanka Navy. This was clearly evident since about 2011 which saw the construction of buildings as well as statutes that augmented the main mythologized story of the temple. On the other hand, the dependence of tourists on the Naga Vihara temple in Jaffna city as a place for accommodation as well as advice and direction changed considerably by the time the second phase of tourism was in full swing by about 2012. Even though people still came to this temple in search of inexpensive accommodation, other accommodation opportunities also opened up in Jaffna to cater for the increased tourist influx in the form of hotels in the formal tourism sector as well as numerous guest houses through the conversion of people's homes as a secondary source of income. Also, bus and tour operators as well as many ordinary travellers had become more familiar with the tourist landscape of the area by this time that the intervention of the temple as a guide to this landscape was no longer a necessity as it was in the earlier phase.

Part of this familiarization emerged from incessant travel as well as from the availability of specialized maps, which I will explore later in this book. On the other hand, compared to the ready acceptance of the mythological vocabulary and narratives of Naga Dipa and Dambakola Patuna temples by tourists, it does not seem that the mythic narratives constructed for the Naga Vihara temple that were in circulation in the earlier phase had been as widely accepted by the incoming tourists which also had an impact on it not becoming a conventional pilgrim or tourist site as opposed to a place for accommodation. The preference of some tourists for alternate accommodation instead of temple accommodation despite its low cost was explained by a bus driver in the following words:

> [T]he temple is a good place to stay and it is cheap. But now we no longer stay there. It is not a place to relax. It can get too crowded. Besides, because it is a temple, we can't even have a drink after a hard day of work. Now I take the people who travel with me to one of two places. In one place, an entire floor has been set up to accommodate people. In the other place, we get the whole house. We simply pay the money and we get the space for ourselves and floor mats to sleep on and a place to cook our meals. This is much more convenient and relaxed. There are places to order food all around too if you want. But it is cheaper to cook. When buses come to Jaffna town, people on bicycles come to meet the drivers and offer accommodation in all kinds of places. These days accommodation in Jaffna is not a problem.[20]

His observations clearly indicate the entrenchment and local institutionalization of warzone tourism.

On the other hand, beyond the expansion of accommodation facilities as well as the increased influx of tourists to the north, since the advent of post-war tourism, travel to these places had become much easier and more comfortable due to improvements in road and transport conditions as well as relative relaxation of security. The travel time between Colombo and Jaffna by road had been reduced from 14 hours or more at the time of the ceasefire to about six hours by 2014. The train service all the way from Colombo to Kankesanturai in Jaffna was also operational by 2014 after an absence of nearly 25 years.

However, the geography and the landscape of war-related monuments that constituted a major source of attraction in the first phase of tourism underwent a radical transformation almost from the beginning of post-war tourism. For example, all the LTTE monuments in and around Jaffna and the cemetery in Koppay which were incessantly visited by southern tourists in the earlier phase were destroyed by the government as a matter of policy. In some cases, such as with regard to the Koppay cemetery, the new headquarters of Sri Lanka Army's 501 Brigade was built on its site. Right now, no physical evidence of the cemetery exists at all. All references to it are in the memories of local people and in the relatively inaudible discourses in the localities and sometimes beyond that. These memories, however, are no longer articulated as such, but are merely whispered. The destruction and the disappearance of all traces of these sites make a very potent statement about the fragility of physical structures of memory in an era of victory and triumphalism. Nevertheless, the ancestral house of the LTTE leader Velupillai Prabhakaran remained a popular site for visitors in the second phase of tourism as it was in the first phase as well. Thousands of visitors flocked to see the small house each day exhibiting the same curiosity they showed before. However, locals and Tamil politicians have said that by April 2010 the Sri Lanka Army had destroyed the house. It appears that the military had stopped people from visiting the site over a period of three or four weeks during which time the house was gradually demolished even though the army has formally denied any knowledge of its destruction.[21] The observations of a southern tourist in his internet journal in March 2010 shed further light on the situation:

> This image taken in March shows the ancestral house of slain LTTE leader Velupillai Prabhakaran. It was a monument maintained by the Tigers soon after 2002 peace deal. When southern visitors began pouring into Jaffna after the A9 was opened in January 2010, it became a tourist magnet. The walls, both outer and inner are full of graffiti, there was even an advertisement for a bake house in the south scrawled on the front part. The military had stopped allowing visitors near the house by late February. They had to take a look from the main road, and from within their vehicles. The soldiers stationed there told us that the house was going be demolished soon when we were there in March.[22]

The popularity of the site itself seems to have irked the army as also observed by a Tamil politician who noted that 'thousands of people were coming and seeing the house every day. This might have angered the authorities'.[23] The final result however is that, despite official denials, the house no longer exists and as a result, one of the most popular warzone tourist sites has been permanently removed from the trail as has a historical marker of Sri Lanka's recent turbulent political history been erased from the landscape.

As a result of the government policy of destroying LTTE monuments and cemeteries as well as iconic civilian structures such as Prabhakaran's ancestral home, the warzone tourist trail in the Jaffna district literally dries up once a person navigates beyond Elephant Pass and enters the peninsula. However, this does not mean that the trail cannot continue beyond Jaffna. After their visit to Jaffna, most people return to the south via Mullaitivu which was not open to civilian traffic until 2010. In the earlier phase of warzone tourism, the LTTE simply did not open this area for southern tourism. In the present phase, the general area of Mullaitivu is more 'interesting' to southern tourists as it offered a more 'real feel' of war until at least 2012 than the relatively sanitized and radically rear-ranged landscape and geographies offered on the way to and in Jaffna post-2010. This is more like what the Jaffna trail offered between 2002 and 2005. It is in the areas around Mullaitivu that the war was most bit-terly and brutally fought in its final stage and also where it finally came to an end when the LTTE's top leadership was decimated by the Sri Lanka Army. When one arrives in Puthukkudiyiruppu from Jaffna, the roads get progressively worse as one leaves the A9 and there is a more pro-nounced military rather than a civilian presence, not so much in numbers as in visibility. The military tourist brochure I referred to earlier in this chapter directs travellers to a number of sites in this area which includes Prabhakaran's last hiding place which consists of a four storey bunker, the site of the Farah 3 ship and the newly built Victory Monument, and the somewhat under-maintained but extremely popular Army War Museum in Pudumathalan, very close to where the war actually ended when the LTTE's leader was killed.

When one arrived in this area and travelled into the hinterland as late as 2012, one immediately got the sense that the almost photoshopped and nearly sanitized environs of Jaffna are already a distant dream. Here, rows and rows of blackened palm trees with their tops blown off, still gently swaying in the breeze attempt to narrate a story of devastation not yet narrated in its complete version elsewhere in the country. One can imagine the kind of firepower that would have brought such catastrophic dismemberment to these once majestic trees. That would also nudge the more perceptive visitors, keen to capture something more nuanced beyond what their mobile phone cameras could record, to wonder what the fate of thousands of people who were in this area when the war ended might have been. But if the blackened palm trees were attempting to narrate a story of death, pain and destruction through their silent sway-ing, it was a story that was not heard by most southern tourists. As late as 2012, when one travelled towards one's destinations, it was possible to see large piles of corroding motor vehicles, motorcycles and bicycles packed on top of each other on either side of the road along long stretches (see Figure 3.11). The larger vehicles were numbered in the sense that crude numericals were painted on them. This was yet another telling symbol of the destruction that was caused just over three years ago. Yet, it was taboo to photograph these dismembered and numbered piles of vehicles. In December 2012, not too far from Pudumathalan town, when I attempted to photograph some of these vehicles, a young soldier came running towards me with his gun shouting from a distance: '[D]on't photograph those; you are not supposed to do this. Keep your camera aside'. He was not threatening me but trying to carry out an order as he later explained when I asked him why I am not supposed to photograph them when the military were encouraging tourists to photograph anything and everything at the sites they had captured from the LTTE all around this area. His answer was simple:

> I don't have a problem with you photographing. But we have been told not to let anyone photograph them. I don't know why. Six or seven months ago there as no restriction. All these have been auctioned off to a rich businessman. It was after that, that the prohibition came.[24]

Figure 3.11

Where the tourist gaze fell: One of the graveyards of war-damaged vehicles, Pudumathalan

Source: Author.

So clearly, this was yet another act of erasure that was already in progress. These remnants of war which offered clear markers to the havoc and destruction that the war caused had become part of a business agreement with a businessman and the government or individuals claiming government affinity. They would have been removed soon afterwards and converted into capital, and with that, yet another set of markers of the pain that was tangible in the vicinity would be removed and a seeming sense of normalcy imposed.

Houses without their roofs and bullet holes in the walls (see Figure 3.12), and in many cases missing houses which had only left the foundations as references to their former selves narrate a tragedy that has been most fully captured in Tamil poetry of the time. As R. Cheran's 2009 poem, 'A Stretch of Sand' notes:

> .... Not a sign to tell
> where the living had been.
> Only, on a spreading palmyra tree
> a torn sari, hanging (Cheran 2013: 115).

Figure 3.12

Where the tourist gaze fell: Bullet-damaged house numerically identified by the military, Pudumathalan

Source: Author.

Articulations such as these and the whispered memories of survivors defy the logic of the Sri Lankan government's notion of a 'humanitarian operation'. Instead, these remnants are the missing pages of a story from the master narrative of victory articulated by the state, which had also been popularly and collectively shared to a large extent by many tourists who came to the north and also saw these sites. As such, why these kinds of elements were missing from the master narrative and the largely sanitized perception of tourists was not based on the actual lack of visibility. It was the result of voluntarily ensuring that the prevalent master narrative could flow without contradictions. People saw the bullet-riddled houses, the blackened palms and rows and rows of abandoned, damaged and corroded motor vehicles; exclaimed over the destruction of war; captured countless images and moved on consuming quite happily the comforting narrative of the 'humanitarian operation' and stories on the 'development' of the north that was already on the way.

Nevertheless, just beyond some of these houses, as late as 2012, it was still possible to see large swaths of land with thousands of abandoned plastic vessels, cooking utensils, clothing, shoes, children's books and other personal items strewn around, some of which were being smothered by the advancing undergrowth (see Figure 3.13). It almost seems if the references to a mournful and terrible past are being erased by nature itself until that process is completed and finalized by 'development' which cannot be too far away. Nevertheless, at least for three years after the end of war, when tourists were flocking to the area in large numbers, they continued to talk of a tragedy that the sanitized TV coverage failed to emphasize. At the same time, if one cared to look around in these areas, it was possible to see in some places solitary men, in their almost skeletal personas, digging holes in the muddied grounds of abandoned compounds in an almost ghost-like fashion. On more than one occasion, the soldiers who are all around told me that they are looking for valuables that the former owners might have buried before their flight to survival or death. As one of them mentioned, '[W]e let them do it. They are trying to make a living. These are difficult times, and some of them had lived well before the war'.[25] If tourists failed to see these realities, it was interesting that the soldiers who had fought the war which created the prevalent state of affairs and continued to live in these areas were far more perceptive. In that sense it was not unusual that one of them donated his military-supplied lunch packet to one of the thin and tired-looking men digging not too far away and opted to share the lunch with his colleague who was on security duty nearby.

Figure 3.13

Swaths of destruction, Pudumathalan

Source: Author.

Navigating through these sites of devastation which offered a more real context to the war, even though they literally remained the invisible pages of a forgotten history for most tourists passing through these areas, one could slowly reach through devastated roads many other sites that had become important destinations for tourists as the second phase of warzone tourism became entrenched. When I asked for the road to the Victory Monument and how to get back to the main road, the young soldiers at the main military checkpoint in Puthukkudiyiruppu, insisted that I should visit Prabhakaran's bunker as it was worth seeing. As one of them noted, '[E]veryone goes there sir; you will like it. It's worth seeing. Our people at the site will explain things to you.'[26] Soldiers often directed curious tourists to a large map publically and prominently displayed at army-run visitor information centre at Puthukkudiyiruppu. Identified in Sinhala and English as 'Important Locations of the Final Stage of the Humanitarian Operation', the map is essentially an enlarged military map that points to places of military and strategic significance in the final stage of the war. On the other hand, it is also a tourist map which directs tourists to nearby LTTE and other war-related sites which the army had decided are places of interest. In addition to Prabhakaran's bunker referred to by the soldier above, they also included the safe house of the commander of LTTE's marine wing known popularly as Sea Tigers, a large swimming pool used for training Sea Tiger members, a submarine construction yard, the destroyed metal remnants of the ship known as Farah 3 and so on. In each of these locations, the army had painstakingly established large explanatory signs in English and Sinhala. Writing in 2012, with reference to Prabhakaran's bunker and other LTTE military structures in the Mullaitivu area, a Sri Lankan journalist noted that the 'Sri Lanka Army had gone to great lengths to preserve for now, all that they had captured from the LTTE' (Ratnatunga 2012). However, the absence of Tamil in the tourist information map in the visitor information centre at Puthukkudiyiruppu as well as the on-site explanatory signs in the army-promoted trophy sites is a clear indication of the ethnicization of the victory narrative. These were affectively for the consumption of Sinhalas and 'others' who were presumably not Tamil speakers.

Within this scheme of politics of inclusion and exclusion and ethnically informed field of meaning, as late as December 2012, the army was actively promoting Prabhakaran's bunker as a 'must see' site. After all, it was one of their most important trophies, an emphatic capture. This part of Mullaitivu was a crucial area in the LTTE's overall strategic planning and institutional network. After relocating to Kilinochchi after their expulsion from Jaffna by the army and making it their capital, the LTTE established fortified defences in the Mullaitivu area as well. This was for long-term defence as well as a location for a last stand, in case Kilinochchi was also lost. In this context, this bunker situated not too far away from the sea, which itself was a potential escape route in the event of defeat, was specifically constructed for the LTTE's leader and his family. Descending four stories underground, the bunker was equipped with air conditioning, an exhaust system, self-contained sound-poof power generation, surveillance cameras, satellite technology and weapons storage along with a collection of photographs of deceased LTTE combatants in a chamber reminiscent of a shrine, a stuffed tiger, cognac for Prabhakaran's personal use as well as his personal correspondence.[27]

While the LTTE ruled these areas, none of these structures were open to the public including to people who lived in the areas. In this context, and also due to the manner in which it entered the popular discourse of warzone tourism through print and electronic media as well as through the less structured and more extensive personal discourses of tourists and the army's own promotion of it as one of its most triumphant trophies, the bunker complex soon became an iconic example of the LTTE's wartime structures. Besides, no one venturing into the area from the south as tourists would ever have seen anything like this before. This was affectively a spectacle. Its popularity further expanded after the ancestral house of Prabhakaran in Velvetiturai was destroyed by the army in 2010. Almost every tourist I have talked to had visited the site and, in fact, it was one of the most consistent predetermined locations in their itinerary.

It was not a place someone stumbled upon by accident, but by choice and as the result of a pronounced sense of eagerness. Local TV and print media had popularized the site with government sanction as a possible site of curiosity almost from the time of its capture in 2009 making references to the slain LTTE leader's opulent lifestyle while his 'people' lived around him in abject poverty and facing the dangers of war. Once the bunker complex was opened to the public, the Sri Lanka Army had spent considerable time and effort in identifying different sections of the bunker and its adjacent structures for the benefit of tourists by installing a schematic map of the entire complex at its entrance and identifying in Sinhala and English language signage each of its four floors as well as the dedicated areas within these floors and beyond. These included the conference room where senior LTTE leaders met, the operational centre from where Prabhakaran is supposed to have monitored and commanded the war effort, bathrooms, an underground vehicle park, a bulletproof sentry post, a shooting range, a collection of armour-plated doors initially installed within the bunker and so on. But the personal items used by the LTTE leader and his followers as well as other moveable objects including furniture that the entire country saw on television at the time the bunker complex fell into military hands are no longer to be seen. They are not in the nearby Army Museum or any other public collection even though the entire complex and what was within it survived the ravages of war. Nevertheless, the effort and the care extended by the army in turning the complex into an organized tourist attraction was quite evident. In addition to the signage (see Figure 3.14), many soldiers on site were willing to be voluntary tour guides. They were both happy and proud to explain the intricacies and mythologies of their trophy; they

Figure 3.14

Site map for Prabhakaran's four-tier bunker, Mullaitivu

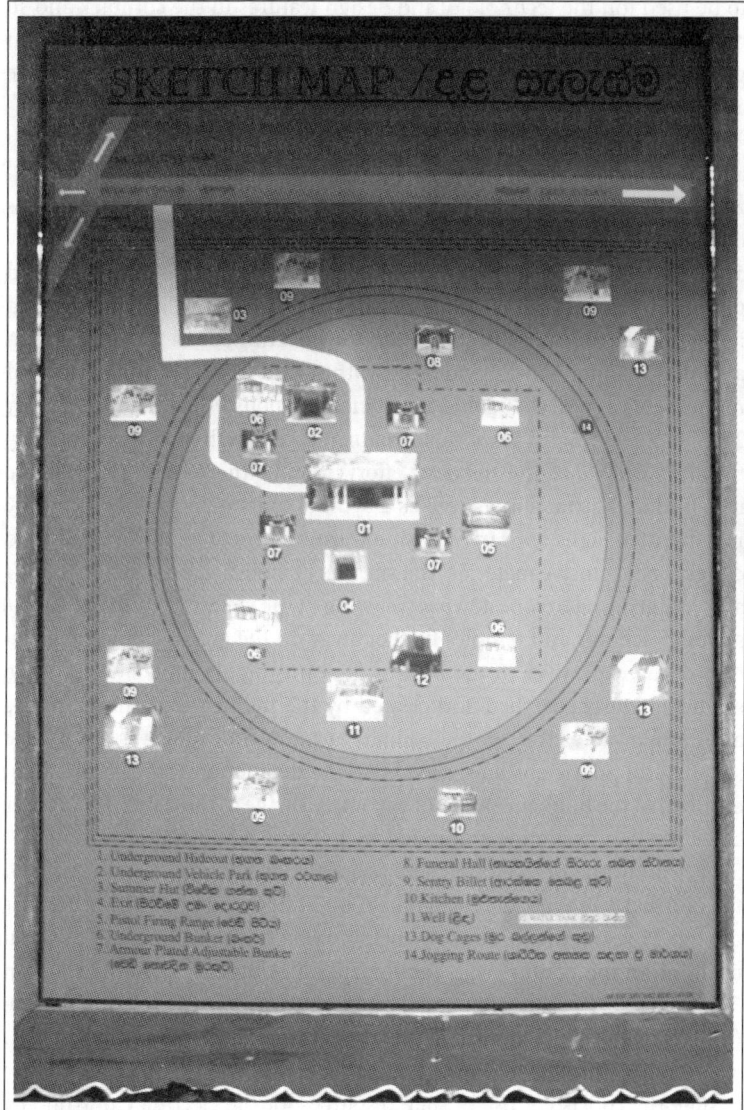

Source: Author.

would describe how they captured the area, how it was first found, what was inside, how the complex was built, what each section was supposed to be used for, the technology and design features in the complex and so on. This kind of public relations role for soldiers would not have been possible if the command structure of the army had not made it possible as a matter of policy.

Unlike more recent military monuments, the bunker complex also attracted visiting members from the Tamil diaspora as well as Tamil citizens settled in the south. This was despite the fact that the signage was only in Sinhala and English and the commentaries from guides was only available in Sinhala. It now appears that this ethnically undifferentiated popularity of the place as well as its direct link to the LTTE in general and its leader in particular discomforted the government in the long run in a similar manner as was evidenced with regard to LTTE cemeteries and monuments as well as Prabhakaran's ancestral house. Since late September 2013, in a seemingly inexplicable manner, access to the site was denied by the army despite all the elaborate efforts it had hitherto taken to promote it as a tourist attraction as well as a symbol of its own military prowess. Handwritten signs appeared outside warning people to stay away due to dangers of explosive material. The site was demolished on 3 October 2013 after the army had requested people living in the vicinity to relocate themselves to schools and temples further away on the grounds that they had discovered explosives in the bunker. It seems highly unlikely that a site so meticulously searched and cleared by the military and showcased as a symbol of its victory would contain unexploded explosives at this late stage. Local politicians have stated that the demolition was carried out to ensure that the bunker would not become a 'shrine to the slain LTTE leader since the area was now controlled by a Tamil provincial government.[28] Significantly, the demolition came about two weeks after the elections to the Northern Provincial Council held on 21 September 2013 for the first time in 25 years, which was convincingly won by the main Tamil political coalition in the country, the Tamil National Alliance (TNA) which won 30 out of the 38 seats of council. The United People's Freedom Alliance (UPFA) which affectively ruled the rest of the country secured seven seats and the Sri Lanka Muslim Congress won one seat. This victory came despite the consistent use of state resources for the election campaign by the incumbent national government as well as the military in favour of the UPFA. The victory also meant that a Tamil-dominated political formation would technically be able to control major aspects of the socio-economic and cultural life of the people in the area even though in real terms it was unlikely that the military's obvious domination of the area would end anytime soon. In fact, this is precisely what happened soon afterwards in a situation when the military and the central government made the popularly elected Northern Provincial Council government ineffective on the ground. It is in this environment that one can understand the comments of irate soldiers who had reportedly chased away Tamil residents attempting to visit the bunker site claiming, '[W]e have done so much for you people, still you went and voted for the TNA.'[29]

Within this overall context, one observer has noted that '[T]he demolition of the bunker at this stage was a tacit acknowledgment by the military establishment that the bunker had been preserved for the benefit of triumphalist Southern tourists rather than aimed at keeping alive the history of the Sri Lankan civil war.'[30] However, unlike in the case of the destruction of his ancestral house, the demolition of Prabhakaran's bunker was formally acknowledged by the army as necessitated by the fact it was on the verge of collapse and also because there was no reason for it to remain standing.[31] In the same context, the military had suggested that tourism at the site was only a 'temporary phenomenon'.[32] Interestingly, the army's anxieties over the possibility of Prabhakaran's bunker becoming a shrine for LTTE memory and heroism in the post-Northern Provincial Council election was given some credence in another development elsewhere in the north about 10 days after the demolition. The recently constituted Chavakachcheri Pradeshiya Sabha (one of the local government units within the Northern Province) passed a resolution on 14 October 2013 'calling for the reconstruction of LTTE cemeteries in the area, coming under the purview of the newly elected Northern Provincial Council' while it also 'decided to commemorate those who died fighting for the LTTE'.[33] The concern among military and government circles was that this resolution might lead to more such resolutions being passed by other local government bodies in the new political dispensation of the Northern Provincial Council. More than the actual possibility of realizing such political objectives, the issue at stake was their potent symbolic value.

Amidst a number of other obvious remnants of war close to the bunker that were popular among visitors was the submarine yard identified by the Sri Lanka Army in two separate explanatory boards as Sea Tiger Submarine Yard and the Mini Submarine Yard (see Figures 3.15 and 3.16). The attempted construction of submarines and other submersible marine vehicles were an integral part of the LTTE's ambitious plans

Figure 3.15

Explanatory sign at LTTE Submarine Yard, Mullaitivu

Source: Author.

Figure 3.16

Remnants of an experimental submarine prototype at LTTE Submarine Yard, Mullaitivu

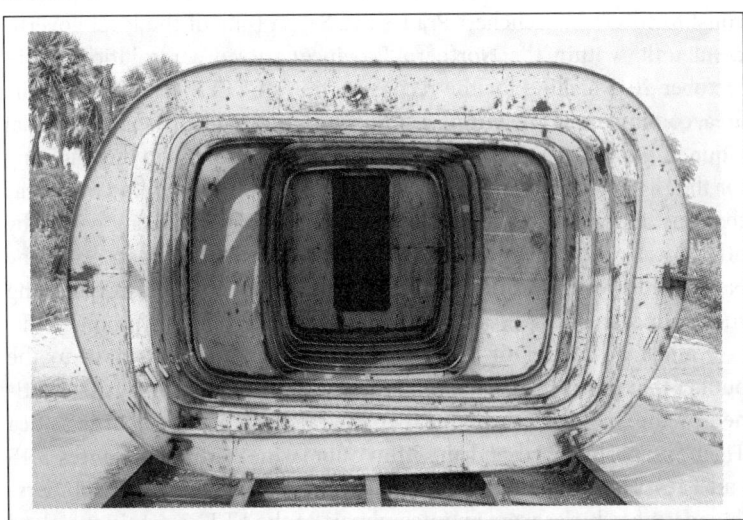

Source: Author.

to dominate the sea in its battle against the Sri Lankan government in general and the Sri Lanka Navy in particular. The site is located very close to the sea. According to the two elaborate signs installed by the Sri Lanka Army, this is where the LTTE had built a number of model submarines on an experimental basis and the nearby large pool was used for pre-testing their stability before they were tested in the sea. A number of partially constructed steel remnants resembling submarines are at the site, which have become popular backdrops for the tourists' relentless appetite for warzone photographs. Despite the material available and the visibility of this site, there is no evidence that the LTTE was anywhere close to constructing a functional submarine with warfare capabilities as opposed to its success in constructing a number of crude but functional aircrafts for its nascent air wing towards the last stage of the war. Nevertheless, an army officer at the site observed,

[G]ood thing we captured this place when we did, and put these people out of business. If these fellows succeeded in building one of these things, the history of the war might have been different. They would have attacked our harbours with more devastating results.[34]

Interestingly, slightly different versions of this observation were narrated by many returning tourists with whom I have had conversations in 2012 and 2013. It seems like a narrative that military volunteers on site shared with tourists who might have paused to listen. Irrespective of the historical and technical accuracy of this claim, it certainly restates the military's heroic and central role in rewriting the country's history from its own perspective.

Another popularly visited site nearby, closely related to LTTE marine operations, is the large pool that has been identified by the army in its main explanatory sign (see Figures 3.17 and 3.18) as a training facility for Sea Tiger divers where they trained in underwater operations and suicide attacks against Sri Lanka Navy crafts as well as coastal installations of the Sri Lanka Army. The massive pool is 83 feet long and 22 feet deep according to military explanations while it was once covered by a camouflaged wire mesh to obscure it from air observation. While the wire mesh has now disappeared, the metal structure that once held it in place remains.

Tourists who visited the bunker, the submarine yard, the pool and other nearby sites also invariably visited the huge metal structure of the Farah 3 ship resting on the beach not too far from where the bunker used

Figure 3.17

Sea Tiger training pool, Mullaitivu

Source: Author.

to stand (see Figure 3.19). Given the almost majestic and haunting presence of the ship on the beach, slightly tilting towards the water, with a giant metal chain extending from the ship well into the beach and a large square section of its hull removed by the LTTE, the remnant was a major attraction on the warzone tourist trail. Not only was it something that was directly related to the war, it was a remnant that narrated the demonized story of the LTTE, which is a crucial component of the state's mega narrative of victory. Farah 3 was a spectacle and had acquired the personality of a movie backdrop. According to the army-installed information sign, the ship was a Jordanian-owned merchant ship. While it was on its way from the coast of Andhra Pradesh in India to South Africa, it developed engine trouble, and had to anchor off the coast of Mullaitivu. LTTE Sea Tigers hijacked the ship and took its crew prisoner in December 2006 and dragged the ship closer to the coast where it ran aground at the present location. Even though the crew were released by the LTTE soon after their capture, its cargo of 14,000 tons of rice as well as electrical items, lights, generators, and all other removable parts and the crew's personal effects were removed by the LTTE.[35] Since that time, the LTTE had used the remnants of the ship to train Sea Tigers for operations against

Figure 3.18

Explanatory sign at Sea Tiger training pool sponsored by holcim cement, Mullaitivu

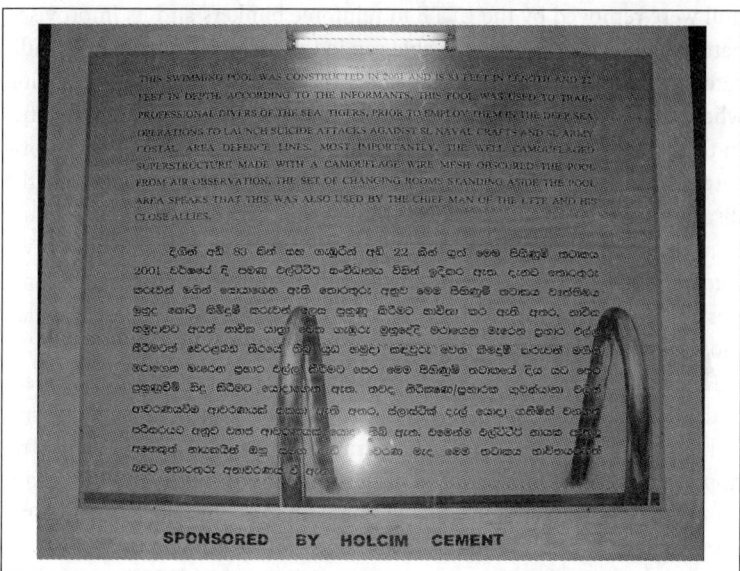

Source: Author.

Figure 3.19

The popular attraction, Farah 3 ship, Mullaitivu

Source: Author.

the Sri Lanka Navy as well as a firing platform and cover against naval movements beyond. More importantly, large sections of the vessel's metal hull were removed by the LTTE to reinforce bunkers and its improvised battle vehicles, as the rather visible gap in the hull demonstrates. As indicated by the information sign set up by the army, this is also the location where the northern and southern formations of the Sri Lanka Army met in their final push against the LTTE on 14 May 2009. Given this historical significance from the point of view of the army and the spectacle the disabled ship on the beach offered, the army had turned the site into a kind of theme park monument supplemented by a picnic area and two cafés which it ran. From the moment civilian traffic into this area became possible in 2010 until 2013, Farah 3 remained one of the most popular, most visited and most photographed sites on the tourist trail.

However, in 2013 the site was closed on the orders of the government and remnants of the ship were sold off as scrap. Unlike LTTE sites closely linked to its military leaders such as Prabhakaran's bunker or his ancestral home, or the safe house of the Sea Tiger leader Soosai and the LTTE monuments and cemeteries, this site did not usher in any specific emotional importance for Tamil visitors and certainly not for Sinhala visitors. It was simply an unmistakable marker to the war and a studio-like backdrop for amateur photographers. As such, the kind of logic that led to the decision to destroy LTTE sites of memory did not apply to this case. In this context and also notwithstanding its popularity as a tourist site, it appears that the only reason why it was removed was due to commercial considerations. That is, like the remnants of vehicles in the same general area were sold off, this metal remnant also became an object of a business transaction sanctioned by the highest levels of the government. In that scheme of things, the beach was erased of an iconic sign of the war and the tourist trail to that part of Mullaitivu District dried up.

Beyond actual remnants of war, the main government-constructed post-war monument in the area, which is also a crucial tourist site, is the Victory Monument[36] at Pudumattalaan, Puthukkudiyiruppu (see Figure 3.20). It was opened to the public on 9 December 2009, merely six months after the end of the war. It marks one of the places where the most intense of the final battles took place. Also, this is the first of the major post-war monuments constructed by the government. The construction of the Victory Monument can be seen as 'an act of tremendous political-military significance' (Balachandran 2009) given its proximity

Figure 3.20

Victory Monument, Puthukkudiyiruppu

Source: Author.

to the Nanthikadal lagoon area where the leader of the LTTE was killed, signalling the effective end of war in May 2009. In 2012, a young soldier from the central hills near the city of Kandy stationed at the monument offered me a sweet and told me during a conversation while gently tapping on his gun, '[W]e built the monument in the place we buried Prabhakaran and the other terrorists who died'.[37] I was quite surprised that he made such an observation to a person he did not even know and had only met 15 minutes ago. The accuracy or the validity of his comment is not very important when what it means is located in the wider context of events that had taken place in this specific place. Often, when a place is politically and emotionally marked as a space of ideological significance, the popular discursive practices that emanate from that definition tend to seamlessly transgress beyond fact and history and enter a realm of conjecture. However, all such discourses and conjectures revolve around some basic facts. After all, we know that Prabhakaran as well as thousands of his followers and civilians died in this area in the final weeks and days of the war and that their bodies were disposed of. Against this backdrop, the soldier's casual observations meant that at least one narrative was in circulation at the time which offered a profoundly morbid significance to the foundation of the monument. That is, the leader of the LTTE and his fellow combatants are literally carrying the burden of the government's victory and their own crushing defeat as well as the chaos of war upon their bodies even after their own gruesome deaths. When located in this field of meaning, the monument has emerged from their bodies and souls by destroying them, their ideals and their politics. It marks an end of a turbulent era and the beginning of a new one. By visiting the monument, the tourists are witnessing by association this end as well as the beginning.

As a structure, the Victory Monument is an uncomplicated and simple edifice. It also does not hold much in the way of elegance. Nevertheless, it communicates the crucial ideal of military heroism and in doing so leaves no room for contradictions or alternate interpretations. The transmission of this fundamental idea is the main purpose of the monument. Its basic form constitutes of the bust of a soldier with raised hands, situated on a high pedestal. This rather visible structure rises from a large lake-like body of water. In this sense, the monument is also an island connected to the mainland by a small bridge. The right hand of the soldier carries an automatic weapon similar to the Chinese-made T-56 assault weapons that were commonly used by soldiers in combat. As a result of the war, its name had become part of popular lore in southern Sri Lanka while most people also knew by experience what this weapon looked like. The left hand carries the national flag. In this sense, the flag and the gun were popularly recognized and potently political iconic references. A white pigeon symbolizing peace is depicted as resting on the gun. When taken in the overall context of the meaning that these symbolic references construct, the general message is one of Sinhala heroism and military conquest in the name of the nation, which has finally brought peace.

Beyond this general message which most visitors would easily understand, there are a number of other, more complex symbolic references which are incorporated within the overall design of the monument. Given the obvious difficulties in easily comprehending these complex systems of meaning, they are carefully explained in Sinhala and English in the explanatory sign situated just outside the monument's main structure on the mainland. No Tamil language explanations are provided on site with reference to the monument itself or to the nearby gallery of maps and images representing the progression of the final stages of the war. The absence of Tamil in the signage, which was also evident in a number of other places already referred to in this chapter, indicates the continuing ethnicization of this narrative despite the government's loftier claims of reconciliation and that the war was not against the Tamil people, but against the LTTE. If this is the case, one wonders why the components of this narrative are not offered in the langue of the people in these localities.

In any event, according to the Sinhala language explanation, the water surrounding the monument symbolizes the ocean around Sri Lanka. This affectively makes the monument representative of the island itself even though this is not part of the overall conceptualization of the monument complex. Instead, the lilies in the water are supposed to symbolize the Sri Lankan nation. Intriguingly however, the lilies seem to die or decrease in numbers when the water level goes down in the drier months of the year, which seem to say much about the fragility of the 'nation'. More importantly, the idea of the nation in this specific context is equated to 'Sri Lanka' as opposed to the more common equation with the Sinhalas. In this sense, the idea of nationhood as articulated here becomes more inclusive. The prominently displayed figures of four lions depicted as guarding the monument are installed in the four corners of its base. This constellation of meaning-embedded structures is expected to symbolically represent the heroes who had come from different parts of the country to ensure the safety of the land. These heroes, the explanation asserts, still symbolically stand guard. The omnipresent icon of lions that has been utilized to construct this specific meaning clearly suggests that the heroes in terms of this understanding are Sinhalas. This becomes self-evident when seen from the context of the well-known symbolic association between Sinhala ethnic identity and the iconic representation of lions. As such, the inclusiveness that was introduced when the idea of the nation was equated with Sri Lanka (as opposed to Sinhala) is negated by juxtaposing the idea of perennial heroism and heroes exclusively with Sinhalas.

The site where the monument is located is specifically identified as the land of victory or *jaya bhoomiya*. This is because it is in this general area that the war actually came to an end, thereby identifying this area more specifically as a site of victory than many other places where crucial battles had been fought and won, which nevertheless did not indicate the conclusion of the war. The explanation presented in very formal and highly Sanskritized Sinhala refers to the hurdles which soldiers had to clear on their march towards the victory that is being memorialized here:

The soldiers who are the guardian deities of the nation came from all four corners of the land. They took no notice whether it was day or night, overcame dangerous jungles, destroyed the death traps set by the enemy and crossed rivers, jungles and other multiple hurdles; they disregarded the rain and the scorching sun and their own personal pain and discomfort; they sacrificed their youth, limbs and lives and completely destroyed the power of the enemy and eradicated terrorism from this land; this monument erected in the land of victory where peace was ushered in for the nation is symbolic of victory in war (*rana vijayagrahana sankethaya*).

Though the monument is the most prominent structure in the vicinity, it is in fact one component of a cluster of three interrelated places of interest situated within walking distance from each other. The other two are the Army War Museum and the gallery of maps and photographs depicting the progression of the final phase of war. Together, these three places narrate the story of the military victory more fully and from the un-confusing and linear perception of the military. In other words, this is the pictorial, monumental and structural manifestation of the mega-narrative of victory that is authored and narrated by the state and the military. All three places are actively promoted by the Sri Lanka Army as important places to visit within the practices of warzone tourism. If the monument established the finality of victory, the gallery of images and maps outlines the path to that victory while the museum presents unmistakable trophies from the recently concluded war. The presently prevailing peace which allows tourists to come in large numbers to the warzone has been made possible by the silencing and the deactivation of weapons and military vehicles presented in the museum. Armed soldiers milling around and usually displaying no tangible signs of stress or anxiety in this post-war environment of relative relaxation, enthusiastically direct people to all three places if they seem to pause. However, given the fact all these places are highly visible and also because they are central components of the post-2009 warzone tourist trail, most tourists do not need this kind of external mediation or guidance to visit these places. Most come here for the specific purpose of seeing all of these, equipped with information given to them by many others who had preceded them.

Many visitors show a keen willingness and enthusiasm to engage in casual conversation with soldiers who are quite ready to share their war experiences as well as explain specificities of nearby attractions. Such banter becomes easy and is a very natural occurrence when one realizes this is essentially a meeting of Sinhala-speaking soldiers with mostly Sinhala-speaking tourists. This is a matter of members of a single linguistic and ethno-cultural community meeting in an ethnic and cultural landscape that was and is different, but has now been conquered and subjected to a new dispensation with which all of them have an affinity. This linguistic affinity of visitors and soldiers manifests very clearly in the formal signage of these places of interest as well. For instance, there are no explanations in Tamil with regard to the monument itself, the gallery of maps and images, and the war museum. It is clear that neither the army nor the government expected this to be a site frequented by Tamils or Tamil speakers. This is quite unlike the post-war monuments established in Kilinochchi and Elephant Pass which explained the relevance of the structures in Tamil as well as in Sinhala and English.

In terms of language at least, the final military victory here is presented very specifically as a Sinhala achievement. As one of the talkative soldiers observed in response to one of my queries, 'Tamil people also come here, but not too many'.[38] As I photographed the monument that evening in early December 2012 while a light drizzle fell across the area, a number of local Tamils silently passed by. They paid no attention to me, the other highly animated tourists, the monument or the other attractions. Their only attention was seemingly on their umbrellas, the firewood and the vegetables some of them carried in plastic bags. They hardly looked up, as if to avoid the sights around them. They simply walked further away from the monument along the gravel path towards a patch of trees made darker that evening due to the hovering rain clouds above, and disappeared from sight while the chatter of southern tourists and their laughter continued well into the evening as did the clicking of cameras.

At some point in that December evening, I followed one of the chatty groups of tourists into the gallery of images and photographs very close to the museum. The space is a simple gallery that combines cartography and photography to vocalize the military's narrative of war, bravery, humanism and victory. The maps offer detailed presentations of the different thrusts of various military units from different directions in the final phase of the war. They indicated where different formations met with other military units, how they progressed beyond that point and so on. In other words, it is essentially a cartography of victory. In fact, the maps are identified in Sinhala as 'the victorious path of the Wanni humanitarian operation'. Wanni is the larger area that includes Kilinochchi and

Mullaitivu which constituted the final battlegrounds. As already noted elsewhere in this reading, the 'humanitarian operation' is the official terminology the government as well as the military used to refer to the final phase of war. This idea of 'humanitarianism' in this discourse emerged from the strong self-articulated notion that the war was under-taken to rescue Tamil civilians trapped by the LTTE. In the final phase of war, civilians were in fact used as human shields by the LTTE even though in the end that did not protect the organization from military shelling and final inhalation. Sri Lanka's post-war difficulties with the international community enveloped in accusations of war crimes stems from what happened in this period and in this general area.

The collection of war photography captured by the army itself presented along with the maps indicates two interrelated aspects of this 'humanitarian' operation. One set of powerful images depict the pictures of civilians in army custody helped, fed and cared for by the army. This collection has been identified in Sinhala as 'civilians held hostage by ter-rorists rescued in the Wanni humanitarian operation'. The other set of images identified as 'weapons, vehicles and ocean craft captured from terrorists in the Wanni humanitarian operation' depicts images of mili-tary trophies form the war. Many of these are presented in the museum situated close by.

Clearly, these maps and images have an integral linkage with the overall narrative that is being constructed by these three attractions. On the other hand, the maps are historically important in understanding the progression of the war. At the same time, while the images, particularly of people, narrate the 'humanitarian' aspect of the war that the army is quite keen to articulate, they also point to silences of human suffering, death and destruction that the war has caused, allowing for additional and less linear interpretations. The audibility of one interpretation has affectively brought silence upon other possible interpretations. It does not appear that these considerations enter the collective consciousness of most tourists who enter this space. In fact, this is the least visited of the three places. And in most cases, even when people visit the gallery, they simply go in and leave quickly. It is not a place for photography or engaged conversations. It is not a place that can capture the imagination of most. The monument and the war museum are far more interesting to tourists than this collection of maps and images.

That evening, as the drizzle continued and the sun was beginning to fade behind the trees and beyond the grey clouds to dive yet again beneath the horizon of the western coast that was not visible from this part of the country, the chatty group of Sinhala tourists quickly exited the gallery of maps and images and started to walk leisurely to the Army War Museum. I followed them, listening to their laughter and banter while some of the younger members of the group were glued to their mobile phones describing in animated conversation to unseen loved ones their adventures. Adventure stories were being spun live. One young woman insisted to her unseen friend back home: 'This place is quite something. You must come and see all this and I don't mind coming again with you.'[39] I had seen earlier on another group of tourists posing in front the simple sign with a small tile roof announcing the presence of the museum (see Figure 3.21). In front of the sign, across the gravel road was a large Coca-Cola advertisement. Coke along with other significations of global capital had already penetrated the warzone, infusing a global sense of 'normalcy' in the minds of tourists and further destabilizing their ability to comprehend the calamites of war. The Museum is a simple long steel structure with a tin roof, half walls and a fence-like low, wooden struc-ture right around allowing for the breeze to come in and cool the interior.

Figure 3.21

Signage near the entry to War Museum of the Sri Lanka Army, Puthukkudiyiruppu

Source: Author.

The floor was rough and cemented, ideal for the kind of heavy tourist traffic and requiring minimal maintenance. Right outside, a sign proclaims loudly that the cement was sponsored by Holcim, a multinational cement company, which maintains a pronounced presence in Sri Lanka. The museum is both a sad and an intriguing place as it is also a very popular place. Both inside and outside the building numerous examples of LTTE military equipment ranging from guns to ammunition to propellers, boats, tugs, prototype missiles and submarines captured by the army are presented in no specific order, following no known cataloguing system and with minimum or no contextual information. The museum generates a personality that varies between an ill-conceived museum and underdeveloped theme park. Nevertheless, it is also intriguing as it is bustling with potential narratives and very real icons of the country's recent turbulent history. It is sad because the leaking roof from multiple places, the drizzles and monsoons often accompanied by winds that furiously invade the museum over its half walls and the numerous militarized boats and other remnants that are more readily exposed to the elements in the adjacent compound beckons the question as to how long and in which manner these artefacts would narrate their stories before they might well disappear from sight and from memory.

But for the moment, none of these issues seem to matter to the flocking tourists. They also do not seem to matter to the soldiers. Some soldiers, with considerably long military experience, are on duty at the museum and have by now become affective and very articulate guides and curators. They know everything in this place and are very willing to speak with interested tourists. The tourists walk among the artefacts, photograph them, chat with each other and more importantly pose near some of the more eye-catching artefacts such as the prototype mini submarines with images of sharks with rows of teeth painted on them as well as the bigger ocean craft outside. Some of these images end up at various corners of the internet, taking the pictorial travel archives of these tourists and their zones of silence much beyond their immediate family and peer circles. When tourists linger at a particular artefact or seem interested, the more enterprising of the soldiers quite happily double up as museum guides (see Figure 3.22) and offered to explain what the equipment are, when and where they were captured and so on in a populist and heroic manner of presentation, sometimes weaving their own war experiences into the emerging narrative, making the overall story all the more interesting and compelling to listeners:

Figure 3.22

Army guide with a group of young tourists, Sri Lanka Army War Museum, Puthukkudiyiruppu

Source: Author.

[T]his is a water scooter. It is like any other scooter that you drive on the road. Come touch this and see. Don't worry, it won't explode now. We have removed the trigger. But these were invented by the LTTE terrorists to launch suicide attacks against navy ships. In the end, none of these were a match for our boys. This was captured not too far from here. If he could have, Prabhakaran would have escaped on this with his wife on his shoulders. But then, we prevented all that. Things that took our lives and maimed our bodies are now safe and in this museum.[40]

Everyone nodded; cameras clicked and some touched the artefact and the soldier posed for photographs too.

He went on to another artefact and narrated an episode from his own experience before explaining the attributes of yet another artefact, and the group of tourists followed him. He was keener to direct his story to the younger members among the visitors: 'You should remember this history well. You are too young to understand all this. But you should not forget. Many of our people died trying to make this place safe'.[41] The animated presentations of soldier-guides almost always captured the attention and the imagination of visitors, particularly the children, and remain the only affective catalogue of the museum, albeit a slightly changing one in the absence of any printed versions. Variations in the narratives come from the personal experiences which different soldiers weave into their presentations. The accuracy of the specific histories that are narrated as well as the technical information offered is not known for sure. But no one is interested and no one complains. What is narrated seem to be taken for what they are by most tourists. Nevertheless, the artefacts tell a much more interesting story if one ponders beyond the military personnel's linear rendition of war and its end. They epitomize the story of an organization with grandiose schemes of statehood, industrialization, notions of a military industrial complex and also how such a grand scheme of things could eventually fail. But then, warzone tourism is not an academic or intellectual enterprise to ponder over such things; it is a practice of leisure and emotion to satisfy the senses and a wayward manifestation of curiosity in the context of which the calamities and pains of war experienced by local people can also be easily and conveniently expelled from the collective conscience of most tourists. I will come to the politics this process unfolds later in this reading.

Beyond the Stops; 'Relaxing' and Staying the Nights in the Warzone

Beyond the specific promotion of post-war monuments built in areas within the trail of warzone tourism in northern Sri Lanka, what exists in the space between the government's interest to eradicate the presence of the LTTE from the northern landscape and the army's interest to promote some of these sites? I have already noted in the beginning of this chapter that the government's official policy with regard to warzone tourism was 'not to highlight former LTTE landmarks for tourism purposes', in the context of which the government had 'already begun to clear some LTTE landmarks in line with the government's view that terrorism, the LTTE and violence which affected the public during the war should be forgotten' (*Tamil Guardian* 2010; see also *Daily Mirror* 2010). This policy was implemented very early in the second phase of warzone tourism. That is why many of the LTTE structures that were popular destinations for southern tourists in the first phase of tourism were not available in the second phase. They had been demolished by the army under clear instructions from the government. For the government, the erasure of the LTTE presence from the landscapes of memory and violent politics was not a simple matter of erasing the memory of the organization from public consciousness per se. After all, the government had no direct control over public consciousness. It was more precisely interested in erasing its heroic image from the physical landscape which was decidedly embedded in LTTE's cemeteries and monuments. In other words, the government did not want to see a situation in which there might be a competition for attention between the wartime LTTE monuments and other structures of memory and the post-war monuments set up by the government itself. It was quite mindful and wary of the popularity of LTTE war remnants among Sinhala tourists in the earlier phase of tourism. An adulation of LTTE's wartime structures among tourists which may lead to a glorification and romanticization of its power in the recent past was something that the government was not ready to deal with. As a police officer in Jaffna town observed,

> [O]nly thing these things (LTTE structures) do is to make our people think how great they were, how efficient they were, how organized they were. This is not what they were all about. They were after all, mass murderers…. So these things should come down like the LTTE itself. Only then can the country reinvent itself…. Partly destroyed buildings are not the only things that can promote tourism.[42]

For him and many others, this was a matter of literally cleansing the north of the LTTE's physical presence and re-establishing the writ of the state as well as civility on that revived landscape.

In so far as the LTTE's formal structures of memory were concerned, there was a clear agreement between the government and the army. That is why cemeteries and monuments set up by the LTTE were quickly demolished and all their traces erased soon after the second phase of tourism began. However, the positions of the government and the army with regard to other LTTE structures which were not designed as objects of memory were not always clear and certainly not mutually complementary. Though not an area of overt tension, this was an area of invisible tension and anxiety. The government's own overall position on tourism in the warzone was clearly spelt out in its policy statement referred to above. Without any ambiguity, it identified all LTTE landmarks for demolition and erasure. But that process initially began with a focus on structures that were specifically constructed for purposes of memory. For the government, it was important to bring all aspects of the political economy of the warzone well into the mainstream economic practice of the country while also keeping the region under strict military surveillance. As such, there is very clear government investment and encouragement of private investment in the north-east for the promotion and development of mainstream tourism with a focus on the culture, religion and the natural-scapes of the region. It is in this context that one could understand the post-war mushrooming of high and low-end tourist infrastructure in the region.

Nevertheless, compared to the government's wariness of warzone tourism based exclusively on war remnants, the military clearly had such an interest. For them, places such as Prabhakaran's bunker, the Farah 3 ship and other related structures described in this chapter were of crucial importance for promotion as places of interest in the tourist trail for a very specific reason. They were clear and iconic examples of its own victorious path; they were essentially unassailable trophies which allowed for its own sense of heroism and triumph to be projected to society and relived through the relentless visits of tourists. This preoccupation is evident in a number of its actions. As already indicated, the Sri Lanka Army took great care to formally identify all the former LTTE locations it wanted to promote as 'attractions'. Towards this end, carefully designed signs were strategically installed and in some cases detailed maps were also provided where needed, as in the case of Prabhakaran's bunker. With regard to other locations such as the Sea Tigers' training pool, LTTE's Submarine Yard, Farah 3 ship and so on, information pertaining to each location was also provided on site. But in almost all cases the information was either in Sinhala or in Sinhala and English, but almost never in Tamil. So Tamil was visibly non-existent and Sinhala was clearly privileged in this discourse. In other words, the post-war power equation was clearly entrenched through language. In the road map published by the Security Forces Headquarters in Kilinochchi, which was in circulation by 2012, four of the 12 sites specifically identified were directly linked to the war, and were its remnants. Three of these were post-war monuments set up by the army and one was the Bulldozer Monument which became an instant attraction under different circumstances in both phases of tourism, and is both a remnant of war as well as a formal military monument. All these point to two interrelated facts. The first has to do with the military's preoccupation with a specific type of war-zone tourism, with selected trophy sites as central attractions. The second pertains to the specific kind of discourse that catered to and sustained this emergent form of tourism through the on-site maps and the constellation of signage which was produced in the process. Harrison describes this state of affairs as part of 'a macabre tourist trail the military have set up primarily for people from the majority Sinhala community to see where their defeated enemy lived'.[43]

There is a great degree of complexity that manifests within two extremes in the context of this kind of tourism centred on these monuments and war remnants, which may not be immediately visible. One extreme is erasure as exhibited in the government's relentless efforts in demolishing LTTE's structures of memory as well as key buildings in recent times such as Prabhakaran's ancestral home and his bunker described earlier in this chapter. The other extreme is relative memory as manifest in the army's promotion of tourism focused on surviving remnants of war in the form of LTTE buildings as well as the multiplicity of equipment in the War Museum at Pudukuduyiruppu. In the discourse that emerges from within these two extremes, even though the effort of the government is to distance the memory of the LTTE as stated in its official policy, LTTE's marginalized post-war presence nevertheless always manifests in all the war sites and practices in the warzone tourist trail. It is after all their buildings that southern tourists come to see; it is their improvised vehicles and boats that they see in the museum and which become the backdrops for their warzone photographs; it is their weapons that soldiers talk about at the museum intertwined with the personal war stories of the narrators. In other words, in these discourses, the LTTE is the point of departure as well as the final point of arrival and the main points of reference within the parameters of the discursive practices at play. True, all of these also point to their final and decisive demise and the military's equally decisive triumph. So the complete erasure of the LTTE on the one hand and limited exposure of it on the other ensures the continued presence of the LTTE in the discourse of tourism which is much more tangible than a mere fading memory. It is a presence without which warzone tourism will have no focus, no stage to be performed, no direction and above all no discourse. It is the nature of this seeming contradiction between presence and absence and the meanings it conjures that Amarnath Amarasingam wonders about when he asks, '[T]he government has destroyed the childhood home of the rebel leader Prabhakaran, as well as rebels' cemeteries, but has kept the Tiger bunkers and constructed war museums. Why? What kind of argument is being made here?'[44] He also affectively provides the answer to his own question when he notes,

> [I]n a strange way, it amounts to a subtle building-up of the Tigers, a kind of glorification of the threat that they posed—openly on display at the war museum in Puthukkudiyiruppu. The government can then point to it and say, 'look what we were able to destroy' and, of course, 'if we're not careful, look what can re-emerge'.[45]

It is within this specific interest of the army that one can understand the building of tourist infrastructure directly by the army at two obvious levels. However, this has been undertaken with the blessings of the government even though its own position on tourism and tourist infrastructure is somewhat different from that of the army. To put it simply, two kinds of infrastructure have been established to cater to low-end as well as high-end tourism according to military perception based on both facilities provided and design preoccupations. It appears that the military in particular has learned well from the LTTE's own experience in investing in tourist infrastructure in the first phase of warzone tourism as was evident in the rest stops it controlled in Kilinochchi. However, given the relative calm of the second phase and the network and manpower the military has in the region, the infrastructure that has come up so far tends to be much more expansive than what the LTTE had to offer in the first phase.

In so far as low-end infrastructure is concerned, the most evident manifestation is the network of army-managed cafés that have been established along the A9 to Jaffna after Vavuniya as well as in a number of internal locations in the north including in and around Mullaitivu. For instance, two such cafés were in operation at the site of the Farah 3 ship until the ship was dismantled and sold for scrap by the government (see Figure 3.24). Until they lasted, they were the only places around the site for a drink or snacks. These kinds of cafés are also located near major checkpoints, specific military monuments such as the Elephant Pass Monument (see Figure 3.23) or other war attractions such as the Water Tank Monument in Kilinochchi. The latter however is not identified as a café but as a souvenir shop selling chocolates, biscuits, soft drinks and a

Figure 3.23

Interior of Sri Lanka Army-run café near Gamini Kularatna Memorial and War Hero Memorial, Elephant Pass

Source: Author.

Figure 3.24

Interior of Sri Lanka Army-run café at Farah 3 site, Mullaitivu

Source: Author.

few other items. On the road to Mullaitivu from the A9, off the Paranthan Junction, there is at least one such nondescript café which offers tea and sweets as well as breakfast, lunch and dinner to road construction workers, soldiers who do not want to eat their military-supplied meals and tourists who do not mind the smoke-darkened, low-ambience interior of the shack where a soldier lives and cooks under very spartan conditions. The food is basic, cheap and tastes more than adequate in prevailing local contexts. In any case, what is provided is an affordable service for people who want it. In general, these are ramshackle structures often with tin roofs and made with locally available material which may range from bamboo to coconut or Palmyra trunks, and are furnished mostly with plastic chairs and tables or rough wooden benches. Floors are made of rough uncut cement or straightened out metal sheets from asphalt barrels or ammunition boxes, depending on what is available in the vicinity.

In many cafés, particularly those off the A9 and in other more visited locations, the intrusion of global capital is hard to miss. Large billboards outside with sexy young female and male models inform travellers of the virtues of Coca-Cola, Sprite and Mountain Dew by semiotic association with notions of youthful exuberance and a sense of style. The contradictions between this idealized lifestyle and the reality of soldiers' routine lives and that of local people do not readily enter the consciousness of travellers. Inside, Coca-Cola-supplied coolers are ever well-stocked to dispense their carbonated and coloured liquids chilled. Those who would prefer hot beverages can of course follow the inclinations offered by the large Nestlé hoardings outside and be satisfied with the sugary and standardized Nescafé and tea dispensed from machines operated by young soldiers and served on Styrofoam cups. Gone are the days of individually made tea served in porcelain cups and saucers, a memory as distant as the time before the war itself.

When it comes to non-ready-made food and their cultural settings, these cafés have also destabilized the local sensibilities of cuisine and the demographics within which they were traditionally located. Many of these cafés are identified almost uniformly as *Jana Avanhala* which in Sinhala means 'people's café' or 'people's place of rest'. Many simply do not have any individualized names at all. Where words like jana avanhala are found interspersed with the global corporate colours and emblems of Coca-Cola and Nestlé, rather than as a name of a specific café, they are used as a category of space. So today, if something is called jana avanhala in the north-east, it is most likely a café run by the military. Often one can also see signs identifying which units of the army operate these cafés, which vary from place to place.

In any case, as this generalized category of name itself amply demonstrates, these are not cafés in the conventional sense of the word, but are simply places that sell sundry eatables and drinks. They are not domains of innocence as one might assume with regard to an ordinary café. Instead, these are ethnicized spaces marking paths of tourist travel deep inside the Tamil heartland which carries an unmistakably Sinhala sensibility in more ways than one. They are also markers of the army's triumphant march northwards and are symbolic of its omnipresent presence in the area as well as a signification of the post-war, state-sponsored cultural hegemony in the region. In this sense, other than the merchandize that come to travellers courtesy of global capital such as Coke and Nescafé, anything that is cooked in these places is very much Sinhala in terms of the raw materials and spices used, the taste and the manner of cooking, catering almost exclusively to a Sinhala clientele. Even when *vada*, the traditional Tamil food is served as a snack in some of these places, the quantities and types of flour and lentils used, the way of cooking and the sauce with which it is served (*sambar* or chutney) have fundamentally transformed due to its pronounced Sinhalization. Only the name with a Sinhala emphasis remains to give it some sense of location within perceivably local cuisine.

Clearly, stopping at one of these places is not a simple matter of satisfying one's pangs of hunger or thirst. It is not that simple given the nature of local circumstances tempered by war and uncomfortable peace, bringing to mind Terry Eagleton's perceptive observation, 'if there is one sure thing about food, it is that it is never just food' and 'like the post-structuralist text, food is endlessly interpretable, as gift, threat, poison, recompense, barter, seduction, solidarity, suffocation'.[46] What scholars like Eagleton with an interest in the theoretical understanding of food and consumption have suggested is that food is not only about satisfy-ing hunger. It is part of a larger discourse with a field of signs that cre-ates meanings, power relationships, status positions and interpretations beyond the mere object of food and the act of eating or drinking. These meanings come from the food as well as where and how you eat it. All these considerations are at play in these cafés.

For Tamil travellers who almost never stop at these places, this food and these cafés might offer interpretive possibilities of threat, poison and suffocation in the sense articulated by Eagleton. After all, they offer culturally unfamiliar food in militarized cultural spaces that conjure meanings of defeat, subjugation and occupation in the context of the recently concluded war and its political aftermath. These cafés are also seen as a network of institutions that deprive much needed economic opportunities to local people attempting to come out of the vagaries of war into the relative stability and economic opportunities of post-war. On the other hand, for many Sinhala travellers already well entrenched in the practice of warzone tourism, resting, eating and drinking in these places represent something altogether very different that would vary from feelings of solidarity and friendship as well as elation over triumph in war. After all, they are Sinhala politico-cultural enclaves serviced by Sinhala speaking personnel who were considered heroes in the midst of war. Besides, some of these places also offer food infused with smells that are more suitable to the Sinhala palette in the midst of a Tamil culinary and socio-cultural landscape. Stopping at these places therefore is not a simple matter of stopping at any café. It is a political act and a cultural practice replete with much interpretive possibilities whether the ordinary tourist is aware of this or not.

Stories that unfold about the handful of military-run hotels or guest-houses at crucial locations in the warzone are quite different from the narratives of and from the shabbily constructed, dimly lit, half-heart-edly served and marginally maintained cafés described above. Literally, they are not places to 'write home about', which is also why they hardly become places where people want to be seen in and photographed in as quite evident with regard to many other sites in the warzone tourist trail. If the cafés were truly utilitarian in their basic objective and were only supposed to provide very rudimentary services at low cost, irrespective of what they might have become in the realms of practice and interpretation, the hotels and guest houses were purposefully located, well-constructed and carefully maintained as permanent structures and were conceived and advertised as centres for high-end or relatively high end tourism when the daily price tags for accommodation and food as well as avail-able facilities and design considerations are taken into account. In this exploration, I will only look into the meanings and politics of three of these kinds of enterprises in the north out of about nine such operations by the Sri Lanka Army and the Sri Lankan Air Force situated in different parts of the country.[47] Of these, approximately five operations are located in the former battlegrounds of the north-east. My focus for this reading is on Lagoon's Edge and Green House at Nandikadal in Mullaitivu and

Thal Sevana at Kankesanturai in Jaffna, all of which are operated by the Sri Lanka Army.

On 28 December 2012, the Sinhala language newspaper *Mawbima* carried an article authored by Sanjaka Prasad Dolewatte with a somewhat unsettling title in the form of a question. It asked the readers, '[W]ould you like to spend a night at the Nandikadal lagoon where Prabhakaran died, for Rs 15,000?'[48] Similarly, on 31 December 2012, *Lanka-C-News*, a website that reports Sri Lankan news, in a brief news item noted that a luxury holiday bungalow[49] had been opened 'at the place where Prabakaran was killed'.[50] Margaret Harrison, writing about the same facility in the *Huffington Post* on 26 December 2012, observed that,

> [T]he Sri Lankan military is advertising a newly constructed hotel in the heart of the killing fields in the north of the island, where tens of thousands of minority Tamils were killed in 2009. The holiday resort, called Lagoon's Edge, caters for Sinhala war tourists who want to see the last bastion of the defeated Tamil Tiger rebels.[51]

It is in Nandikadal that the LTTE leader was killed in May 2009 and the war finally came to an end. He is supposed to have waded across the lagoon along with other LTTE operatives and civilians to the army-controlled side of the lagoon where he met his violent and inglorious end, which also marked the end of the war itself. Now, as evidenced by these three entries in the media, it appeared that the site had already acquired a price tag of LKR 15,000 to spend a night of luxury courtesy of the Sri Lanka Army in the vicinity of not only Prabhakaran's violent death but also of incredible human suffering, death and destruction. The *Mawbima* article notes that the paper's own interest was to explore the place after seeing an earlier newspaper advertisement perceivably placed by the Sri Lanka Army this was decidedly not at all macabre compared to the title of the *Mawbima* article unless of course one was aware of the location and its associations. That advertisement was essentially an invitation: '[C]ome to enjoy the serenity of the Nandikadal lagoon'.[52] Known officially as Lagoon's Edge, the *Mawbima* article describes the location of the bungalow in the following words:

> The Nandikadal lagoon was the location of the final victory of the human-itarian operation launched four years ago by the three armed forces. Thousands of Tamil civilians were kept as hostages at the further end of Nandikadal lagoon by the terrorists [LTTE]. It was across the waters of

the Nandikadal lagoon that these people were brought to the safety of the other side of the lagoon with the help of the extended humanitarian arms of the Army.[53]

Clearly, there is no difference in the narrative of the Sri Lanka Army and the state on the one hand and the newspaper on the other about the end of war. Quite simply, it was a humanitarian operation launched to rescue civilians from terrorists. There appeared to be no contradictions or grey areas in this narrative. It was a master narrative of power and victory that needed to be accepted in its totality. In this context, the ensuing human suffering, death and destruction hardly enter the narrative even from its margins. Interestingly, that counter narrative on the end of war emerges in the essay by Harrison on the opening of the bungalow when she observes,

> [R]ight in the heart of what was rebel territory, the hotel overlooks the stretch of water that became the frontline during the final bloody months of the conflict, in which it's now estimated by the United Nations 40,000 or possibly 70,000 civilians died in a few months. Tamil survivors describe wading through the neck-high water, passing floating corpses and dodging bullets. Several children and injured or elderly people drowned in the water in the struggle to escape. On the far side of the lagoon from the hotel built by the army, lies the sandy spit of land, which is considered Sri Lanka's killing fields.[54]

Taking about seven months to build, and designed and constructed entirely by soldiers, the hotel's main claim to fame other than its location is the fact that everything in the entire structure from the roof and the ceiling to the floors and internal walls as well as all the furniture and wall decorations have been turned out from giant teak tress felled from the nearby jungles which had survived the vagaries of war.[55] Providing accommodation for eight people at a time, the two-storeyed structure also has an antique car as one of its main attractions in a separate open enclosure, which according to soldiers on site had been abandoned by the LTTE in the area.[56] According to the Facebook page of the bungalow maintained by the Sri Lanka Army Headquarters in Nanthikadal, it consists of,

> three fully air conditioned bedrooms with attached bathrooms, a living area, pantry and garden area for outdoor activities while all meals and services are supplied by the Sri Lanka Army and the bungalow is available for reservations for a maximum of 6 adults (above 12 yrs) who are recommended by a Sri Lanka Army official.[57]

The slight discrepancy between the maximum occupancy at the bungalow between the army-run Facebook page and the *Lakbima* article is of no significant concern.

Interestingly however, of all the possible areas where a leisure site of this kind could have been located in the northern Sri Lanka, the specificity of this place is self-evident. As already noted, this is because the Sri Lanka Army considers this place its own site of victory. This factor was clearly elaborated in the newspaper article:

> Nandikadal area, which saw the final historic victory of the thirty year war, is significant due to a number of reasons. Velupillai Prabhakaran breathed his last breath close by. The homes of many LTTE leaders are also located in the vicinity while this is also the area where many of the families of LTTE's great heroes lived. This is also where many LTTE terrorists who fought for the organization until their final defeat, surrendered to the government's military. It is also a place where many lives were lost at the height of war. Now, in this land, a holiday bungalow has been built. The special feature in this resort is that everything in it has been built of teak wood.[58]

The last three sentences in this description are quite intriguing. The first sentence recognizes this to be a place where great many people had died; the next simply observes that a holiday bungalow has been now built on this place; the final sentence observed as a matter of fact that everything in the place has been turned out in teak wood. The tragedy of human destruction and pain noted in abstract is soon lost in the matter of fact statement referring to the construction of the holiday bungalow and its special feature pertaining to teakwood structure and interiors. This description is symbolic of the way in which the human tragedy of war has been eclipsed and expelled clinically from the omnipresent master narrative of victory. Admittedly however, almost as an afterthought borne out of guilt, the idea of tragedy emerges again briefly later in the article. But it is unmistakable how easy it was for the article to slip from the mere mention of tragedy at one moment to mundane construction details of the building itself at the next moment. Then, the article presents a brief notation on how the building is symbolic of the discipline of the Sri Lanka Army and how this has contributed to its excellent maintenance and cleanliness.[59]

This bungalow is one of the army's premier on-site accommodation facilities to cater to the kind of warzone tourism it had promoted since the end of war. In fact, one of the soldiers in the bungalow had noted,

'[W]e take everyone who comes here to the Nandikdal lagoon and many other LTTE sites in the Mullaitivu jungle.'[60] The article further elaborates the places of interest that tourists who might stay here could visit while enjoying the taste of good food: The Farah 3 ship, the swimming pool of the terrorists, the house of the Sea Tiger leader Soosai, weapons of terrorists, the place where Prabhakaran died, the orchard owned by Prabhakaran and so on.[61] Indeed, the success of the bungalow does not simply come from the fact that it is located in the place where the war ended but also because from there one could engage in sightseeing with a great degree of comfort and with the guidance of the military. The mere idea that the bungalow is located in the final battleground cannot attract tourists and sustain their interest beyond a point. But when that fact is associated with a number of sites which had already become popular attractions, the bungalow's popularity is guaranteed.

In addition to numerous visits of individuals who embark on the warzone tourist trail on their own, the bungalow had already become an integral part of more formal tours of warzone tourism, at least with regard to one tour company. Sha Lanka, a company that specializes in tours in Sri Lanka, has a specialized tour over seven days and nights identified as the 'Battle Field Tour'. It is designed as a motorcycle tour for an added sense of adventure. Essentially meant for foreign visitors, the tour includes everything from airport transfers, hotels, meals, transport, tour mechanics and baggage handling as well as translators for any language.[62] The tour is explained as follows, which combines sightseeing around the war remnants in Mullaitivu with a focus on Nandikadal and Pudukuduyirippu areas and relaxation at Lagoon's Edge:

> The main focus of the tour is Mullaitivu (Pudukuduirippu) area where the Sri Lanka Army defeated the LTTE. The tour takes in the 12 most important attractions, namely Vishwamadhu area (Prabhakaran's hospital bunker, fruit farm and torture chambers) in addition to Farah 3, the Jordanian ship pirated by the LTTE, Soosai's house, submarine boat yard, the swimming pool, submarine testing tank, Prabhakaran's 4 tier bunker, vehicle graveyard, SL Army Victory Monument and memorial for 1,600 slain SL Army soldiers. An officer from SLA will accompany us as a guide to all the sites. We will stay for two nights at Lagoon's Edge hotel (overlooking Nandikadal) maintained by the Sri Lanka Army Mullaitivu Camp with sumptuous Sri Lankan meals served by the Army chefs. On this tour the group will cover towns and villages that came to prominence during the 30 year war. With the horrifying

battle field atmosphere in our thoughts we move on to the famous Cultural Triangle to enjoy the page (sic) & pageantry and ancient beauty of Sri Lanka.[63]

The tour takes tourists to the most clearly identified sites in the war tourist trail. And its claim to 'cover towns and villages that came to prominence during the 30 year war' indicates the voyeuristic nature of the tour. After all, these towns did not come into prominence due to their natural beauty or any other such mundane attributes but due to their central involvement in the war, either because of the almost total physical destruction and loss of human life they experienced or because they had supplied some of the combatants to the LTTE, or both. On the other hand, the description outlines quite well how the Sri Lanka Army has become an integral service provider for the kind of tourism it had conceptualized and promoted. In this particular case, the army provides 'sumptuous' Sri Lankan meals, accommodation at the Lagoon's Edge and army officers as guides to a warzone tour organized by a private company. As in the *Mawbima* article about Lagoon's Edge discussed above, in the Sha Lanka tour description also, the shift from a fleeting thought on the destructions of war to the pleasures of leisure is magically rapid. It is a simple matter of 'horrifying battle field atmosphere in our thoughts' at one moment to making the emotional shift to enjoy the 'pageantry and ancient beauty of Sri Lanka' at the next moment. Whatever remains in the emotional space between these two emotive registers must necessarily disappear into the recesses of lost memory as mere collateral damage.

The Lagoon's Edge is important for three other significant reasons. First, it was opened to the public by the president of Sri Lanka in September 2012 in the presence of the commander of the army at the time and other high ranking military and political leaders. This indicates the very obvious political patronage the project received from the highest levels of the politico-military hierarchy in Sri Lanka. This patronage comes irrespective of the tension between the army and the government with regard to their interpretations of warzone tourism. Here, the government is directly supporting the army's understanding of warzone tourism. However, it is noteworthy that on the instructions of the government, the army facilitated the removal of two important sites in the warzone tourist trail of which Lagoon's Edge was a part, particularly for the more affluent travellers as well as the military officers and their families. This action, which took place less than one year after the bungalow was opened, saw the removal and selling of the Farah 3 ship for scrap metal and the demolition of Prabhakaran's bunker in 2013.

Second, this is not just any bungalow of the kind one would find all over Sri Lanka's regular tourist trails. It is not a domain of innocence where politics have little or no role to play and can be understood in terms of simple economics of profit located within the well-established hospitality industry. More clearly, Lagoon's Edge is a Sinhala politico-cultural space of leisure with its own ideological makeup in the way it has been conceived and presented. Its main stakeholders and regular workers are Sinhalas most of whom are from the army while most of its patrons are also Sinhalas, or foreigners in general or military personnel and their families. It is in this context that one could understand the significance of the cultural pageant with Kandyan drummers and dancers who greeted the president when the bungalow was officially opened to the public. Since Independence in 1948, Kandyan dance among other cultural elements drawn from the wider repertoire of Sinhala culture have come to represent the Sinhalaness of the nation state in both socio-cultural and politico-emotional terms. As such, though situated deep in the Tamil cultural heartland, that opening indicated without confusion the very Sinhala political and cultural identity of this place of leisure.[64] Besides, one of the wall decorations in the resort is a wooden replica of the Victory Monument situated nearby.

Third, Lagoon's Edge with all its claims to glamour and uniqueness came into being merely three years after the end of war even though the most basic living conditions of local people that were so completely disrupted by the war had hardly been addressed at the time. Margaret Harrison describes this contradiction in the following words:

> And this luxury teak hotel for tourists from the south of the island to view the spoils of victory must be little comfort to local people who shelter in flimsy tents. According to an article in *Time* magazine in May 2012, the UN estimated 100,000 houses were destroyed in the final phase of the war but only 16,000 had been rebuilt. An International Crisis Group report this year said most Tamils returning home after the war live 'in makeshift and inadequate shelters and many struggle to afford food, with few jobs or economic opportunities and little or no savings'.[65]

In this sense, facilities like Lagoon's Edge can only exist in the realm of extreme contradictions when unpleasant memories of the recent past can somehow be expelled from one's consciousness. This is something, as I have already noted, that north-bound tourists have been able to do as a matter of routine.

Along with Lagoon's Edge, the Sri Lanka Army Headquarters in Mullaitivu runs another holiday bungalow called Green House close to the lagoon, which is a slightly smaller and less glamorous operation compared to Lagoon's Edge. Its own Facebook page operated by the Sri Lanka Army cantonment in Nanthikadal introduces Green House as 'a remote get-away from the day-to-day hustle and bustle of the city life, situated in the shores of the Nanthi Kadal (sic) lagoon in the secure premises of Security Forces Headquarters, Mullaitivu, Northern Province, Sri Lanka'.[66] So unlike Lagoon's Edge, Green House is well within the army headquarters' premises. Smaller than Lagoon's Edge, Green House 'consists of two fully air conditioned bed rooms with attached bathrooms, a living area, pantry and garden area for outdoor activities' while 'all meals and services are supplied by the Sri Lanka Army and the bungalow is available for reservations for a maximum of 8 adults (above 12 yrs) who are recommended by a Sri Lanka Army official'.[67] As we can see, reservations in both places are technically not open to anyone, but through the recommendation of a Sri Lanka Army officer. However, given the massive expansion of the army during the last 30 years, almost every Sinhala middle class person is more than likely to know someone who could make that introduction. Besides, the reservation details are available publically online with no information on strict restriction to military personnel. In that sense, for all practical purposes, the two bungalows are open to everyone who is willing to pay the money and is able to ensure a formal introduction. Compared to Lagoon's Edge, however, Green House has not yet attracted the kind of popular attention in the media, even though it is also often used by tourists who want to stay overnight in the region who also have the required connections. The main claim to fame in both places is that they are situated squarely within the place where the war ended amidst much chaos, death and destruction. In this sense, if one is to stay in either of these places, one has to be able to come to terms with that carnage and deal with it. The easiest way to do so of course is to be an uncritical contributor to the mega narrative of the victors already referred to. The same general conditions and contradictions explained with reference to Lagoon's Edge also applies to Green House.

But additional details of Green House available on its own Facebook page shed more light on the cultural politics of the space, which also allows for the rethinking of the larger politics in post-war northern Sri Lanka. The menus for breakfast, lunch, dinner and dessert offered by Green House read like a post-structuralist text open to interpretation in the realm of the ethno-cultural politics of exclusivism and hegemony.[68] I have already noted the Sinhala politico-cultural identity of Lagoon's Edge with reference to its workforce, clientele, presentation and the discourse within which it is located. The same cultural dynamics are at play when it comes to Green House. Its Sinhala cultural sensibility becomes quite apparent in its four menus. In the context of the larger Tamil culinary discourses and practices located in the rolling landscapes beyond the facility, what it offers is mostly Sinhala culinary favourites with a smattering of universalized food often generically referred to as 'Western' or 'Chinese' in South Asia, including in Sri Lanka. The breakfast menu offers four options. Out of these, three are specifically identified as 'rice and curry' or 'string hopper[69] and curry' combinations (Menu Nos. 1, 3 and 4). These are 'typical' of breakfast possibilities in the Sinhala south. I say 'typical' here to denote the fact that like all cultural facts food also changes and transforms their elements over time, and in this context many Sinhalas would eat bread and more Western oriented cereal also for breakfast. Nevertheless, within the commonsensical discourse of nationalism and the popular sense of tradition that pervades the society as a matter of routine, most people would agree that the kind of food in Green House's breakfast menu are the kind of breakfast foods which denote a sense of 'tradition' and 'authenticity' within a Sinhala cultural sensibility despite the polemics and problematics of these terms. It is precisely within this understanding that such foods have been offered to the visitors by the army in this bungalow.

Menu No. 2 offers bread, butter, jam, bull's-eye eggs and sausages. While this is certainly not an unfamiliar combination of breakfast food for the average middle-class palette in today's contexts of unmitigated globalization and standardization of numerous cultural practices as well as tastes, this would nevertheless be considered 'Western' or 'non-traditional' by most Sinhalas. Its inclusion is to cater to presumably 'westernized' tastes of some local tourists as well as for the benefit of anticipated foreign visitors. Similarly, the four choices in the lunch menu are also very much Sinhala in their orientation though some of them indicate a certain degree of 'innovation' in their preparation. Interestingly, Menu No. 1 also offers chicken *Kuruma*, a North Indian dish combining chicken and yoghurt as its main ingredients and known in India as Chicken *Kurma* or *Korma,* along with more typical Sinhala favourites. While this inclusion seems somewhat strange, the overall menu for lunch, like breakfast, consists of Sinhala favourites. Nevertheless, over the last decade or so, one could see certain adaptations of North Indian foods within the middle class and the mostly urban clienteles in Sri Lanka, which might partially explain this inclusion even though it is very much camouflaged by the accompanying dishes and curries. Of the four choices in the dinner menu, two are clearly Sinhala foods. Even so, Menu No. 1 includes string-hopper *buriyani*[70] which is the Sinhalization of the original preparation made famous in north Indian and particularly Mughal cuisine, which is no longer considered an importation from the subcontinent in terms of popular Sinhala imagination.

Menu No. 3 offers *paratha,* a North Indian bread that has become popular in the urban and more cosmopolitan parts of the country over the last decade or so, while Menu No. 4 offers noodles, which by now has become very much a part of popular Sinhala cuisine. In both these menus, besides the obvious imported cultural elements, all other accompanying curries and dishes are clearly Sinhala foods. They also mark in no uncertain terms the localization of the imported foods. The dessert menu by comparison is a more cosmopolitan if relatively uninspiring offering, more due to convenience than by design. It offers ice cream, jelly with ice cream, biscuit pudding, bananas and curd with treacle. Only the last two items are associated with a sense of traditional Sinhala deserts while all are common and uncomplicated desert offerings in many average restaurants today.

What does all this mean in terms of cultural politics when located in the context of wider post-war politics in Sri Lanka? Terry Eagleton has perceptively if somewhat mischievously observed that 'food is just as much materialized emotion as a love lyric' and food is 'actually a relationship' though it might look like an object.[71] These observations make contextual sense if one were to critically read what these menus mean in terms of culture and politics. These are not mere menus that indicate without contractions the kind of food that is offered in this establishment. They constitute the narrativization of emotions in the manner suggested by Eagleton. Very clearly, given their somewhat obvious manifestation in terms of Sinhala cultural sensibilities, the menus and the food they offer are indicative of the post-war Sinhala emotions of post-victory nationalism that have flowed across the country, which also followed the warzone tourists along their trail. They are the culinary embodiment of the emotional make-up of the victors. In this scheme of things, it is evident that Tamil food of any kind is simply not available in these menus. If what is absent could be thought of as the emotions of the defeated and the deprived people still trying to eke out a living not too far from this Sinhala cultural oasis, then, like their absence in the menu, their emotions are not part of the equation of power, culture and hegemony under the prevailing dispensation. The relationship that more localized foods might have been able to construct with the outlying localities and their structures of feeling in cultural terms simply does not take place here. Such possibilities, like the defeated, suspicious and anxiety-ridden people living in the margins not too far away are at best marginalized or driven into nonexistence.

To state it more simply, the design of these menus also suggests that according to the army's thinking, only or mostly Sinhala people were expected to visit these facilities. Even so, many of them who would have been quite familiar with Tamil food might well have partaken of these if they had the option. But the removal of that option itself shows the relative completeness of the cultural hegemony that is in place. In this sense, these facilities have to be perceived as ethicized Sinhala comfort zones in a larger zone of political and cultural discomfort marked by the demographic realities of the area and the aftermath of the war. In this context, when a person travels to one of these places, spends his or her time of leisure there and enjoys these politically 'sensitive' foods that are on offer, it is no longer a matter of private choice in a private space. It is a matter of becoming part of a larger public discourse and contributing to a particular ideology and a way of seeing the realities around you. That is, the reality of the world according to the victors. Clearly, even something as seemingly innocuous as food is not immune from the discourse of victory.

However, similar culinary tendencies can also be seen in other institutional settings that are not controlled by agencies of the state, but are nevertheless located in the realm of the larger post-war economy. Though a focus on this emergent and dynamic economy has not been an emphasis in this book, I believe a brief deviation to describe some manifestations of this specific culinary tendency makes contextual sense. This is because these tendencies have emerged as a result of responding to market realities, ushered in by warzone tourism. Let me give two examples from Jaffna and Pudukuduirippu. In December 2012, I stayed a few nights in one of the new post-war hotels in Jaffna which had very quickly acquired a booming business. The dominant conversations I heard during my stay were in Sinhala except for the few exchanges between local hotel workers who obviously spoke Tamil. That gave an idea of the kind of clientele this hotel attracted at the time. At breakfast one morning, I was surprised to see bread, string hoppers (known as *idi appa* in Sinhala), coconut salad or *pol sambol* and a fish curry prepared in a typically southern Sinhala fashion known as *embul tiyal*. Idi appa known in Tamil as *idi appam* itself was not the most typical northern breakfast food though it was known in much the same way as bread was also known. Both were sometimes consumed for breakfast depending on circumstances. But *dosa, idli* and other kinds of breakfast foods that one more typically expected to see on a breakfast table in a place like Jaffna were missing in this Tamil-run hotel. According to the waiters, as most people who came to the hotel were Sinhalas, the hotel management had decided to specifically cater to them. Towards that end, they had also recruited cooks and Sinhala-speaking waiters from the southern town of Matara. In this case, even if one wanted to taste something from the region, it was not possible. Considerations of the post-war market and particularly the massive warzone tourist influx had ensured that.

A few days after the incident described above, I was looking for breakfast near Pudukuduirippu, having left Jaffna too early to have breakfast. But rain and bad road conditions had ensured that I had reached the devastated town relatively late for breakfast. Clear signs of war and a heavy military presence were all around. It was just after noon. The young soldiers in the main military checkpoint in the town directed me to a recently built post-war hotel. They also had no local food and said they can only give noodles and 'Chinese' food, which also had to be cooked. No Tamil cuisine was available here either. Not wanting to wait too long for the perceived Chinese food in this part of the country, I ventured to the main road leading to the town from the A9, and started looking for any place that might sell something that could address basic issues of hunger, quickly. I found a small kiosk run by a man in his forties who had just returned from a refugee camp. The military had allowed him to set up this small kiosk on government land. His wife and small daughter were helping him run the place. He offered a typically southern form of bread known in Sinhala as *roast paan* along with pol sambol and dhal curry. In my conversation with him in broken Sinhala and a smattering of Tamil what emerged was a simple fact. The people who came looking for food to his kiosk were soldiers stationed in nearby areas and tourists coming in large numbers to see the LTTE-era remnants in the vicinity and the Victory Monument set up by the government. Again, he was catering to their perceived taste. In both cases, individuals running local businesses—a relatively large hotel in one case and a small kiosk in the other—had taken what might be called a rational economic decision in ensuring the wider availability of Sinhala food assuming that this is what the tourists would have preferred. However, most Sinhalas are familiar enough with mainstream Tamil food. As such, many of them might well have consumed them if available. But it appears that none of these individuals were willing to experiment with the idea. The kiosk owner's young daughter was also seen eating the same food, affectively ensuring that the kind of breakfast or lunch her parents might have eaten not too long ago was not readily available to her now. In this sense, without government regulations or state-level institutional compulsions, individual market decisions had ensured the radical alteration of the local culinary landscape at least in some pockets. Of course, to what extent and for how long this might continue remains to be seen and would be decided only by the future of warzone tourism in the region.

Let me now return to the analysis of military-run hotels in the warzone tourist trail. The Thal Sevana Holiday Resort in Kankesanturai managed by the Security Forces Headquarters in Jaffna with over 30 rooms was opened to the public in October 2010. The narratives that emerge from there are somewhat different from the two tourist enterprises in Mullaitivu described earlier. It is also a much larger operation compared to the two bungalows in Mullaitivu. The coastal town of Kankesanturai was best known in the pre-war times as the location of a large cement factory that the state had established there. This was one of the few major government-owned industries located in the Tamil-dominated north-east. Significant parts of the factory were destroyed during the war and lay abandoned for nearly three decades. In fact, it epitomized the widespread physical destruction of the war and more specifically its economic fallout. Seen from this perspective, it is obvious that the new resort—like the other two—is situated in a former battle zone which had seen considerable military action, destruction and human suffering. However, Kankesanturai does not have the kind of morbid claims to fame as Nandikadal does. The word Thal Sevana in Sinhala means 'Palmyra grove'. The name of the resort has been coined with reference to the most iconic slender tall trees which are typical of the area. Nevertheless, it is in Sinhala and not in the local language which is Tamil. Clearly, at least with regard to the name itself, if not for its reference, the post-war, Sinhala cultural power holds sway in this context too. But at the same time, unlike the two bungalows in Nandikadal which saw their genesis only after the end of war, Thal Sevana can trace its beginning to an earlier pre-war reality which was nevertheless associated with the hospitality industry owned by the state. That is, the site where the resort is located was the former location of the Kankesanturai Rest House, which itself was destroyed as a result of war.[72]

Rest houses, like the circuit bungalows of various government agencies, were initially set up in the British colonial period for colonial officials to rest while they were visiting different parts of the country on official duty. The rest houses, which essentially operated like small nondescript hotels, were later opened to the public and were part of the network of government-owned 'hotels' frequented by middle-class travellers, many of whom were government officers and their families. By the late 1970s, many of these had become dysfunctional or had simply closed down while others were handed over to private-sector operators to run for profit, well below the standards they were initially known for. A handful however continued to offer quality service under another government-owned agency called Ceylon Hotels Corporation. For many years, the Kankesanturai Rest House was a popular location for southern travellers to rest during their visits to the Jaffna peninsula in the pre-war period. A southern traveller who had seen the reinvention of the old rest house as Thal Sevana brings to her nostalgic recollection its earlier incarnation as part of her own holiday experience in the pre-war period:

> Often when siblings and families got together to share a meal, my husband would suggest a holiday and the loudest shout for destination would be Jaffna. We have stayed in the circuit bungalow of the Cement Corporation; at Elephant Pass and Kankesanturai rest-houses, those old post-colonial bungalows that offered excellent food—pol sambal and deep fried red chilies inevitably part of the meal—OK rooms and dignified service.[73]

Her references to food in these recollections bring out another important factor with regard to some of these rest houses. Pol sambol, as already briefly noted, which she refers to is essentially a coconut-based salad that constitutes of a mixture of scraped coconut, red chilies, salt, onions and dried fragments of fish typically associated with Sinhala cooking and culinary practices. Though located deep in the Tamil Hindu heartland, places like Kankesanturai Rest House regularly offered typical Sinhala food along with local specialties. This was because they were frequented by Sinhala officials on official duty as well as other travellers from the south. But local foods were always available as an option, which many visitors opted for.

The military's reinvention of the rest house as the Thal Sevana Resort took place over a number of years and in two phases, initially as a leisure location for members of the armed forces and their families, which was later expanded for the use of the wider public as attested by the declaration of the Sri Lanka Army itself:

'Thal Sevena', the former rest house building which was in a ruined condition due to terrorists' occupation for years and tsunami disaster was renovated to a holiday resort in 2010 on a concept of the incumbent Commander SF-J [Security Forces-Jaffna], especially for the members and their families visiting Jaffna after the war ended. It was later expanded to the present condition with intention of providing accommodation to civilians making pilgrimage and holiday destination to Jaffna. Within a short span of time, it became popular not only among the people from the South but many Jaffna residents and foreigners.[74]

Some care has been taken to preserve selected components of the old rest house in the process of reinvention. Despite the expansion and new additions in the post-war period and an entirely new layout, the reception and restaurant have been constructed by refurbishing the earlier building, a fact that talkative military members would quite willingly inform any tourist who might show some curiosity. This also shows a certain institutionalized willingness to link Thal Sevana to the pre-war period of relative calm than to the war era of chaos.

Unlike the two army-run resorts in Mullaitivu, it appears that an attempt was made to operate Thal Sevana as a professional hotel from the earliest time of its resurrection and reinvention. As the army explains,

[S]oldiers who were given professional training on the field are serving at the hotel. 'Thal Sevana' is a mirror of discipline and capability of Sri Lanka Army soldiers who soon got adapted to the postwar situation of the country. It provides service to local dignitaries, foreign diplomats and ordinary people equally catering to their needs. Many Jaffna families now select 'Thal Sevana' as the venue to hold their official meetings, birthday parties, get-together functions and weddings.[75]

In this sense, rather than as a site to relive victory and the brutal end of the LTTE's leadership as in the case of the two bungalows in Mullaitivu, Thal Sevana focuses on post-war reconstruction as well as the army's own attempts to reinvent itself in a non-combative and commercial role in the post-war period. In this sense, rather than reliving the war, here, the attempt seems to be on moving on. However, that is also done by erasing the calamities and destructions of war within the premises and perhaps very soon from the surrounding neighbourhoods as well. This erasure, as already noted, is an integral part of the post-war mega-narrative. As one traveller to the resort in 2012 observed,

> [D]uring a recent visit to Jaffna after thirty long years of separation of the Peninsula from the rest of the Island, we had lunch at the newly opened resort hotel—Thal Sevana. It was a memorable event in our two days in Jaffna. I will briefly expand on the statement I have made on the two hours spent at Thal Sevana being a high point of our stay in Jaffna. Firstly we were impressed by the warm welcome we received at this newly built, obviously functional hotel. Situated on a picturesque spot on the coastline of Kankesanturai, it was balm to the emotions made raw by the sight of deserted, desolate, bullet pocked houses and yellow taped areas declaring mine-danger. It was a hope-inspiring experience and one that proved the benefit of the army's presence in Jaffna. Here was a project of the army additional to its main function—that of peace maintaining and patrolling the Peninsula which could still harbour Tigers in hiding.[76]

What narratives such as these indicate is the linear and non-contradictory approach to the history and perception of post-war reality; development erases all evils of the causes and impacts of war. Additional commentary in the same narrative adds further emphasis to this position:

> The holiday resort was a luxurious oasis in the shambles of a civil war against a terror group which had destruction of humans, fauna and flora, buildings and the very fabric of life as their way of claiming Eelam. The polished floors and clean walls, good toilets, cool within the dining area and rooms with the soft lapping of the waves as gentle background music was complemented by the happy smiling faces of the service personnel. The very fact of its normalcy gave hope for the situation of Jaffna being improved by the Army.[77]

What is interesting is the fact these narratives, in their own way, relocate Thal Sevana well within the war itself via numerous passing references despite the military's own effort, at least in this instance, in distancing its enterprise from the fogs of war.

What is clear is that Thal Sevana, while still catering to the warzone tourist trail as well as the emerging regular leisure and pilgrim tourism, does not depend on the memories of war or its physical remnants for its legitimacy and survival. Instead, its sense of identity and pride seems to come from its own sense of professionalization and seeming mastery of the fundamental virtues of the hospitality industry. Naturally, this is a far cry from the active combat role played by the army as late as 2009. This transformation is manifest by it winning the 'International Star for Leadership in Quality Award' after competing with hotels in 188 countries.[78]

Another army-run leisure spot known as Nature Park Holiday Resort in Chundikulam, opened to the public in January 2012, is quite different from Thal Sevana even though it too caters to a kind of tourism that has nothing to do with the war or its remaining artefacts. Managed by the 55th Division of the Sri Lanka Army, its focus is on nature. Geographically, it is situated within the Chundikulam bird sanctuary, which had already been demarcated as a sanctuary before the war, and is located at the south-eastern tip of the Jaffna peninsula bordering the sea and lagoon stretch of Elephant Pass. In 2012, a high ranking military official had explained to a group of local journalists the army's perception on what the resort was supposed to achieve: 'Nature Park Holiday Resort has a different atmosphere. It is for those who love nature and are interested in birdwatching. If a guest wishes to go to the sea they can do that too. This place is out of the world'.[79] In this sense, even though constructed three years after the end of war and at the height of warzone tourism, the Nature Park Holiday Resort does not bank on promoting warzone tourism for its existence, but on providing a commercially viable forum for the perennially exclusive and very selective middle-class pastime of birdwatching. In addition to a cottage that has two bedrooms, a dining room and a hall, the resort also offers eight additional rooms. The idea of nature at the centre of its design is emphasized in a 2012 write-up of the place in a local magazine focused on tourism:

> The entire design of the holiday resort is to ensure that guests are truly one with the environment. The bathrooms in the eight separate rooms are open air, thus providing the night sky as the roof. There are no corridors connecting the buildings. The pathways wind through neatly landscaped gardens that are not artificial but in line with the surrounding environment.[80]

Nevertheless, for those interested, it can be a base for warzone tourism in Jaffna and Mullaitivu even though its overall design and sense of management does not overtly cater to this.

There are fundamental differences in the way various army-run leisure locations in the former warzone are designed and operated. The army's formal advent into the hospitality industry in the former warzone began at the height of warzone tourism and well after the end of war in 2009. It was at this time that such ventures were initiated as a matter of a definite policy. Though historically all three armed forces in Sri Lanka as well as the police did have holiday bungalows or circuit bungalows for their officers like many other government organizations, none of these entities had entered the wider tourism market until the end of the war. Moreover, they were not conceived as commercial operations. After a policy decision was made to enter the commercial hospitality industry, all army-run holiday bungalows and resorts which were open to the public were built or reinvented after the war ended. All such places in the north-east are established amidst places where the violence and destruction of war were experienced at close quarters.

In this sense, the location and landscaping of tourist facilities of this kind embed and signify possible sources of locational violence as suggested by Sally Ness (Ness 2005). However, beyond the generality of locational violence associated with these places by virtue of being established in a former warzone, the specificities of the signification and the depth of embeddedness of violence in these places vary significantly from place to place depending on the contextual history of each place. This difference, I suggest, also impacts the personality of each establishment. So the enormous violence in the surrounding areas and the brutal end of the LTTE leader define the existence and the character of Lagoon's Edge and Green House to such an extent that without these references and the possibility of visiting fast-disappearing LTTE sites in the vicinity, these places become de-contextualized. Without such associations, they would lose their meaning and relevance as well as their specificity. Without such references, they will simply become like any other circuit bungalow owned by the army even though they were located in the veritable epicentre of the warzone where the war actually ended. Comparatively, Thal Sevana and Nature Park, while also located in the warzone, do not depend on the narratives of the war and references to war-related locations such as specific battles or where war remnants might be seen to manifest their public personalities and sense of relevance. Instead, they are focused on more mainstream interests of emerging tourism in the area also shared by private-sector operators as well as issues such as nature, natural beauty and so on, almost to the extent of erasure of memories of war. Nevertheless, both kinds of leisure sites will continue to cater to warzone tourists while the trail itself lasts. The decisions to associate some of these establishments more closely with war while others focus on nature and natural beauty are taken on the basis of the interests of specific area commanders as well as the proximity of specific places to wartime incidents and the relative proximity of these places to context-laden locations.

Though not the main focus of this book, perhaps a brief note on the larger implications and global repercussions of the military's advent into the hospitality industry as well as the underlying interests of the military itself in this involvement should be placed in context. These non-combat, post-war initiatives include vast and expanding interests in holiday sites, travel trade, farms, urban planning and management, private security and so on. These initiatives and particularly those related to tourism have been identified and condemned as unethical tourism by organizations such as Sri Lanka Campaign for Peace and Justice.[81] This has come about as a result of the allegations by international human rights organizations of the Sri Lanka Army's and the Sri Lankan government's involvement in war crimes at the final stages of the war. These allegations, which implicate the military and the government centrally in committing war crimes, have been routinely rejected by both entities and remain effectively unresolved.

However, from the military's own point of view, the decision to involve itself in the hospitality industry and other post-war ventures has implications well beyond the interests of warzone tourism. This has to do with the maintenance of a combat-ready and battle-hardened military machine in peacetime. While the Sri Lanka Army and the other branches of the armed forces have not yet affectively looked at the possibility of demobilization, they have looked towards ventures such as tourism, travel and urban development as possible avenues to which its personnel could be diverted to in peacetime. However, these ventures have specific negative undercurrents which have to do with the hurdles they place against local people gaining access to the post-war economy of the north-east. As such, all the resorts run by the army in the north are manned, maintained, supplied and served by the military itself. Given the resources at its disposal, this makes perfect economic as well as management sense, and also helps improve the margin of profit from these ventures. However, this also means that these entities do not generate local employment beyond a point while they also restrict large expanses of local land to ordinary people from the area. The grey area between these two realities is a domain of considerable tension and anxiety, which the Sri Lankan state has hitherto not addressed in any serious manner. It is also an area where a more nuanced understanding of the dynamics involved is needed which has to necessarily go beyond the rhetoric of the international human rights discourse.

Nevertheless, what is clear is that some of the tourist and travel infrastructure provided by the military which was initially set up to cater to warzone tourism is quite likely to be a long-term presence that would become part of the mainstream hospitality industry in the country over time. They are clearly a part of the region's post-war economy which one has to deal with even if warzone tourism itself comes to an end. As the cases of Thal Sevana and the Nature Park clearly indicate, some of these have already become an integral part of regular tourism in the region. Whether the army and the government loosen this closed system even at the cost of profit to include local citizens in these ventures as a principled position on long-term economic inclusion of local interests in times to come remains to be seen.

Notes

1. The best examples of this trend are the various Facebook and Wikipedia pages of General Shavendra Silva. For more information visit, https://www.facebook.com/pages/Brigadier-Shavendra-Silva/42853263463 (accessed on 30 September 2013); https://www.facebook.com/Major.General.shavendra.silva (accessed on 2 February 2016); http://en.wikipedia.org/wiki/Shavendra_Silva (accessed on 2 February 2016). Interestingly however, many of the more active sites at the time of war seem to have been disabled in more recent times depending on the changed circumstances of their promoters as well as the natural progression of time and the resultant distance from the events of war.
2. Milk rice, known in Sinhala as *kiri bath* consists of rice cooked in coconut milk. It is often cooked to denote auspicious moments. Such as the new year, weddings, offerings of alms to monks and so on.
3. Excerpt from interview conducted in Nawala, Nugegoda on 16 May 2009.
4. Excerpt from interview conducted in Attidiya, Ratmalana on 16 May 2009.
5. The claim has been made in the website 'Journalists for Democracy in Sri Lanka'. For further details, please visit: http://www.jdslanka.org/index.php/2012-01-30-09-30-42/human-rights/274-navi-pillay-highlights-denial-of-tamil-right-to-commemorate-war-dead (accessed on 8 December 2013).

6. Source: http://www.jdslanka.org/index.php/2012-01-30-09-31-17/reflections/422-genocide-resistance-and-the-politics-of-remembering (accessed on 8 December 2013).

7. For more information, please see *Tamil Net* (23 March 2010).

8. http://www.tamilguardian.com/article.asp?articleid=6495 (accessed on 15 March 2014).

9. Excerpt from interview in Kilinochchi, December 2012.

10. For a more detailed description of the Kilinochchi War Hero Memorial and its politics, please refer to Perera (2015).

11. Official Website of Ministry of Defense and Urban Development, Government of Sri Lanka; http://www.defence.lk/new.asp?fname=20100506_05 (accessed on 15 September 2013).

12. BBC; http://www.bbc.co.uk/news/world-south-asia-14183579 (accessed on 15 September 2013).

13. Excerpts from interview in Kilinochchi, December 2012.

14. Excerpt from interview in Kilinochchi in December 2012.

15. Approximate translation from the Sinhala original.

16. Excerpt from an in interview, December 2012, Elephant Pass.

17. For a more details on the Elephant Pass War Hero Memoria, please refer to Perera (2015).

18. For a detailed account of the debacle, the best account available is Jayatilake (2008).

19. Lanka Puwath; http://www.lankapuvath.lk/index.php/latest-news/security/7023-elephant-pass-adorn-historic-war-hero-memorial- (accessed on 15 September 2013).

20. Interview conducted in Gampaha, Western province in December 2013. This driver had taken tourists to Jaffna in the first as well as the second phases of tourism. By 2013, such travel had become very regular and easily organized as a result of familiarity with the places visited, relatively easy travel and facilities that had become available post-war.

21. For more information on the destruction of the house and related issues, please visit the following websites: http://news.bbc.co.uk/2/hi/8652136.stm and http://www.hindustantimes.com/world-news/SriLanka/Tourism-takes-toll-on-Prabhakaran-s-home-army-steps-in-to-guard-it/Article1-518691.aspx (accessed on 25 October 2013).

22. For information and images of the house, please visit, http://www.flickr.com/photos/perambara/4564845336/in/photostream/ (accessed on 25 October 2013).

23. http://news.bbc.co.uk/2/hi/8652136.stm (accessed on 25 October 2013).

24. Excerpt from interview near Pudumathalan, December 2012.

25. Excerpt from an interview, December 2012, Pudumathalan.

26. Excerpt from interview in Pudumathalan, December 2012.

27. http://www.bbc.co.uk/news/world-asia-24402355 (accessed on 26 October 2013).

28. https://www.colombotelegraph.com/index.php/prabhakarans-bunker-destroyed-in-wanni/ (accessed on 26 October 2013).

29. https://www.colombotelegraph.com/index.php/after-we-did-so-much-for-you-you-voted-for-tna-military-tells-wanni-residents/ (accessed on 26 October 2013).

30. https://www.colombotelegraph.com/index.php/prabhakarans-bunker-destroyed-in-wanni/ (accessed on 26 October 2013).

31. https://www.colombotelegraph.com/index.php/after-we-did-so-much-for-you-you-voted-for-tna-military-tells-wanni-residents/ (accessed on 25 January 2016).

32. http://www.bbc.co.uk/news/world-asia-24402355 (accessed on 26 October 2013).

33. http://www.island.lk/index.php?page_cat=article-details&page=article-details&code_title=90283 (accessed on 26 October 2013).

34. Excerpt from interview in Pudumathalan, December 2012.

35. For more information, visit, http://srilankanews.wordpress.com/2007/05/02/sea-tigers-have-looted-14000-tons-of-rice-from-jordanian-ship-farah-111/ (accessed on 30th March 2014).

36. For a more details on the Victory monument, please refer Perera (2015).

37. Except from interview in Pudumathalan, December 2012.

38. Excerpt from conversation recorded at Pudumathalan, December 2012.

39. Excerpt from filed notes, Pudumathalan, December 2012.

40. Excerpt from narrative to visiting tourists at the War Museum, Pudumathalan, December 2012.

41. Excerpt from narrative to visiting tourists at the War Museum, Pudumathalan, December 2012.

42. Excerpts from interview in Jaffna in December 2012.

43. http://timesofindia.indiatimes.com/world/south-asia/Row-in-Lanka-as-govt-turns-Tamil-killing-fields-into-tourist-hot-spot/articleshow/18083064.cms (accessed on 08 April 2014).

44. http://timesofindia.indiatimes.com/world/south-asia/Row-in-Lanka-as-govt-turns-Tamil-killing-fields-into-tourist-hot-spot/articleshow/18083064.cms (accessed on 08 April 2014).

45. http://timesofindia.indiatimes.com/world/south-asia/Row-in-Lanka-as-govt-turns-Tamil-killing-fields-into-tourist-hot-spot/articleshow/18083064.cms (accessed on 08 April 2014).

46. For more details on Terry Eagleton's ideas on the interpretive attributes of food, one could read Eagleton (1997).

47. For more information on military-run hotels, resorts, bungalows, cafés, catering services and travel services, please visit, Sri Lanka Campaign for Peace and Justice at: http://www.srilankacampaign.org/LinkedBusinesses.htm#hotelsandresorts (accessed on 8 April 2014).

48. http://www.mawbima.lk/54-10427-news-detail.html (accessed on 8 April 2014).

49. The facility has been identified by the Sri Lanka Army itself as a holiday bungalow while in other media discussions in Sinhala and English it has been referred to as a hotel and resort.

50. http://lankacnews.com/english/main-news/a-luxury-holiday-resort-at-the-place-where-prabakaran-was-killed/ (accessed on 8 April 2014).

51. For more information read Margaret Harrison (2014).

52. http://www.mawbima.lk/54-10427-news-detail.html (accessed on 8 April 2014).

53. http://www.mawbima.lk/54-10427-news-detail.html (accessed on 8 April 2014).

54. http://www.huffingtonpost.co.uk/frances-harrison/sri-lankas-killing-fields-tourism_b_2356247.html (accessed on 13 April 2014).

55. http://www.mawbima.lk/54-10427-news-detail.html (accessed on 8 April 2014).

56. http://www.mawbima.lk/54-10427-news-detail.html (last accessed on 8 April 2014).

57. https://www.facebook.com/pages/Lagoons-Edge/466660380052525 (accessed on 12 April 2014).

58. http://www.mawbima.lk/54-10427-news-detail.html (accessed on 8 April 2014).

59. http://www.mawbima.lk/54-10427-news-detail.html (accessed on 8 April 2014).

60. http://www.mawbima.lk/54-10427-news-detail.html (accessed on 8 April 2014).

61. http://www.mawbima.lk/54-10427-news-detail.html (accessed on 8 April 2014).

62. http://www.negombo-motorcycle-tours.com/motorcycletour/battlefield/ (accessed in 8 April 2014).

63. For more information, tour details and images, please visit: http://www.negombo-motorcycle-tours.com/motorcycletour/battlefield/ (accessed in 8 April 2014).

64. For more information, location maps and images of Lagoon's Edge including mages of the official opening of the resort, please visit its official Facebook page maintained by the Sri Lanka Army Headquarters in Mullaitivu at: https://www.facebook.com/pages/Lagoons-Edge/466660380052525 (accessed on 25 January 2016).

65. http://www.huffingtonpost.co.uk/frances-harrison/sri-lankas-killing-fields-tourism_b_2356247.html (accessed on 13 April 2014). For the *Time* article ('Three Years After War's End, Sri Lanka Is Only Beginning to Make Peace') referred to in the quotation please visit: http://world.time.com/2012/05/18/three-years-after-wars-end-sri-lanka-is-only-beginning-to-make-peace/ (accessed on 14 April 2014); for the International Crisis Group report ('Sri Lanka's North II: Rebuilding under the Military' / Asia Report No. 220, 16 Mar 2012) referred to in the quotation please visit: http://www.crisisgroup.

org/en/regions/asia/south-asia/sri-lanka/220-sri-lankas-north-ii-rebuilding-under-the-military.aspx (accessed on 14 April 2014).

66. For more information, location maps and photographs of the location, please visit the official Facebook page of Green House maintained by the Sri Lanka Army Headquarters in Mullaitivu: https://www.facebook.com/pages/Green-House-Holiday-Bungalow/369841146395064 (accessed on 12 April 2014).

67. https://www.facebook.com/pages/Green-House-Holiday-Bungalow/ 369841146395064 (accessed on 12 April 2014).

68. For illustrated renditions of the breakfast, lunch, dinner and desert menus of Green House as well as other related images, please visit: https://www.face-book.com/pages/Green-House-Holiday-Bungalow/369841146395064?id=3 69841146395064&sk=photos_stream (accessed on 20 April 2014).

69. String-hoppers is the anglicized word for the noodle-like food known in Sinhala as *idi aappa* and in Tamil and Malayalam as *idi appam*. Though originally a cultural importation from Kerala, string-hopers has been well adopted into the Sinhala culinary practice and hierarchy, and is now never considered as an import from South India. It is often presented as a typically Sinhala food.

70. *Buriyani*, pronounced *biryani* in North and most other parts of India is a rice-based fried dish (often as a meal by itself) which also contains vegetables and meats that originated in Turkey, Iran or in that general region. The word, buriyani/biryani comes from the Persian *beryā*(n) which literally means fried or roasted. This food was brought to India in particular and South Asia more generally by Muslim travellers most possibly in the Mughal times, and became one of the most popular foods in Mughal courts. Taking into account the similarity of the local name and the Indian rendition as well as Sri Lanka's close cultural affinities with India, in all probability this was introduced to Sri Lanka via India by Muslim traders. In the Sri Lankan context, it has undergone many changes in terms of materials used as well as more specific localization of taste. One of the transformations is the use of string-hoppers instead of rice as the main ingredient in one version. Rice however remains the main ingredient in most other local preparations. Interestingly, it is this more localized version that uses string-hoppers which the Sri Lanka Army decided to include in its menu at Green House.

71. http://www.timeshighereducation.co.uk/features/edible-ecriture/104281. article (accessed on 20 April 2014).

72. http://www.cimicjaffna.com/Cimicnews_2013_07_04.php (accessed on 25 April 2014).

73. http://island.lk/index.php?page_cat=article-details&page=article-details&code_title=25367 (last accessed on 25 April 2014).

74. http://www.cimicjaffna.com/Cimicnews_2013_07_04.php (accessed on 26 April 2014).

75. http://www.cimicjaffna.com/Cimicnews_2013_07_04.php (accessed on 26 April 2014).

76. http://island.lk/index.php?page_cat=article-details&page=article-details& code_title=25367 (accessed on 26 April 2014).
77. http://island.lk/index.php?page_cat=article-details&page=article-details& code_title=25367 (accessed on 26 April 2014).
78. http://www.cimicjaffna.com/Cimicnews_2013_07_04.php (last accessed on 26 April 2014).
79. http://exploresrilanka.lk/2012/07/in-the-shade-of-the-palms/ (last accessed on 26 April 2014).
80. http://exploresrilanka.lk/2012/07/in-the-shade-of-the-palms/ (last accessed on 26 April 2014).
81. For more information, please visit Sri Lanka campaign for Peace and Justice at: http://www.srilankacampaign.org/LinkedBusinesses.htm (last accessed on 27 April 2014).

4
Photography and Cartography in Warzone Tourism

'What is the use of a book', thought Alice, 'without pictures or conversations?'

—Lewis Carroll

This is what Lewis Carroll's little fictional character Alice ponders at the very beginning of the book, *Alice's Adventures in Wonderland*.[1] Indeed, what is the point of a yarn without the pictures to make the connections: pictures of 'authenticity', pictures of exploration, pictures of triumphs and adventures, pictures of excitement and pictures of conquest, among others? Scholars familiar with the history of ethnography would also know the crucial narratives that images of 'exotic' places, often with the ethnographers in the foreground posing with 'exotic' objects and subjects, did to enhance and embellish the credibility, authority and 'authenticity' of the narratives that our academic forefathers were weaving. Both Alice's words and our intellectual forefathers' preoccupation with image-creation and narrative-making came to my mind when I initially witnessed in 2002 the rush of tourism from southern Sri Lanka and Tamil diasporic centres mostly in Europe and North America to war-ravaged northern parts of the country, which I have described in Chapter 2. I could see that photography was a major preoccupation in these travels which continued in the second phase of warzone tourism also, which I have described in Chapter 3. But my concern here is not on images per se. The narratives that emerge within warzone tourism and the emotions that temper these travels make more contextual sense when situated in the realm of easy-to-capture images. It is not an accident that we live in a time where clicking a photograph is possible with almost every mobile telephone. As such, warzone tourism necessarily involves a significant preoccupation on the part of travellers with photography. In the Sri Lankan context which I described in the previous two chapters, this preoccupation included print photography as the present millennium arrived, which has since then been completely taken over by digital photography.

Logic of Photography in Contemporary Warzone Travels

So far in the book, I have outlined how warzone tourism emerged and expanded in Sri Lanka. In this context, both photography and cartography have played a significant role though the implication of the latter is not overtly evident. Comparatively however, the presence of the practice of photography throughout the warzone trail in both the first and the second phase is very obvious. In this chapter, I will focus on the twin occupations of photography and cartography in warzone travel, beginning with photography. Photographs do not constitute a single category. They vary significantly on the basis of contextuality: who captured the images, when, how, for what reason and so on. Some may capture images as part of an aesthetic exercise in order to create an artwork within a sense of pleasure. Yet others might capture images to formulate an illustrative record, as in the case of news photography as well as travel photography. At the same time, it is self-evident that 'aesthetically satisfying' images captured by people such as tourists or even professional photographers and academics in the field may not be seen as a reliable source of knowledge in many formal academic contexts (Collier and Collier 1986: 165). Many of the images that warzone tourists in Sri Lanka have captured in their numerous travels fall within the first category. Even so, their interest to create an illustrative record of their own travel does not fall within more formal ventures such as news photography, which nevertheless shares some basic similarities.

What these tourists have captured are images taken in the contexts of pleasure, leisure and curiosity, with no serious interests in sequencing or analyzing, and have nothing to do with research as such in terms of their overall intent. It is with regard to such situations that Collier and Collier have noted, 'we can responsibly analyze only visual evidence that is contextually complete and sequentially organized' because 'no matter how rich our photographic material is, quantitative use of evidence is limited to that which is countable, measurable, comparable or in some other ways scalable in quantitative forms' (Collier and Collier 1986: 163). Colliers' position is quite restrictive and not particularly useful when situated in today's academic contexts influenced by the inroads made by cultural studies and post-structuralist ideas among others, which take ordinary images that cannot be quantified as a serious source of research worthy of interpretation. On the other hand, Colliers' observations make very little sense when an academic pursuit perceives photographs beyond the rigid restrictions of quantification. As Susan Sontag has noted, a photograph simply cannot provide an interpretation by itself (Butler 2005). Such images, such as the ones captured by warzone tourists in Sri Lanka, have to be given a context and, through that, a sense of wider relevance and meaning through the work of scholarship. By doing so, scholars will transform such imagery and their immediate meanings from the realm of relatively private consumption to the domain of formal scholarship which would be available publicly. It is in such a context that I will locate photography in warzone tourism as a potential source worthy of a wider reading. As I shall explain later, these images have stories to narrate which make considerable sense when attempting to understand warzone travel and its wider implications.

At the beginning of this chapter, I referred to our academic forefathers' preoccupation with photography and the possible association this activity had with Sri Lankan warzone tourists' consistent interest in capturing contextual images of their travels, mostly in digital form. Given the importance of the 'visual' in narrating the annals of warzone travel, in which digital photography has a special place, it is crucial to revisit even briefly this historical relationship with photography and travel along with the association that numerous early colonial and postcolonial characters had with the photography in particular and image-making more generally when attempting to figure out what contemporary tourists to northern Sri Lanka have to do with photography.

I have already noted in Chapter 1 that irrespective of Urry's de-emphasis of sight as the most superficial of the senses when dealing with tourism, it does carry enormous discursive power when situated in the context of capturing and freezing certain sights through photography, which manifests very clearly when dealing with warzone tourism in Sri Lanka. Also as

Barthes has noted, '[P]hotography mechanically repeats what could never be repeated existentially' (Barthes 1981: 4) thereby ushering in events and moments of the past to the present and connecting them with wider realities than those associated with the immediate circumstance of the images themselves. In fact, when tourists capture images, while they might be superficial in Urry's terms because of the casualness in which many of these are captured, they nevertheless become records of travels of individuals and collectives. They create cartographies of not only where they go but also what kind of objects and places capture their imagination and attention. They also would inform us where they do not go and what they seem not to focus on even in the places they do visit, thereby offering considerable interpretive possibilities of these systemic absences.

In the Sri Lankan context, many of the tourists who travelled to the north in the first phase of warzone tourism and more clearly since the second phase, were armed with digital cameras in their mobile phones. Others carried regular digital cameras as well. This ensured a cheap and very accessible technology for both capturing and storing images as well as the possibility of sharing them with wider audiences later. It is in this context that images captured in this manner were shared among family members and friends in print form as well as digitally via email, Facebook, Twitter, on blogs and so on. All of this meant that thousands of casual images had become part of a much larger discourse that was in constant circulation. In this sense, images such as these were not only connected with the moment of photography (the past) but also to the present and through sources like the internet, to an eternity whose lifespan cannot be determined.

When photographs are seen in this sense, there is one crucial common thread between these historically and spatially distinct preoccupations with photography. That is, the photography of colonial characters and early anthropologists on one hand and the photography of contemporary warzone travellers in Sri Lanka on the other. In the case of early anthropology and colonial travel, photography (and before that sketches and engravings) was used to authenticate the nature of travel and the contextual validity of the ethnographer's and the colonial traveller's presence in a specific place at a specific time. They became part of the discourse which legitimized and authenticated a traveller's presence in a unique, exotic, weird or dangerous place at a specific temporal moment. Images, therefore, are closely linked with three interrelated elements: place, temporality and authenticating presence.

For a colonial missionary of the 18th century, posing with 'fierce' looking tribesmen was a matter of authenticating his presence in the midst of uncivilized and possibly cannibalistic lands where the word of god needed to be spread and hordes of heathens civilized. It established his passion and faith and convinced his well-wishers to spend the necessary funds for the work of god and the expansion of the European empires. In Sri Lanka's warzone tourism of both phases, to pose with LTTE combatants or in front of war remnants was a matter of authenticating one's travels through a gruesome warzone which was closed for civilian travels for nearly three decades. They were authentic markers of an adventure trail. As a 62-year old man who had visited Jaffna in the first phase of tourism once told me showing his collection of colour prints, '[S]ee this is Kamalini. She was in the LTTE's political wing. There [in the north], she is like one of our ministers. She was quite friendly towards us, not like our politicians.'[2] Indeed, it was an image of Kamalini[3] who had become a familiar face in the Sinhala south during the ceasefire period due to the considerable press coverage she received at the time. In the image, she was dressed in the 'civilian' uniform of the LTTE which was prevalent the time. Her beaming presence in the photograph added much credibility and authenticity to the senior tourist's travel story. After all, it was not only a document which offered proof of travel but also evidence of meeting the 'exotic' in this particular 'orientalist' experience. This specific practice and the associations that travellers attempt to make are not too different from the posed images of early colonial travellers and anthropologists with fierce-looking tribesman and purported 'cannibals'. In both the colonial and recent Sri Lankan experiences referred to above, the images bound together the conditionalities of place, temporality and authenticating presence. In both contexts, these visuals introduced these once 'uncharted' places to a larger and receptive public albeit through very different mediums.

As we know, these kinds of images played a significant part in creating the idea of the Orient as an exotic, mysterious and sometimes dangerous place in the context of the Orientalist discourse as outlined by Edward Said (1979). Pinney (2011), when discussing the parallel evolution of both photography and anthropology from the latter part of the 19th century to the first part of 20th century, notes that many anthropologists considered photography as a way of reflecting the reality of social life and cultural practice of their contexts of research. However, more than examples of authenticity of a research context, we know today that the anthropological images of the late 19th and early 20th centuries were essentially posed for the benefit of the anthropologists and others like them, which nevertheless did not preclude them from arguments of authenticity in the popular discourse. But as in the case of colonial travellers, such images also marked an anthropologist's presence in an unusual place not very different from the contextual relevance of photographs from the Sri Lankan warzone. More specifically in this context, Wolbert has observed that an '"anthropologist as photographer" is both an amateur and professional: as a rule, anthropologists are not trained photographers, but even when they photograph without training—they do make photographs in a professional context' (Wolbert 2000: 321).

Similarly, the kinds of tourists I am concerned with in this book are also mostly amateur photographers and, more importantly, unlike the anthropologists that Wolbert refers to, they do not work in a professional context, but in a situation of leisure. So the images they capture, often in digital technology in today's contexts, are not expected to enhance their professional lives. Instead, they merely record the annals of their travels, identify where they have been and authenticate the things they have seen. In the annals of contemporary warzone tourism in Sri Lanka, photography is considered 'irrefutable' proof, particularly of a person's presence in a particular place. That is why tourists were very keen to pose near recognizable remnants of battle, with uniformed LTTE personnel, at specific monuments and long-inaccessible pilgrim sites, and so on.

The work of photography in contemporary warzone travels in Sri Lanka is closer to photography's association with the life trajectories of early colonial travellers. Despite this preoccupation over the authenticity of presence that a photograph is supposed to provide, a photograph cannot be seen simplistically as a document that authenticates a fact, an event or a person's presence in a specific place beyond all possible doubt. As Shell has noted, 'a photograph captures everything in that it reveals nothing' (Shell 2012: 9). Much of today's warzone travel photography in the Sri Lankan context falls into this category. We need to note that many of these images constitute 'posed' photographs of historically liminal events within which warzone travel is located. Therefore, one simply cannot capture events of the war itself even though in the initial period of travel it was possible to capture images very clearly related to the consequences of war. Besides, in the first phase of travel, war was in the background; battles were fought away from the gaze of the tourists and skirmishes continued to be reported in the press. One had to travel through LTTE-held territory where their writ was clear and their armed presence quite obvious and aspired for by tourists as photo opportunities. So the presence of the war was very much evident as a narrative backdrop while travel continued. So when tourists posed in front of LTTE monuments, they were not simply immortalizing an image but referencing a signification to a state of affairs that paralleled but opposed and negated the state in other parts of the country. However, in terms of tourist sensibility tempered by a heightened sense of adventure, this kind of interpretation was not necessarily part of the tourists' own discourse. However, the moment such images ventured into public space through the internet and other forums, the possibilities of generating other discourses and more politically nuanced interpretations became possible and inevitable.

However, in general, the kind of photography that warzone travellers are engaged in is very different from capturing the ravages of war itself even though their images have been captured within a once-active warzone. In most cases, these were simply trophy photographs. With reference to violence and photography, Susan Sontag (2002) notes that photography is rhetoric for the victims and survivors of war since photographs of war situations narrate their experiences and are supposed to evoke a sense of public concern of the calamities of war as well as to produce 'the illusion of consensus' as to what has happened (Sontag 2002: 83). She further points out that since its very beginning, photography has been somewhat proximately associated with death, killing and war due to its clear ability over many other forms of expression to graphically represent pasts that have disappeared and deaths that have occurred (Sontag 2002). Further, discussing Sontag's ideas on photography Butler notes that 'contemporary notion of atrocity requires photographic evidence' (2005: 824). However, when a tourist engaged in warzone travel captures an image, none of the attributes of photography in the contexts of war and violence that Sontag has outlined seem to come into play. Instead of contextualizing war or even creating an illusion of consensus, this kind of image-making decontextualizes war and removes its calamities from the consciousness of the picture-taking and picture-consuming public. This is particularly so in the second phase where travels are taking place in an atmosphere of victory and triumphalism. Also, since most tourists do not meet the locals who have experienced and witnessed the deprivations of war, the silence about war in contemporary photography tends to get further entrenched. So, as photography in warzone travel relentlessly continued, the pain and destructions of war found no resonance in the minds of travellers.

As warzone tourism expanded to its second phase, even posing amidst remnants of war such as LTTE monuments became more difficult due to the dismantling of many war-related structures as this reading has already documented. So, if image-making among clusters of LTTE monuments and with its uniformed personnel allowed for a secondary albeit less visible discourse of politics and history to emerge in the first phase, that possibility was completely negated as the second phase advanced. If LTTE structures and other remnants directly related to war were the sentinels that marked the first phase of warzone travel, in the second, that position was taken by post-war military monuments constructed by the state and the Sri Lanka Army. As such, the monuments in Elephant Pass, Kilinochchi and Pudukuduyiruppu became sites for consistent photography, particularly after the more popular and the last remaining LTTE buildings were destroyed by the government. Photographs taken near these recently constructed war monuments narrate a specific story of victory that the state has constructed with which many travellers readily agree. This is why they want to pose for photographs near such locations and thereby become a pictorial index in the post-war master narrative. But as in the first phase, these images too are silent about how the war actually touched the local people who are usually invisible in these images and are also not present at these sites but can only be seen in the distance. But tourists are usually not interested in conversations with them given their propensity to disrupt the master-narrative. That is why these individuals are almost never within the frames of warzone photographs.

This does not mean however that 'posing' is inauthentic in the minds of the people who practice them, be they tourists or professionals. As historians of ethnography might argue, the work of Edward Curtis has become legendary due to his extensive attempts to 'stage manage' a romantic representation of the 'dying native American culture' (Pinney 2011: 90–92). It is in this constructed context that we can view today the many stoic photographs of hunters, farmers, warriors and others who emerge out of the pages of colonial travel literature and early ethnographies. This practice is also linked to the attempt of pictorially articulating a sense of what was considered 'exotic'. But at best, visual imagery of this kind offered incomplete narratives. In this context, such imagery sometimes seemed 'disquieting' in the sense 'they appeared to show everything and yet, like the physical body, remained annoyingly mute' (MacDougal 1999: 276).

Despite these kinds of critiques that can be presented to argue against the contextual 'authenticity' of what is presented in an image, a photograph nevertheless is popularly supposed to bring 'facts' into a specific context. So, the people who engaged in photography in warzone travels did so enthusiastically as they travelled through the warzone simply because they expected their photographs to narrate certain stories usually for themselves and for their immediate circles of friends and kin. Much of their interest had to do with their own perceived authenticity of their experiences as well as the authenticity of what their gaze had seen and the images captured by their cameras. It seems to me these kinds of experiences frozen in time as photographs can be referred to as 'visual narratives' following Pimenta and Pooviaah (2010) who have suggested the term to identify the manner in which narratives are presented through visual aids, including photography. This is also quite similar to what Murray (1995) has called a 'narrative illustration' which deals with pictorial events that takes place over a period of time.

Besides, intellectual and academic reservations about the possible inauthenticity of photography have nothing to do with its relentless, popular practice at the ground level, often moved by a very powerful sense of authenticity and an urge to preserve memories. And many travel stories accompanied by such images were indeed narrated in numerous living rooms, offices, schools and quite often in various corners of the internet as well. This narrativization became more possible, it's discursive reach wider and its longevity much greater due to the ability to digitize images which pictorially contextualized what the written and spoken words narrated and the ability to place many of these images online for wider circulation. As such, irrespective of the contradictions this practice of image-making might entail in theoretical and philosophical terms, it nevertheless needs to be explored as an important aspect of the overall practice of warzone tourism which took place on the ground and what it means when taken as a complex web of activities.

As I have noted elsewhere, from the beginning of the first phase of warzone travel, there was a significant consistency in framing photographs among tourists (Perera 2005). Irrespective of the differences in terms of the actual individuals in these images and sometimes the locations where they might have been taken, the kind of backgrounds which people preferred, who they posed with (often with LTTE sentries) and the stories they were expected to narrate tended to be strikingly similar (Perera 2005). This means that the nature of photography in this particular context had already been institutionalized and routinized by popular practice within a very short period of time without any kind of formal external intervention (Perera 2005). It was simply a matter of consistent popular choice and practice. In a sense, this is quite similar to what Urry has referred to as 'the pursuit of the exotic and the diverse ends in uniformity' (Urry 2002: 8). The most common frames of these photographs include individuals posing in front of the defaced and bullet-riddled but still surviving place name at the entry point to Elephant Pass, the formal entry to the Jaffna peninsula, which narrates irrefutably that a person had actually visited the north during the first phase of tourism. In the second phase, the practice continued with entire families, other groups as well as individuals often posing in front of the newly established and standardized green signboards at the entry to Elephant Pass as well as the former LTTE bastions of Mullaitivu and Kilinochchi. These new post-war government-established location signs prominently presented the place name in Sinhala on the first line, no longer defaced as the LTTE had done in the previous era.

When people pose in front of these signs, the photographs they take become part of a wider discourse. In that discourse, they narrate additional stories beyond signalling an entry of a person to the area concerned. They also narrate the dismantling of the LTTE's power, the entry of a new dispensation of power and authority spearheaded by the military, and the politico-cultural domination of Sinhalas in the post-war period. In both phases of tourism, this kind of image also constitutes a foolproof certificate of authenticity quite similar to that well-known secular ritual which most first-time visitors to Disneyland in Anaheim and Universal Studios Hollywood perform (Perera 2005). They pose outside the entrances to these institutions so that their images can be captured with the name boards of the places in the background. In this specific travel discourse, Elephant Pass had acquired in the local context what Disneyland and Universal Studios had already achieved in the US context many years before. The Sinhala tourists' eagerness to pose with unknown but uniformed LTTE combatants was not so different from the eagerness shown by visitors to Disneyland to pose with popular characters created by Walt Disney, ranging from Mickey Mouse, Snow White and Donald Duck to Goofy. This was also a matter of capturing the 'exotic', something specific to the war and different from the everyday lives of the tourist. Yet, the pursuit of this kind of exoticism by almost everyone who ventured into the warzone ended in creating a somewhat obvious uniformity in photography.

In a related context and with reference to European tourist travel and photography, Urry notes that 'if there are any non-white faces in the photographs it would be presumed that they are the 'exotic natives' being gazed upon' (Urry 2002: 139). In the local context, metaphorically, the 'non-white' faces of exotic value were those of the LTTE cadres in uniform and preferably with guns. There is no clear evidence that Sinhala travellers were as keen to pose with ordinary Tamil civilians or even LTTE cadres not in uniform given their lack of reference to an obvious sense of the exotic or 'authenticity'. In the Sri Lankan context, what was needed instead of Disney's funny costumes were men and women wearing recognizable LTTE uniforms while those bearing weapons were even more sort after. Given the eager flexibility shown by LTTE members in this new practice of pictorial adventure, despite the organization's reputation as a no-nonsense battle-hardened entity, it was quite clear that they must have been ordered by their commanders to play this role. Interestingly however, the eagerness shown by Sinhala tourists to pose with LTTE members did not extend to members of the Sri Lankan military beyond the very first months of the second phase. Perhaps due to their familiarity with the travellers in terms of language, culture and ideology, the kind of exoticism offered by the LTTE was not present with them.

In addition to the kind of photographs and their contexts referred to previously, tourists have also shown great eagerness to pose in recognizable locations associated with established and emergent pilgrim sites during both phases of travel. In both the first and second phases, most Buddhists who visited the Naga Dipa Buddhist Temple have shown a marked propensity to pose in front of its silver coloured stupa as well as at its ornate entrance. It was simply a matter of indicating their entrance to the temple, a long-established pilgrim centre, which had been closed to most pilgrims for over three decades. In the first phase, civilian entry to the temple signalled the limited travel possibilities of the cease-fire and the re-blossoming of a religious practice that had been dormant as a war-induced necessity for 30 years. In the second phase, when people flocked to the same temple in incredibly larger numbers than before, it symbolized the end of war and the opening up of the north to southern tourist travel in general, which also meant the total annihilation of the

LTTE and the re-emergence of state control in the north. In other words, it was due to these radically changed politico-military circumstances that travel had become possible in this scale. On the other hand, specifically in the second phase, people were also eager to visit the Dambakola Patuna temple which indicated a massive infrastructure expansion during this time and a popularization among people and an acceptance as a legitimate pilgrim site. Almost as a ritualized practice, many wanted to be photographed at its very recognizable signboard just outside the temple premises, featuring the Buddhist flag and the name of the temple in Sinhala as well as near its small stupa and the statutory, but particularly in front of the statue of Teri Sangamitta. Collections of images such as these at a simple level are obviously part of the personal travel documentation of individuals and families. On the other hand, they also indicate in cultural terms, the post-war expansion of institutionalized Sinhala Buddhism in the area, and the association of the state and its numerous agencies in this revival. What the seemingly innocuous family pictures show is the dawn of a new era and the eclipse of the older one with the LTTE and Tamil nationalism at its helm even though it is not the stated objective of tourists to make such political interpretations.

One could make the same argument about the wider narratives that emerge from tourists' photographs of popularly visited 'regular' tourist sites in the north such as the famous hot water well in Kiramalai, the 'bottomless' well in Puttur and many beaches that have been identified in recently produced tour maps. Many Sinhala tourists (particularly those in the age group of 35 and below) who would have not visited the north prior to the onset of warzone tourism due to the entrenchment of the war would not have even heard of many of these places. After all, these sites were not directly associated with the war and were mostly local attractions. Information about such places would have come to them after warzone tourism began as part of the warzone travel discourse itself. The information about these places and the ability to visit them as well as capturing images of their travel activities became possible for tourists only because the war ended the way it did. As in previous cases, the photographs taken by countless tourists indicate the new possibilities and the changed political landscape of the north. In other words, as the second phase of warzone travel continued, warzone photography became a constantly asserted and consistently repeated practice of generating a pictorial cartography of the post-war politico-military and cultural dispensation in the north, which nevertheless does not usually accommodate within their frames the pain and destruction of the region as felt and seen by locals. After all, as Sontag has accurately observed, 'the memory of war, however, like all memory, is mostly local' (Sontag 2002), which does not necessarily pierce the conscience of others beyond the immediate localities of experience.

Logic of Cartography and its Practice in Contemporary Warzone Travels

Cartography has much to do with Sri Lanka's civil war as well as the second phase of warzone tourism even though its presence in the practice of politics and warzone travel is not as overtly visible compared to the obvious and recurrent visibility of photography. Instead, cartography is a relatively invisible and taken for granted presence in the twin contexts of war and warzone travel. However, maps are simply not rational technical documents providing abstract information on travel even though they provide consolidated information on the geography of a place which may vary from layouts of roads to information on the topography of swaths of land to cultural landscapes. As such, they have their own dynamics and politics which need to be taken into account when attempting to understand how maps have an impact upon people's decisions to travel and in their process of planning as well as in their imaginings of nationhood and place. Elaborating on the deeper and non-obvious attributes of maps, Lacoste has noted that the map, as the central referent to geography, is fundamentally an instrument of power (Lacoste 1973: 1). Tagore attempted to outline some of these complications of geography and maps in his famous line in the novel *The Home and the World* when his fictional character noted, '[T]he geography of a country is not the whole truth. No one can give up his life for a map' (Tagore 2011: 38). True enough, geography does not constitute the complete narrative of a country. Nevertheless, people do give up their lives often for that geography—for that map or territory, contrary to the misgivings of Tagore's fictional character. One can argue that the genesis of Sri Lanka's civil war was essentially over the ownership of a map. At a very basic level, a map is an abstraction derived from certain concrete realities designed and motivated by practical concerns which includes both political and military interests (Lacoste 1973: 1).

In this sense, the perceived and real discrimination of Tamils in Sinhala-dominated society meant that some Tamils opted to react to this experience in non-violent forms since the late 1970s. Over time, these actions gave politico-military meaning to the idea of Eelam and came to determine much of the relationships between Sinhalas and Tamils. Eelam, of course, is the name Tamil separatists gave the land they hoped to carve out of the existing territory of Sri Lanka. This goal was to be achieved via the idea of 'traditional Tamil homelands', which was also at a very basic level, a cartographic contextualization. What was perceived as 'traditional Tamil homelands' was a reference in the Tamil nationalist discourse to areas of Sri Lanka where Tamils predominated, which was believed to be a historically consistent fact. The past however is never a concrete fact in any nationalist discourse, as was also the case in this instance. Nevertheless, this categorization was a conscious cartographic imagination with considerable emotional power which referred to a clearly identified area in the contemporary map of Sri Lanka. This imagination or reference was indicative of the independent country that was expected to be established through armed struggle. Seen in this sense, the Tamil nationalist imagination of Eelam as well as the Sri Lankan state's and Sinhala nationalists' conception of integral territory of Sri Lanka can be understood as two cartographic imaginations exercising considerable power as suggested by Lacoste (1973: 1). As instruments of power, both renditions could mobilize the emotions of large groups of people who were willing to sacrifice their lives for the carving out of one imagination in the hope of making that imagination a political reality while yet others were equally as willing to do the same thing to ensure that the integrity of the imagination of Sri Lanka as a non-bifurcated territory remained as such. Seen from this perspective, the armed confrontation between the Sri Lankan state and the Tamil guerrilla groups and the ideological conflict between Tamil and Sinhala nationalists were essentially a confrontation over these two cartographic imaginations. Furthermore, the map is a way of 'representing space which facilitates its domination and control' in the context of which mapping refers to a formal act of defining space 'along the lines set within a particular epistemological experience' (Lacoste 1973: 1–2).

As already noted, both the idea of Eelam and the opposition to it was a contestation between two very different imaginings of maps based on vastly divergent epistemological experiences that were mediated by mutually oppositional nationalist politics which were tempered by very different perspectives on the past. As recent Sri Lankan history would indicate, it was the LTTE which took the Tamil nationalist assumptions and arguments for the creation of a separate state (country) to its most destructive end. In that journey, the political map of Tamil Eelam (see Figure 4.1) consisting of large areas of land from the north-western, northern and eastern parts of Sri Lanka indicated the territory of the perceived state of Eelam. As such, prominent renditions of this map became an integral part of numerous LTTE propaganda materials, flags, monuments and proposed postage stamps and an essential presence on many pro-LTTE websites. This map along with the ferocious-looking LTTE emblem consisting of a growling tiger became the most iconic markers of the LTTE itself and its project of building an imagined independent state.

But it also became more than a map once the war began and expanded from the late 1970s onwards. With its expansion, the map was affectively redrawn on the ground based on the military successes of the warring parties. Though the LTTE could never fully exert its control over all the areas it had outlined in its map of Eelam on the ground itself, for a long time many of these areas became closed zones for people from the south. In other words, while the war lasted, swathes of land from the north-east of the familiar tear-shaped map of Sri Lanka became inaccessible to many people except for those who lived in these areas, thereby changing the political complexion of the regular map of Sri Lanka while a de facto map of Eelam took root on ground. In this sense, the Sri Lankan government's war with the LTTE was a matter of attempting to bridge the two parts of this bifurcated map and re-establish its former integrity. As a military officer once told me,

> [O]ur country looks like a mango no? But then, these LTTE fellows took an entire slice off it. They defaced it with the idea of Eelam. What is the point of a mango with an entire slice cut off? So our fight was to reclaim what was lost.[4]

Clearly, his narrative was also about the loss of integrity of the map of Sri Lanka and the urge to reclaim it while the idea of the map was referenced by implicating the image of a mango. Sri Lanka is often equated to a pearl, a tear drop or a mango in casual conversations.

This focus on maps was a crucial preoccupation during the war itself on the part of the Sri Lankan military and police units as well as the LTTE. The entire war effort had to do with which part of the map one would be able to control and at what cost. Besides, all formal battle plans

Figure 4.1

Cartographic imagination of 'Tamil Eelam'

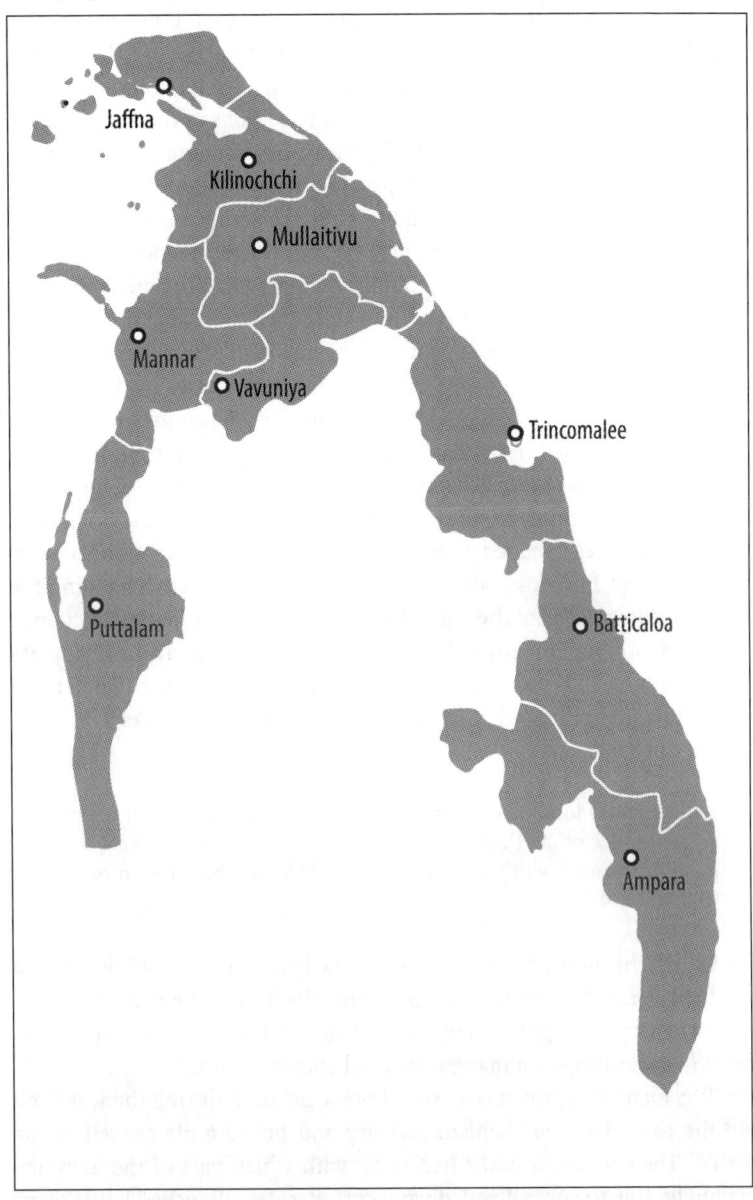

Source: Cartography by Janananda Laksiri, Colombo.

of the warring factions were based upon initial plans worked out through military maps. As far as ordinary people were concerned, at the height of war, the map that was constantly redrawn on the ground in terms of military abilities and battleground successes of the warring parties meant the emergence of zones of exclusion and inclusion. As such, for many people who became enthusiastic travellers to the warzone in the first and second phases of warzone tourism, the areas they visited were areas of mystery and exploration by virtue of being closed to them for a considerable period of time. If the possibilities of discovery were limited in terms of this cartographic reality in the first phase, in the second, it became literally limitless as we have already seen in the previous chapters. In both cases however, in practical terms travel meant tracing the contours of a map once restricted, on the ground.

Within this general understating of cartography, I will explore what maps had to do with warzone tourism, not simply as abstract documents of 'facts' but also as a discourse on nationalism and emotional understating of a contested space. In this exploration, I will look at three specific maps that figure centrally in this kind of travel:

1. The Sri Lanka Road Map published regularly by the Sri Lanka Survey Department;
2. The postwar map of Kilinochchi District with twelve specifically identified 'tourist' sites published by the Security Force Headquarters in Kilinochchi and
3. The map of north Sri Lanka published privately in Jaffna after the war ended.

All these maps were supposed to help travellers while the latter two were specifically focused on travel in the warzone. In the first phase of warzone tourism, maps in the formal sense hardly had any place in the overall context of planning and implementing travel given the significantly limited itineraries of travel, a limitation brought upon by non-conducive road conditions and, more importantly, because the war itself had not ended but was merely experiencing a lull in the areas where tourists were allowed to travel. In this context, the main roads were already known to drivers and travellers and many simply referred to the standard road map published regularly by the Sri Lanka Survey Department which predated the war and had been published at least since the 1960s. It was not unusual for many long-distance drivers to have this reasonably priced map known for its accuracy in their vehicles even though most would not consult it on a routine basis. This was particularly the case with tourist vehicle operators. Similar maps were also published by a number of private-sector publishers and were widely available in the market by the mid-1990s. The popularity of the survey department map as an innocuous but accurate travel aid continued well into the second phase of warzone tourism. As one bus driver who had driven more than 125 tours into the warzone after the road opened in the second phase noted, pointing to his tattered and faded survey department map which he had pulled out of the glove compartment of his bus,

> This is always here. Not that we look at it all the time. We know the roads. But we look at it if we get lost and also when we turn to unfamiliar interior roads from the main roads. We sometimes look for shortcuts. Even if we ask people for directions, sometimes we look at the map to be sure. Sometimes we show in the map where we are going to the people who are travelling with us.[5]

In this sense, the maps were fulfilling a similar role as images of deities which are often installed in the front interior of busses and trucks and smaller versions in cars. They were a taken for granted presence, a kind of insurance against unforeseen calamities.

If issues such as borders are taken for granted, in most contexts, states tend to impose a 'disenchanted' perception on national territory and 'see' it simply as empty homogenous space, politically and culturally speaking. In this context, what the state sees in an uncomplicated map such as a road map is merely a 'techno-rational-grid devoid of emotions' (Pinney 1997: 855–60; Scott 1998). Republished intermittently since at least the 1960s, the Survey Department road map[6] needs to be understood in the above sense as a 'disenchanted' technical document. It indicates roads in the country without political commentary from before the war, at the height of the war as well as after the war ended. The only additions are when major new roads had been added to the road network on the ground. So, the 2013 edition shows the new Southern Expressway as well as the Airport Expressway, indicating completed and under construction sections. However, from the late 1990s up to 2009, the maps published at the time still prominently indicated the A9 to Jaffna though it was affectively closed along with all other roads in the north for civilian and vehicular traffic from the south for over a decade.

As explained in Chapter 2, it was via this once-closed road that the pioneering warzone tourists in the first phase had anxiously travelled to the north, with nothing much to guide them except for their spirit of adventure, blessings from their favourite deities and the Sri Lanka Road Map in the possession of the better organized among them. At the time, a government entity such as the Survey Department simply could not indicate in their map that the A9 and all other major and minor roads in the LTTE-controlled areas were closed to southern traffic. Such an indication would have simply changed the shape and personality of the map itself. It would have been a formal indication of the government's loss of control over significant parts of the country. So, while the ground situation changed drastically as the war expanded and the state's writ was seriously challenged, on the map, the integrity of the territory remained unchanged. But that was the only place where these changing geophysical and politico-military contexts remained static.

But the place of cartography changed in the second phase quite visibly as a result of the enhanced possibilities of travel, improved road conditions and relative rapidity with which destinations could be reached in the post-war context as well as due to the emergence of specific maps catering to warzone tourism. Even so, cartography in the post-war era also remained a less obvious affair compared to photography though its presence is manifest and omnipotent in practice. Travel in the warzone is a matter of constantly retracing a cartographic reality that was once lost and therefore emphasizing its recovery. Of course, it is another matter if the 'sacrifices' of those who died for these different interpretations of maps are embedded or not in post-war geographies and their cartographic renditions. The territory no longer precedes the map, nor does it survive it. It is nevertheless the map that precedes the territory— precession of simulacra—that engenders the territory (Baudrillard 1994: 1). Therefore, it is not a surprise that both the Sri Lanka Army and a small private sector outfit in Jaffna found it pertinent to produce maps with a focus on warzone travel. In this sense, for many travellers to the post-war north, these maps preceded territory. They traced on ground what the maps had drawn on paper.

Compared to the unemotional Sri Lanka Road Map of the Survey Department, the post-war map officially known as 'Travel Guide Kilinochchi' with 12 specifically identified 'tourist' sites published by the Security Force Head Quarters in Kilinochchi is a very different genre of map, hitherto not known in the country (see Figures 4.2 and 4.3).

Accompanied by small-scale road maps of the Kilinochchi District and Sri Lanka, the document also presents images of the sites specifically identified and snippets of advice for travellers. In this sense, this cartographic rendition is not a simple combination of two maps, but has to be read along with the images and the words it accompanies. More importantly, going by the use of language, it seems to be meant specifically for the use of Sinhala tourists who are travelling to the warzone. The site locations in the map are in English and are difficult to read due to the small scale. However, the roads are easy enough to fathom and the locations are obvious enough to work out. The Kilinochchi map which receives more prominence compared to the Sri Lanka map identifies 12 locations which the Sri Lanka Army considers as important sites for tourists to visit. There are images of all the 12 sites with captions in Sinhala and English. One page consisting of advice to travellers is only presented in Sinhala. The

Figure 4.2

Cartographic and text details of the brochure, 'Travel Guide Kilinochchi' distributed to all north-bound tourists

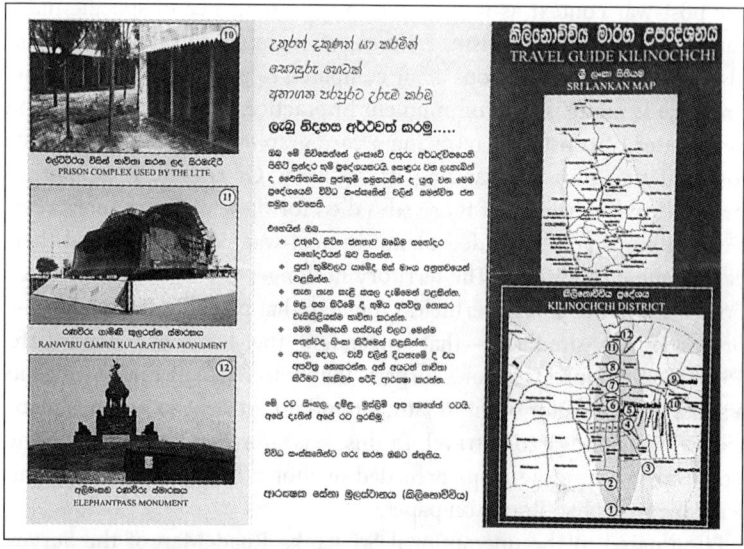

Source: Sri Lanka Security Forces Head Quarters, Kilinochchi.
Disclaimer: This figure is not to scale. It does not represent any authentic national or international boundaries and is used for illustrative purposes only.

Figure 4.3

Images of recommended sites in the brochure, 'Travel Guide Kilinochchi' distributed to all north-bound tourists

Source: Sri Lanka Security Forces Head Quarters, Kilinochchi.
Disclaimer: This figure is not to scale. It does not represent any authentic national or international boundaries and is used for illustrative purposes only.

document contains no writing in Tamil. The smaller Sri Lanka map indicates the major roads in the country including the A9 which leads to Jaffna. Published for free distribution, it was available as early as 2012. As briefly referred to in Chapter 3, soldiers at military checkpoints distributed this guide map while they were dispensing their regular duties. Often, they also advised travellers which places are more interesting in their view and how to get to these places. In terms of the categories they represent, the 12 sites can be identified as given in Table 4.1.

The basis upon which the Sri Lanka Army has identified some of the 12 places on the map of Kilinochchi and proceeded to provide photographs of these sites is not immediately clear.[7] However, a closer reading of the Kilinochchi map itself and the kind of meanings these places acquire in the context of the Army's written statements as presented in

Table 4.1

Summary of cartographic information from maps, text and images in the brochure 'Travel Guide Kilinochchi'

S. No.	Site number and site identity	Category (Directly war-related structures are in italics)
1.	Kokavil Monument and Transmission Tower	*Post-war monument built by the Sri Lanka Army in memory of Captain S.U. Aladeniya and a number of other soldiers killed in battle in the 1990s. Behind the monument is a telecommunication transmission tower also referred to in the accompanying description and map. The tower is included in the map as a sign of post-war 'development' in the area.*
2.	Thirumurukkandi Kovil	Well-known Hindu shrine in the area.
3.	Iranamadu Tank (reservoir)	Irrigation reservoir deep in the former LTTE controlled area, considered to be one of the largest in the north.
4.	Kilinochchi Monument	*Post-war monument built by the Sri Lanka Army.*
5.	Water tank in Kilinochchi destroyed by the LTTE	*Pre-war government-constructed water tank for the city water supply destroyed by the LTTE in 2009. Presently converted into a museum by the Sri Lanka Army.*
6.	Lumbini Temple	Minor pre-war Buddhist temple destroyed during the war. At present rebuilt and expanded with military and state sponsorship.
7.	Karadi Culvert	Part of pre-existing irrigation system.
8.	Paranthan Chemical Factory	Pre-war government-constructed chemical factory destroyed in the war.
9.	Abandoned bunker of Prabhakaran	*Wartime LTTE structure.*
10.	Prison complex used by the LTTE	*Wartime LTTE structure.*
11.	Gamini Kularatna Monument	*Wartime LTTE monument converted into a Sri Lanka Army monument in memory of Corporal Gamini Kularatna in the post-war period by the Sri Lanka Army.*
12.	Elephant Pass Monument	*Post-war monument built by the Sri Lanka Army.*

Source: Generated from maps, images and text in the brochure, 'Travel Guide Kilinochchi'.

the document shed more light on the epistemology of the entire document as an integrated symbolic field of meaning. This is particularly so when one considers this as a guide to Sinhala tourists who travel through the former warzone. Nevertheless, seven of the sites clearly and directly relate to the war. While the map is meant for the use of Sinhala tourists, the advice given to travellers by the army and the public position it has taken in this document merits further exploration. In the back flap of the document, the following statements are presented in bold:

> Let us gift a wonderful tomorrow to future generations by linking the north and the south; Let us make the freedom we have achieved meaningful.

The first statement is indicative of an aspiration to link the once-separated northern and southern areas of the country which has been made possible as a result of victory in war. Though it is essentially crafted in cartographic terms, this statement is not simply a reference to re-linking territories. It is also a wish for a better future through that linkage. The second sentence is a direct reference to victory in war. However, that too is not articulated in a simple militaristic or triumphalist register. Rather, it is a more open invitation requesting that the freedom that has been achieved through victory is made meaningful. Interestingly, the word 'victory' does not emerge directly in the text. It only manifests contextually with reference to the idea of freedom as its corollary. These two statements serve as the main ideological anchor of the document and are followed by a brief contextualization of the place where the tourists would arrive in their tour (Kilinochchi), accompanied by a series of other statements framed in the form of advice:

> You are now coming to a beautiful area situated in the northern part of Sri Lanka. This area which consists of beautiful forests and historic places of worship is also the home to many people of different cultures. Therefore:
>
> * You must consider the people in the north as your own brothers and sisters;
>
> * You should refrain from consuming meat and fish when you visit religious places;
>
> * You must not recklessly dump garbage.
>
> * When you are relieving yourselves, do not do so in open ground. Always use a toilet;

* Refrain from harming the flora and fauna as well as the animals that inhabit this land;

* When you are bathing in rivers, streams and reservoirs, ensure that you do not pollute them. Use them and protect them in such a way so that others also can use them.

This country belongs to all of us: Sinhalas, Tamils and Muslims. Let us protect our country with our own hands.

We thank you for being respectful towards diffident cultures.

Security Force Headquarters (Kilinochchi)

Taken in this sense, the map, the accompanying images and the written text constitute a specific, publicly articulated ideological position that the Sri Lanka Army has taken within its Kilinochchi command. It wants to be seen as the protector of life and of flora and fauna of the area as well as the overall guardian and conscience of the area identified as a multicultural space. So despite the massive destruction in war and the deprivations experienced by many people in the region soon after the war ended, in so far as the public position taken by the Sri Lanka Army in his document is concerned, Sinhala tourists entering Kilinochchi must be mindful of their actions and should consider all peoples in the land as a family. As evident in the previous chapter, particularly with reference to signage at many key Sri Lanka Army monuments as well as war sites the army has identified as tourist attractions, all explanations are in Sinhala or in Sinhala and English. Such an obvious absence of Tamil leads one to assume that the army's official position has no reference to the multicultural and multi-ethnic realities of the country. As far as the present map under discussion is concerned, Sinhala predominates as the main language of discourse while Tamil is clearly absent. But then, most tourists who would have made the trip in the post-war period were Sinhalas. It appears that the army had them in mind as the main consumers of this document and its concern seems to have been to make an ideological statement about the need for a multicultural ethos on the one hand and discipline the travellers with regard to their routine practices on the other. When situated in the larger context, what is unclear is whether this document reflects the policy of the army, or its Kilinochchi Command or the benevolent views of powerful officers who were able to take this position via the public articulations in this document.

Nevertheless, when the overall context of the document is taken into account, the logic of identifying these specific sites as worthy of tourists' attention becomes clearer. The Thirumurukkandi Hindu shrine and the Lumbini Buddhist temple have been incorporated into this tourist scheme of things in order to give credence to the idea of multiculturalism that the accompanying statements in this cartographic exercise had attempted to establish. After all, the document informs travellers that this area is the home to 'many people of different cultures'. However, despite the fact that the Thirumurukkandi shrine is well-known in the area, it is not particularly significant in the scheme of the Hindu religion of the area while it is also not architecturally significant. In other words, it is simply one among the many other Hindu temples in the area, which the army had decided to feature on its tourist map. On the other hand, when compared with many major Buddhist temples of the pre- and post-colonial eras in different parts of the country, the Lumbini temple is mostly an uninspiring post-war structure, architecturally speaking. It is also not historically significant. While the temple had a minor presence in the area prior to the war, its present expansion is a post-war phenomenon with the sponsorship of the state and the army. Seen in this sense, the two temples representing Hinduism and Buddhism have been introduced into the map and the discourse of tourism the document represents, as indicative of the multi-religiosity in the area as well as the country in terms of how these concepts are understood by the Sri Lanka Army. In other words, they are two symbolic and linear references to two temples representing Hinduism and Buddhism, rather than being based on a historical or cultural understating of the practice of these religions in the area.

The Lumbini temple is hardly of any significant interest in tourist or cultural terms. Also, the overwhelming Buddhist presence in Kilinochchi today constitutes of military and police personnel rather than local citizens. In the pre-war past, it would have been frequented by the handful of Sinhala Buddhist merchants in and around Kilinochchi and the police and military personnel stationed in the vicinity. However, according to a May 2009 news item on government-owned Independent Television Network, the temple was a regular stopover for Buddhist pilgrims in the pre-war era, on their way to Naga Dipa further to the north, and the temple supposedly had a large dormitory for their use at the time.[8] However, the LTTE had systematically destroyed the temple while the area was under its control as it considered the temple a sign of Sinhala presence and expansion into the 'traditional Tamil homelands'. The reconstruction of the temple began with military sponsorship as a matter of priority soon after the Sri Lanka Army captured Kilinochchi from the LTTE in January 2009, about four months prior to the conclusion of the war. It was ceremonially opened in early May 2009 even before the war came to an end by the end of the same month. The rapidity of this renovation shows the politico-cultural significance that the army had attached to the temple.[9] The news bulletin specifically noted that the temple could be seen as a symbol of Buddhist and Hindu coexistence as the renovated structure also contained a Hindu shrine within its premises clearly in keeping with the multicultural ethos the army's tour map was referring to.

However, there are some indications that this is not a simple resurrection and renovation of a war-damaged temple. Kandasamy Sivakumaran, a local resident of Kilinochchi who was displaced and living in the camp for internally displaced people set up during the final battle for Kilinochchi in 2009, claims that the land where the present temple stands belongs to him and two other friends. According to him,

> [T]his land belongs to the three of us. Earlier we used to have a spare parts shop here. And now we do not have a place to live or a land to pursue our livelihood. The land where the Temple is being built is now an empty land because the shops have been demolished. This land is ours. They have built this Buddha statue and the temple in the year 2009. Because this land was like this when I returned I could not settle back into my land.[10]

Despite these claims, there is adequate information that a small-scale temple did exist in the vicinity prior to the escalation of war, even though it seems to have lapsed from the memory of many local residents as it had been demolished by the LTTE quite early during its occupation of Kilinochchi. On the other hand, it also appears that in its enthusiasm to renovate and expand the temple, the Army might have encroached onto adjacent land which remained unclaimed in 2009 due to the displacement of its owners. In any event, the emerging cluster of narratives point to a contested recent history for the temple rather than a linear longer history devoid of contradictions.

Despite the assumed intentions of the map and in the context of its contested history, the presence of the Lumbini temple in Kilinochchi and its rapid expansion in the post-war period narrates another story which has nothing to do with multiculturalism. This is the story of institutionalized Buddhism as the religion of the state and that of the majority of the people in the country who think of themselves as the victors in the recently concluded war. In this context, it appears that institutionalized Buddhism with state patronage is establishing a significant public presence in the former LTTE-controlled area where there was hardly any visible local Buddhist presence prior to 2009. In terms of this understanding, the map published by the Sri Lanka Army's Kilinochchi Headquarters also refers to the post-war cultural expansion of the Sinhala Buddhist dominated state into the Tamil Hindu heartland. In this case, even though the temple existed prior to the war, it is significant that it was singled out for renovation ahead of all other large-scale renovations in the area including civilian housing. As such, beyond the notion of multiculturalism, by locating the temple in its guide map of Kilinochchi, the army is also attempting to nudge tourists in the direction of the reawakened temple symbolizing the enhanced post-war power of the state and the Sinhala Buddhist people. After all, it is a matter of inviting tourists to visit a politico-cultural religious complex that the army itself has created.

The inclusion of the Iranamadu reservoir and the Karadi culvert, which are part of the pre-war irrigation system still operational in the area, makes sense more easily when perceived as indicative of local scenic 'beauty'. In the description of Kilinochchi which accompanies the map, the army informs tourists that they 'are now coming to a beautiful area situated in the northern part of Sri Lanka' with 'beautiful forests and historic places of worship'. In the context of this beautiful landscape, pointing people in the direction of the Iranamadu reservoir which is one of the largest bodies of water in the north and to Karadi culvert with its cascading waters flowing towards recently opened up rice cultivations is simply pointing tourists in the direction of objects of perceived scenic beauty in the same way that tourists in the North Central Province further south might have been directed towards similar bodies of water such as Tisa Weva and Parakrama Samudraya as part of the popular travel discourse on landscapes of scenic beauty and heritage. At another less visible level, the functioning of these irrigation systems also indicates the arrival of relative 'normalcy' and 'peace' in the area where agriculture has resumed after the war ended and guns were silenced. These are also recent post-war outcomes in the area for which the new dispensation led by the Sri Lanka Army takes credit for. These indicators fall well within the rather vocal public discourse on 'development' that the government and the military establishment had initiated soon after the end of war, in the context of which it was expected that the deprivations of war itself should be forgotten. As such, the inclusion of these sites is also a reference to the emerging power and omnipresence of the rather linear and ahistorical development discourse promoted by the state.

Beyond these sites, all the other places are directly linked to the war or are associated with it. The Paranthan Chemical Factory was one of the largest government-owned industrial venture in the north employing many local residents before it was destroyed by the LTTE and was abandoned in the late 1980s. Soon after the war ended and when the first groups of tourists started on their northward journeys, it appeared like a ghost town spread across a land area exceeding 200 acres of mangled concrete and steel structures overrun by trees and other kinds of vegetation. It was a clear sign of the destruction of war. It was a standing and unmistakably ghostly narrative of war and destruction. Similarly, the water tank in the town destroyed by the LTTE was also indicative not only of the destruction of war but more specifically the 'brutality' of the LTTE since it was destroyed to ensure no civilians could inhabit the town after the group retreated towards the eastern coast of Mullaitivu as Kilinochchi fell. It is to ensure that this message could be narrated convincingly that the crumpled water tank was converted into a museum by the army. So both these remnants are in the map to narrate the story of destruction in war and the culpability of the LTTE in this destruction, while they also narrate at a secondary register the military's role in bringing peace to the area. The two LTTE structures identified in the map, the abandoned bunker used by Prabhakaran and the prison complex used by the LTTE, are essentially trophies of the army symbolizing its capture of the one-time capital of the LTTE and its domination in terms of military power and the annihilation of the LTTE.

Finally, the five post-war monuments featured in the map and also discussed in detail in Chapter 3 are indicative of the conclusion of the army's long march to a decisive victory through 30 years of battle and considerable institutional and personal losses. As monuments, they are expected to be testimonials to the victory of the Sri Lanka Army in particular as well as the state more generally. Taken in this sense, the 'Travel Guide Kilinochchi' as an amalgamation of maps, images and written text expects to take visiting Sinhala tourists from the south on a tour that narrates the army's own story through war, the destructions the war has brought about, the defeat of the LTTE, the valour of the army in battle, its own final victory and the arrival of peace and what it sees as 'normalcy' in the backdrop of the scenic beauty and cultural complexity in the area. As already noted, the kind of story that sites like the Lumbini Temple narrate is not overtly obvious on the map or in the grand narratives of the state unless its location in these kinds of documents and its post-war revival is more cautiously probed. The nuances of such inaudible stories will always remain at the margins of defeat and in the domain of the private voices of local people often not heard by tourists.

The next map I would like to focus on has been locally published tri-lingually in Jaffna and has been popular among tourists and bus drivers since about 2013 (see Figure 4.4). The non-formal and often inaccurate use of Sinhala in the map indicates that it has been put together by a group of Tamil-speaking entrepreneurs. While the map has no name or any indication of the publisher, it offers a number of mobile phone numbers for further information, particularly for ordering copies. Priced at LKR 70.00 the map has at least two editions, one available in 2013 and the

Figure 4.4

Tourist guide map for warzone travel available in 2013

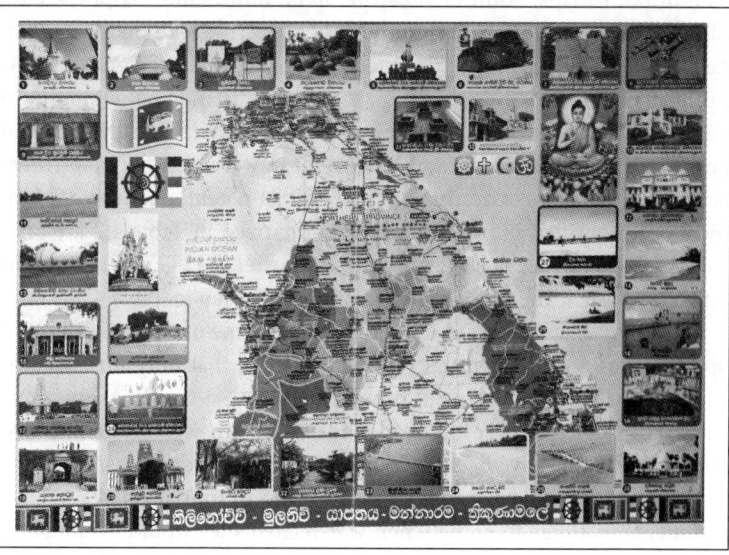

Source: From field material provided by the author.
Disclaimer: This figure is not to scale. It does not represent any authentic national or international boundaries and is used for illustrative purposes only.

other in 2014 carrying minor but important variations. According to the formal identification of the major places of reference, the 2013 edition focuses on Kilinochchi, Mullaitivu, Jaffna, Mannar and Trincomalee districts while the 2014 version focuses only on Kilinochchi, Mullaitivu and Jaffna districts. Produced specifically for the use of post-war tourists, the 2013 map identifies 32 places and the 2014 map identifies 26 places as important sites to visit. The reduction in the number of sites from 32 to 26 from the 2013 to 2014 editions mostly emanates from the latter edition focusing on two less districts compared to the 2013 edition. That is, Trincomalee and Mannar Districts had been dropped from the latter edition, which also meant that sites from these two districts were no longer available in the new map. The identified sites in both versions can be summarized as given in Table 4.2.

As a map with at least two editions specially produced for the use of tourists to the warzone, the cartographic and political narratives shed much light on the nature of warzone tourism and its associated dynamics. As already noted, the maps have been produced in Jaffna by a group of small-time, Tamil-speaking entrepreneurs interested in making some inroads into the profits of the post-war tourism industry. On the reverse side of both maps, additional cartographic information is provided in Sinhala and Tamil. These include a list of access roads to the sites identified in the maps as well as distances from Jaffna and the A9 road to a number of selected sites. In addition, a list of islands belonging to Sri Lanka is also provided, while their names are given in English, Sinhala and Tamil. What is much more important however are the maps themselves and the kinds of destinations they direct potential tourists to. If the locations identified in both maps as summarized in Table 4.2 are taken together, one can see that they belong to a cluster of 12 general categories. At a very basic level, these can be identified as given in Table 4.3.

What the maps indicate immediately, in terms of their directions to specific sites and their visual representation, is that only nine sites are directly related to the war out of which six are Sri Lanka Army monuments constructed after the war while three are war remnants. Even though the maps have been produced to facilitate war tourism, the producers have also taken into account the kind of tourism that was likely to emerge in times to come when war-related sites would no longer be available except for military monuments. In fact, that time has already arrived; this is why, as explained in the previous chapter, some of the

Table 4.2

Cartographic data and site information from 2013 and 2014 map editions

	Site name	Category of site (Directly war-related structures and places are in italics)	2013 edition	2014 edition
1.	Naga Dipa Viharaya	Buddhist temple and long-established pilgrim site in Jaffna District referred to in detail in Chapter Two and Three.	Identified in 2013 edition.	Identified in 2014 edition also.
2.	Naga Vihara	Post 1960s Buddhist temple in Jaffna town referred to in detail in Chapter Two and Three.	Identified in 2013 edition.	Identified in 2014 edition also.
3.	Lumbini Viharaya	Buddhist temple in Kilinochchi which has been renovated and expanded post-war referred to in detail in Chapter Four.	Identified in 2013 edition.	Identified in 2014 edition also.
4.	Kadurugoda Viharaya	Archaeological remains purported to be from a Buddhist monastery or burial site.	Identified in 2013 edition.	Identified in 2014 edition also.
5.	*Elephant Pass War Heroes Monument*	*Post-war military monument at Elephant Pass referred to in detail in Chapter Three.*	*Identified in 2013 edition.*	*Identified in 2014 edition also.*
6.	*Gamini Kularatna Monument*	*Monument at Elephant Pass incorporating a militarized bulldozer in memory of Corporal Gamini Kularatna referred to in detail in Chapter Three.*	*Identified in 2013 edition.*	*Identified in 2014 edition also.*
7.	*Kilinochchi War Heroes Monument*	*Post-war military monument in Kilinochchi town referred to in detail in Chapter Three.*	*Identified in 2013 edition.*	*Identified in 2014 edition also.*
8.	*Victory Monument*	*Post-war monument in Pudumathalan commemorating Sri Lanka Army's victory over the LTTE referred to in detail in Chapter Three.*	*Identified in 2013 edition.*	*Identified in 2014 edition also.*
9.	Mosque at Naga Dipa	The third main religious site on Naga Dipa island after the Buddhist and Hindu temples.	Identified in 2013 edition.	Identified in 2014 edition also.

(Continued)

Table 4.2
(Continued)

	Site name	Category of site (Directly war-related structures and places are in italics)	2013 edition	2014 edition
10.	*Denzel Kobbekaduwa Monument*	*Post-war monument set up by the Sri Lanka Army off the coast of mainland Jaffna to commemorate the assassination of General Denzel Kobbekaduwa and others by the LTTE.*	*Identified in 2013 edition.*	*Identified in 2014 edition also.*
11.	*Nandikadal Lagoon*	*The general area in Mullaitivu where the war finally came to an end in 2009.*	*Identified in 2013 edition.*	*Identified in 2014 edition also.*
12.	*Jaffna Library*	*Public library in Jaffna destroyed in 1981 and referred to in detail in Chapter Two.*	*Identified in 2013 edition.*	*Identified in 2014 edition also.*
13.	*Water Tank, Kilinochchi*	*Water Tank in Kilinochchi blown up by the LTTE in 2009 and converted into a museum by the Sri Lanka Army after the war; referred to in detail in Chapter Three.*	*Identified in 2013 edition.*	*Identified in 2014 edition also.*
14.	Satti Beach	Stretch of coast in the north known locally for its scenic beauty.	Identified in 2013 edition.	Identified in 2014 edition also.
15.	Madhu Church	Well-known Catholic Church in the Mannar District which was a popular pilgrim destination for Sinhala and Tamil Catholics prior to the war and continues to be so after the war.	Identified in 2013 edition.	Not identified in the 2014 edition after Mannar District was dropped from the 2014 edition.
16.	University	University of Jaffna, Tirunelveli established in the 1970s.	Not identified in the 2013 edition	Identified only in the 2014 edition.
17.	Kiramalai Hot Water well	Well-known large hot water well in the extreme north adjacent to the sea in Kiramalai. Regionally important tourist site prior to the war.	Identified in 2013 edition.	Identified in 2014 edition also.

18.	Naga Amman Hindu Temple	Historically important Hindu shrine in the Naga Dipa island and one of the two most important religious sites in the island along with Naga Dipa Buddhist temple.	Identified in 2013 edition.	Identified in 2014 edition also.
19.	Bottomless Well, Puttur	An ancient deep well in Puttur, Jaffna District where the bottom is not supposed to be visible to the naked eye. Regionally important tourist site prior to the war.	Identified in 2013 edition.	Identified in 2014 edition also.
20.	*Jaffna Fort*	*The old Portuguese Fort and later renovated by the Dutch which was once the main city camp of the Sri Lanka Army; almost completely destroyed by the LTTE prior to the end of war.*	*Identified in 2013 edition.*	*Identified in 2014 edition also.*
21.	Nallur Temple	One of the best known and most revered Hindu Temples in the Jaffna District	Identified in 2013 edition.	Identified in 2014 edition also.
22.	*Bunker House*	*The bunker complex in Pudukuduyirippu, Mullaitivu District known to be LTTE leader Prabhakaran's last stronghold.*	*Identified in 2013 edition.*	*Identified in 2014 edition also, but with a different image*
23.	Children's Park, Jaffna	The municipal park in Jaffna town set up for children had been converted into a monument for LTTE leader Sathasivam Krishnakumar (Kittu) at the time of the first wave of warzone tourism and was known as Kittu Children's Park. Referred to in detail in Chapter Two. It has been reconverted to its municipality-designated use after the war ended.	Identified in 2013 edition.	Identified in 2014 edition also.
24.	Kinniya Bridge (Trincomalee District)	Long bridge across the sea in Kinniya, Trincomalee which has been a local attraction for a considerable period of time.	Identified in 2013 edition.	*Not identified in the 2014 edition (as sites in the Trincomalee District have been excluded in this edition).*

(Continued)

Table 4.2
(Continued)

	Site name	Category of site (Directly war-related structures and places are in italics)	2013 edition	2014 edition
25	Point Pedro	The northern-most point of Sri Lanka facing the Indian subcontinent marked by a post-war concrete sign with an image of the Sri Lankan national flag.	Not identified in the 2013 edition.	Identified only in the 2014 edition.
26.	Karainagar Beach	The sea shore at Karainagar in Kyts island known for its scenic beauty close to a major Sri Lanka Navy base.	Identified in 2013 edition.	Identified in 2014 edition also.
27.	Sangupity Bridge	Well-known bridge across the sea at Sangupity, Jaffna District connecting the road from Pooneryn in the South with the Jaffna Peninsula. The present bridge has been built post-war by the government with ADB funds.	Identified in 2013 edition.	Identified in 2014 edition also.
28.	Dambakola Patuna Buddhist temple	Buddhist temple of recent origin in Jaffna District sponsored by the Sri Lanka Navy and referred to in detail in Chapter Two.	Identified in 2013 edition.	Identified in 2014 edition also.
29.	Long Ship	*Farah 3 ship hijacked and grounded by the LTTE and later converted into a tourist attraction by the Sri Lanka Army; referred to in Detail in Chapter Three.*	*Identified in 2013 edition.*	*Not identified in the 2014 edition.*
30.	Kokavil Military Monument	*Post-war monument established by the Sri Lanka Army to commemorate Captain S.U. Aladeniya and others killed by the LTTE in 1990.*	*Identified in 2013 edition.*	*Not identified in the 2013 edition.*

No.	Site	Description	2013 edition	2014 edition
31.	Nilaveli Beach (Trincomalee District)	Beach and shallow waters in the Trincomalee District with a number of resorts. Popular as a holiday destination for middleclass local tourists before the war.	Identified in 2013 edition.	Not identified in the 2013 edition (as sites in the Trincomalee District have been excluded in the 2014 edition).
32.	Allirani Kotte	A cluster of ruins in Silvaturai in Mannar District known locally as a fort but more likely an early British period Bungalow.	Identified in 2013 edition.	Not identified in the 2013 edition (as sites in the Mannar District have been excluded in the 2014 edition).
33.	Hot Water wells in Kinniya, (Trincomalee District)	A cluster of seven well-known hot water wells in the Trincomalee District which has been a popular site for Sri Lankan tourists from different parts of the country since before the outbreak of war	Identified in 2013 edition.	Not identified in the 2013 edition (as sites in the Trincomalee District have been excluded in the 2014 edition).
34.	Koneswaran Temple (Trincomalee District)	Well-known Hindu temple located within the Dutch Fort in Trincomalee, which is also a major military base in the east.	Identified in 2013 edition.	Not identified in the 2013 edition (as sites in the Trincomalee District have been excluded in the 2014 edition).

Source: Genearated from maps, text and images from the 2013 and 2014 map editions.

Table 4.3

Summary of site types in map editions 2013 and 2014

Category of sites	Number of sites identified on maps
1. Sri Lanka Army monuments	06
2. LTTE structures and war remnants	03
3. Buddhist temples/archaeological sites	05
4. Hindu temples	03
5. Mosques	01
6. Churches	01
7. Colonial period structures	02
8. Pre-war tourist sites	03
9. Beaches	05
10. Iconic pre-war government buildings in Jaffna	02
11. Bridges	02
12. Parks	01

Source: Generated from map, text and images from the 2013 and 2014 map editions.

army-run hotels and resorts in the north such as Thal Sevana and Nature Park Holiday Resort had already begun catering to a type of northern tourism disassociated from war. As the descriptions in Chapters 2 and 3 suggest, the victory in the war meant a rapid and total dismantling of LTTE monuments that were abundantly visible in the northern landscape during the first phase of tourism. Other non-monumental remnants of war which continued to stand when the second phase of tourism began and were often celebrated and promoted by the army as its trophies have also gone through an almost complete wave of dismantling in more recent times as already described. By the time the 2014 map came into circulation, Prabhakaran's bunker, clearly identified in both editions and which had become one of post-war tourism's most visited attractions, had been dismantled. Similarly, the Farah 3 Ship, which was also a popular destination and prominently identified in the 2013 edition was removed from the 2014 edition because that too had been dismantled by the army. On the other hand, all major post-war military monuments set up by the Sri Lanka Army remain centrally identified in both maps. To a certain extent, the two editions indicate the cartographic tracing of the changing ground conditions in the domain of attractions in the warzone.

But beyond these obvious details, some of the other sites which seem like routine places of interest also narrate stories of war and post-war politico-cultural realities. Of the five beaches identified, Nilaveli had an island-wide reputation as a holiday destination for middle-class people prior to the onset of war while three of the remaining ones had local reputations as scenic places. But the Nandikadal Lagoon had no such pre-war reputation. As explained in Chapter 3, it acquired notoriety as a place of immense destruction, death and pain in the last stages of the war as the place where the war finally ended amidst its ruins. That is why this location is marked in these maps. But now, when tourists follow these maps and come to Nandikadal, they will not see many of the initially promoted major war remnants, which have been systemically dismantled by the government. They will only see the Victory Monument and the adjacent War Museum and a sanitized place of death and destruction. As already explained, many tourists will not converse with locals who could still narrate the horrors of their recent past. But then, that is the nature of tourism.

On the other hand, the maps also direct tourists to five Buddhist temple sites, which include the archaeological site at Kandarodai, now known as Kadurugoda Viharaya among Buddhists. As explained in Chapter 2, the identification of Naga Dipa as a potential tourist site is understandable given its longstanding reputation as a Buddhist pilgrim site. All the other temples however are of no archaeological or historical significance even though some of them had a pre-war presence on a smaller scale (e.g., Naga Viharaya, Jaffna and Lumbini Viharaya, Kilinochchi). But all of them experienced significant restoration, expansion and reinvention (as in the case of Dambakola Patuna Sangamitta Viharaya) after the war ended with state and military patronage. As already explained, this has come about as a result of the Buddhist identity of the state and Sri Lankan military forces being established and expanded in the physical and cultural landscape of the Tamil Hindu heartland of northern Sri Lanka. This is why some of these relatively recent and historically insignificant sites have entered the list of 'must see' sites in these maps.

The site known as Kadurugoda has different significations, which I will explain in more detail in the next chapter. But for the moment, it has a place in the maps due to the widely held belief among the Sinhalas that the site is indicative of a historically ancient Sinhala Buddhist presence in the contemporary Tamil Hindu geophysical space, even though the historical and archaeological merits of this thinking have not been adequately resolved. Taken in this sense, the fact that the two maps point tourists towards these locations is not a simple matter of directing them to a handful of local temples. More crucially, by visiting these sites, consciously or otherwise, tourists are essentially visiting long-established pilgrim locations as well as sites of recent cultural demarcation and expansion on the basis of which the cultural geography and the physical history of the north is being rewritten and reinterpreted.

It is also significant that between them, the two maps have identified three Hindu temples, one mosque and one church as worthwhile places to visit. This has mostly come about due to the rather obvious multi-ethnic, multi-religious and multi-linguistic approach that the two maps have attempted to adopt in their overall presentation. Almost all the place locations in both maps are in Sinhala, English and Tamil while all image captions are in Sinhala and Tamil, in that specific order. On the other hand, both the 2013 and 2014 editions carry the national flag of the country as well as the Buddhist flag and the main emblem of institutional Buddhism, the *dharma chakra*, very prominently along with one uncaptioned and relatively prominent image of the Buddha in each map. In addition, both maps also present the immediately recognizable emblems of Christianity, Islam and Hinduism, though relatively smaller in size compared to the more prominent national and Buddhist symbols. Interestingly, official government maps published by the Survey Department carry none of these ethno-cultural or religious significations. What is clear is that the publishers are attempting to create a multi-ethnic, multi-religious and multi-linguistic discourse through the map in terms of the places identified as well as the use of imagery and symbols. At the same time, they are reiterating the 'national' and the 'Buddhist' credentials of the overall geographic space signalled by the somewhat overt use of imagery and symbolism as referred to above. This is also a matter of creating a 'safe haven' in discursive terms in post-war Sri Lanka where the national public sphere has been dominated by a vocal sense of Sinhala Buddhist militancy with the tacit approval of the state. Given the fact that the maps have been produced in the north and by Tamil-speaking entrepreneurs, it is clear that they did not want any accusations of treason and lack of patriotism directed towards them which was entirely possible in the prevailing circumstances. This is also why all the major post-war military monuments and the better known Buddhist temples of post-war resurrection have also been prominently identified in the maps.

On the other hand, the maps also cater to the government's post-war mega-discourse on development which holds that 'development' is the key to reconciliation in post war north-eastern Sri Lanka to the extent of excluding issues of justice. In this discourse, the resurrected and expanded A9 road to Jaffna and the restored railway line to Jaffna are supposed to be symbolic of this developmental drive. This perspective is also shared by many tourists who make use of these facilities in their travels. It is in this context that the Kinniya Bridge identified in the 2013 edition and the Sangupity Bridge identified in the 2014 edition make sense.

Except the map published by the Survey Department of Sri Lanka, the other three I have focused on in this section do not perceive territory as something 'disenchanted' while they also do not present the geographies represented in these maps as simple, empty, homogenous spaces as part of a simple 'techno-rational-grid (Pinney 1997: 855–60; Scott 1998). Instead, through markings on the maps themselves and the associated imagery, they purposefully guide people to destinations in the north-east as part of the post-war discourse on tourism to the former warzone. The narratives that emerge from the maps and the discursive practices they lead to cannot be seen as domains of innocence. Rather, they are a part of the overall practice of reimagining and redrawing both the cultural and political landscape of post-war northern Sri Lanka, with their own fields of meaning open to interpretation. Interestingly, the privately published maps also do not contradict the mega narrative of the state. However, they do offer a glimpse of the region's multicultural reality, while at the same time offering due political recognition through pictorial representation to the hegemony of Buddhism as well as the nation as imagined by the victors of the recently concluded war.

Taken in this sense, both photography and cartography as discussed in this chapter need to be seen as two aspects of a larger discourse on post-war travel, with their own manifestations of hegemonic politics, silences, vocalities and zones of exclusion and inclusion. Together, the travel maps published for north-bound Sinhala tourists and the photographs they capture of their travels construct a larger cartography of the political and social landscape and the new dispensations of power in post-war northern Sri Lanka.

Notes

1. http://sabian.org/alice_in_wonderland1.php (accessed on 24 October 2013).
2. Excerpt from interview conducted in Colombo in June 2003.
3. Kamalini's real name was Subramaniam Sivagami. At the time of her surrender to security forces she was a senior LTTE leader in its Political Division.
4. Excerpt from a casual conversation in Kandy, March 2010.
5. Excerpt from interview in Colombo in August 2013.
6. The map was initially known as the 'Road Map of Ceylon', and after 1972 it was formally known as the 'Road Map of Sri Lanka'.
7. Nine of these 12 places along with the corresponding images which accompanied the map are also presented in the official website of the Security Force Headquarters in Kilinochchi under 'Emerging Kilinochchi': http://220.247.214.182/sfkilinochchi/p_place_visit.php (accessed on 13 May 2014).
8. For more information, please visit: http://www.youtube.com/watch?v=mX7ks6dxeN8 (accessed on 14 May 2014).
9. For more information on the renovation of the temple presented from the perspective of the state and the Sri Lanka Army, one can view the news bulletin of the state-owned Independent Television Network dated early May 2009 and posted on You Tube on 9 May 2009: http://www.youtube.com/watch?v=mX7ks6dxeN8 (accessed on 14 May 2014). The news bulletin specifically noted that the temple could be seen as a symbol of Buddhist and Hindu coexistence given the fact that it also contained a Hindu shrine within its premises.
10. For more information and Kandasamy Sivakumaran's interview in Tamil, please visit: http://vimarsanam-vimansa.org/report/temple-displaces-family-livelihood-2/ (accessed on 14 May 2013).

5

Tales from Darker Places in Paradise:
Towards a Logic of Warzone Travel

The mind is its own place, and in itself can make a heaven of hell, a hell of heaven.

—John Milton in *Paradise Lost*

In the previous chapters, I have attempted to achieve a number of interrelated objectives. These included the description of the dynamics, emotions and politics of the first and second phases of warzone tourism in Sri Lanka and to work out the place of cartography and photography in these travels. In these descriptions, it would have been self-evident that what emerges in the form of travel is in fact a complex discourse of multiple narratives that make overall sense only if it is possible to understand the nuances of the various voices and zones of silence. But what does all this mean as a series of practices that people had routinely undertaken? What does it mean in terms of ideology? What do these travels achieve beyond the mere act of individuals' progression across space? These are some of the issues I would like to address in this concluding chapter.

In Search of Paradise

As the previous chapters have demonstrated, there should be no confusion that the kind of travel I have described is a form of tourism even though it is a very different form of tourism in terms of its gaze as far as Sri Lanka is concerned. Since the most prominent idea used in Sri Lanka's tourist promotion activities is the notion of paradise, to begin with, I would like to explore the relevance and the location of this idea in the context of warzone tourism. More precisely, how can one situate the tales of paradise that might emanate from the warzone trail of the country and how might these tales entrench or destabilize the idea of paradise itself? In general, officially and formally, Sri Lanka has been obsessive in promoting itself as 'paradise' by focusing on its abundance of natural beauty as well as its archaeological remnants from the distant past.

More specifically, Sri Lanka's tourist promotional authorities have at different times used notions of paradise and its extensions in promoting the country's image as a tourist destination, particularly in the context of international travel.[1] The imagery used in promotional films, posters and brochures of the country's two main airlines, Sri Lankan and Mihin Lanka, as well as the publicity material of individual hotels and the Sri Lanka Tourism Promotion Bureau also routinely take this idea as their point of departure as well as the central argument in all attempts to attract global tourism into the country. On the other hand, the notion of the country as a paradise is an idea that has enormous popular appeal and local currency in general which goes beyond the limits of international and local tourist trade. It is an idea that has been consistently presented to young students through their classroom activities and popular cultural constructs. This ideological thrust continued despite the change in governments over the last three decades and despite the fact that the calamities brought upon by the war were self-evident all around, which in practical terms ruptured all idealized notions of paradise. This proximate affinity with the idea and the word paradise is more pronounced in southern Sri Lanka and more specifically among the Sinhalas, such as the countless tourists who had toured the warzone in the two phases of tourism explored in earlier chapters.

As a word, 'paradise' is laced in layers of Sinhala nationalist pride as it camouflages numerous realities and practices on the ground which might under most normal circumstances contradict the ideal of paradise. However, as a political and ideological category which does not necessarily derive its meaning from surrounding realities and the extended experiences of the polity, the contradictions of the idea of paradise on the ground make little or no sense in the manner in which the word is used in the discourses of global and local tourism and in forms of nationalist rhetoric. In this all-encompassing and un-contradicted sense, the country has been called 'paradise island', 'a land like no other' and, more recently, 'the wonder of Asia' by entities formally promoting tourism. Like all trademarks and merchandising slogans, these words rhetorically stitched together do not necessarily reflect ground realities, particularly those pertaining to the war and its calamitous consequences. Even the three maps which included pictorial references that were explored in the previous chapter, paid considerable attention to places of 'natural beauty' and to cultural and archaeological sites in their serendipitous sensibility along with remnants of war. Nevertheless, thirty years of war had robbed the island of many of its attributes of paradise, unless one refers to the paradise that was lost in the Christian sense of the word.

Despite the hegemonic popularity of the idea of paradise in the tourist discourse on the country, as well as more generally in popular discourses of Sinhala nationalism, politics, culture, the arts and so on, it has also been publically contradicted and questioned at times, even though these efforts are at best marginal and not audible beyond a limited circle of critics. One can take T. Shanaathanan's 2003 installation, *Paradise Bed*, as an example. It consisted of an elegant, striking and seemingly luxurious velvet-like bed and pillow in dark red. It was installed in the midst of a natural backdrop of luxurious and spectacular beauty offering a large expansion of rolling green grass, slender tall trees, blue skies and flowing blue water. This landscape and the artwork situated in the midst of it instinctively recreated in viewers' imagination the taken-for-granted notions of paradise (Perera 2011: 33). However, the seemingly obvious renditions of paradise were fundamentally deceptive. As soon as a person sat on the bed or touched it, its extremely hard surface became clear, ushering in the binary opposite of popular imaginings of paradise (Perera 2011: 33). With that important realization, the artist brought the viewer from the dreamland of paradise to the realities of Sri Lanka and made a crucial point about the country: despite appearances, nothing is what it seems to be. Not surprisingly, Shanaathanan, hailing from the warzone of northern Sri Lanka, had seen the war and its devastations at first hand and also the manner in which such experiences were eclipsed in numerous hegemonic discourses such as the post-war development and war-tourist discourses.

Similarly, Sanath Kalubadana's 2003 installation, *Charcoal Dinner Table*, also offered an emotionally similar narrative contradicting the popular notions of paradise. Set in similarly spectacular natural settings as *Paradise Bed* at the same venue, the installation presented an elegantly and meticulously laid dinner table with a white cloth along with plates and glasses which contained blackened charcoal, which obviously could not be consumed. The individuals who were asked to sit for 'dinner' around the table simply could not eat anything as everything was essentially destroyed beyond consumption despite the visual 'beauty' of the presentation and the overall setting. Again, what was clear was that seeming notions of beauty and paradise could not be taken for granted in broader, local socio-political contexts. Within the general ideas of beauty and paradise which the artwork presented, the specific symbolism of burnt matter and charcoal suggested ideas of destruction, fear and anxiety closely associated with war, which immediately provided a sense of the 'other' of the idea of paradise. As both artworks clearly established, 'notions of paradise could, and in fact actually do, camouflage the larger realities of violence, pain and other contradictory meanings' (Perera 2011: 33). However, these and similar kinds of public contradictions of the idea of paradise and its affinity with local conditions have not expelled the popularity of the notion in general and certainly not from the annals of the hegemonic tourist discourse of both the state and private operators.

Nevertheless, if Sri Lanka is considered a paradise in the sense it is popularly articulated, then the post-war northern warzone needs to be understood as constituting of darker places in this paradise where its conventional meanings have been compromised and unraveled as a result of war. So the tales that emerge from returning travellers from the two warzone tourist trails I have described are literally the stories from these 'darker' places. These are particular kind of stories which come to family circles and broader popular discourses in the public domain, having first gone through the lens of selection tempered by a sense of Sinhala nationalism and euphoria over victory. As such, in the long run, these stories do not contradict the popular imaginings of paradise. It is in such a context that Milton's words from *Paradise Lost* which I had quoted at the beginning of this chapter make sense: 'The mind is its own place, and in itself can make a heaven of hell, a hell of heaven'. As such, most travellers only saw an extension of paradise even when they were travelling across 'hell'.

As I have suggested elsewhere in this book, the way most tourists travelled, ensured that they did not come into regular and sustained contact with local people. As a result, this ensured that their stories which might have described the illusive and liminal sense of the prevailing paradise as their own experience would have shown did not become a significant component of these stories from the darker places of paradise. However, this is also not a simple matter of 'not' seeing what had taken place and what was evident in the landscape. After all, despite the constant rearranging and erasing of geographies and landscapes of memory in the warzone, particularly in the second phase of travel, the deprivations of war were easy enough to see. The cursory gaze of tourism and, more importantly, the frame of mind with which most tourists travelled ensured that local pains did not transmit in a serious manner into the realm of tourist discourses. As such, the kinds of fleeting stories from the darker places in paradise that typified this specific travel discourse did not contradict the idea of paradise. If at all, they suggest that the deprivations of war was a short-term aberration of paradise brought upon by terrorism.

However, much of what has happened in these places and what their inhabitants have seen and felt cannot be openly articulated and are not often voiced in contemporary public contexts in the country, or even in the north and east where much of the war actually took place. It is in this sense that I have referred to the destination of these travels and from where travel narratives emerge—spread across northern Sri Lanka—as darker places. That is, places from where narratives of local personal experiences of pain and loss do not often emerge into the country's wider public discourse. These are places where pain and truth has no public recognition. These are places where ideals of truth and justice have no tangible value. These are darker places in this otherwise widely articulated and accepted sense of paradise because its own stories have lost their audibility when it comes to the wider public discourse in the country. It is in this context of relative silence, where darkness castes a long shadow over the landscape and the collective conscience of the country, that Tamil poetry becomes a different kind of voice, a constellation of stories that percolates out of these darker places of paradise into the south and the world even though many tourists who have returned to their homes with digital images of their travels are still quite unlikely to encounter these stories:

In their onslaught
the lies
the malicious sleight of hand
now joins the smoke

words dissemble
structures crumble
life's blood oozes out.

The shell explodes
A child wounded,
Barely two and half years old;
The doctor
Now a god
Without an anesthetic
Amputates the hands.
The mother screams
Tearless eyes
Now demon (Cheran 2011: 155).

These kinds of stories constitute a fundamental reality of north-eastern Sri Lanka marked by war. However, as already noted, such stories do not generally emanate from the memories and narratives of most returning tourists. It is in this discomforting silence that the notion of paradise might truly find its end. *Resplendent Sites; Discordant Voices*, the perceptive title of Malcolm Crick's (1994) book on international tourism and its relationships with Sri Lankans, though written in a very different context, articulates the possibility of paradise and its inherent contradictions very well. With a closer look at the stories of the darker places marked by war, death and destruction told by local people in the midst of the consistently sanitized but very much audible tourist chatter, and when one peers beyond the frames of the photographs of tourists, it would be possible to confront a very different set of narratives far removed from the ideal imaginings of paradise.

Logic and Structure of Warzone Travels

But what is the logic and structure of the travels I have described so far? How can they be historically located? What I have described is clearly a new kind of travel made possible only by war and its consequences. In the first instance, such travel became possible during a respite from war marked by a faulty ceasefire and in the second instance, it became possible due to the clear end of war marked by a very brutal and decisive victory over the LTTE by the Sri Lankan armed forces. In this specific context, which was not prevalent at any other time in recent history, people travelled to satisfy their curiosity about what war had brought as well as to see a part of the country that had been inaccessible for a long time. That long-term inaccessibility had meant that pre-war sites of interest, most of which were religious sites, had not been accessible to people for a long time. It is precisely due to this latter reason that pilgrim sites invariably became a part of most people's standard itinerary during both phases. At the same time, warzone tourist travel in general has structural features in common with conventional pilgrimages. In any event, this genre of travel make more contextual sense when situated within wider structures of meaning which informs dominant ideas of travel in the broader Sinhala cultural contexts which people have come to perceive on the basis of pre-existing traditions and practices.

On one level, these travels were undertaken within a meaning of pilgrimage in the Buddhist scheme of things, which itself had undergone tremendous transformation over hundreds of years. The traditional sense of pilgrimage is usually brought to contemporary Sinhala consciousness through long-term practice as well as via narratives from ancient historical texts written in Pali such as the *wamsas*,[2] temple paintings and images crystallized in the Sinhala language verse literature of the 1400s written during the Kotte Period known as *sandesa kavya*. The more versatile of these verses mostly described the progression of a bird from the capital of the time to a specific temple bearing a message as it proceeds to describe what can be seen in terms of both nature and culture. The progression of the bird from the capital to a specific temple was a kind of pilgrimage. The basic ideas of pilgrimage that emerge from these sources describe a kind of travel to specific religious sites in different parts of the country for the decisive purpose of merit-making. Structurally, this form of travel was not any different from the idea and practice of pilgrimage in other major religious traditions which includes Christianity, Hinduism and Islam.

According to the Buddhist canonical text, the *Digha Nikaya,* or the long discourses written in Pali, the Buddha is believed to have suggested on the last day of his life that pilgrimages could be undertaken to four places associated with his life, which included the place where he was born, the location where he attained enlightenment, the site where he preached the first sermon and the place where he died or attained *nibbhana* in the Buddhist scheme of things (Weerasinghe 2002: 1). It is in this general context that the Buddhist idea of pilgrimage finds its genesis and initial legitimacy as a recommendation from the Buddha himself. However, these specific locations mentioned in the *Digha Nikaya* are within subcontinental South Asia, and more specifically in present day India and Nepal, which nevertheless continue to be sites of pilgrimage for Sinhala Buddhists.[3] It is within this general structure of meaning that pilgrim sites in the Buddhist spiritual landscape historically emerged in Sri Lanka. According to references in the *Mahavamsa,* the main historical chronicle of Sri Lanka people from southern parts of the country came to Anuradhapura in the 3rd century BCE, to witness the planting of the sacred 'bo' sapling brought from India. It also records a number of royal visits to important Buddhist sites in the island (Weerasinghe 2002: 1). These references are indicative of the historical evolution of the idea and practice of pilgrimage within the Buddhist tradition in the country.

It was believed that such visits and rituals undertaken in each place will help individual travellers to accrue positive *karma* or *pin*, which will ensure a better and religiously sanctified life for the individual traveller in his present life. More importantly, in terms of Buddhist notions of merit-making, karma and rebirth, it was also believed that such pious acts would benefit the traveller in achieving a dignified life after death. On the other hand, despite the absence of a formal scheme of confessional or any other forms of absolving an individual of the *karmic* consequences of his negative action, there is a strong popular belief that pilgrimages to particularly holy shrines will absolve an individual of his sins or *pau*. However, this idea exists beyond canonical realms of legitimacy, purely in the domain of popular belief, which nevertheless acts as an important individual incentive for many people to undertake pilgrimages to specific shrines. In any event, this kind of travel was historically undertaken within a very clear discourse of piety which, as a result, did not include any indulgence in comfort or trivialities of fun which would indicate further loss and unenviable entrenchment in *samsara* or the cycle of birth, death and rebirth that is considered the main source of sorrow in terms of Buddhist belief.

However, this long-term tradition of pilgrimage has undergone significant transformations over the last 100 years or so, which has become more visible over the last 60 years. This has to do with the improvement of road networks and transport systems in general, which made travel more predictable, quicker and safer. On the other hand, radical changes in lifestyles in more recent times and individuals' day-to-day entanglements in systemic forms of formal work and secular activities also ensured that the meanings and forms of pilgrimage had to necessarily transform. Individuals continued to undertake pilgrimages to the same places of worship as hundreds of years before, and also to more recently emerged holy places. However, pilgrimages in more recent times were not always undertaken with the same degree of piety as was once expected. In the new transformed form, travel itself had become more comfortable and also imbued with ideas of entertainment, particularly when groups of travellers included young individuals, while the ritual practices at holy places continued within an idiom of religiosity. In other words, in more recent times, pilgrimage as a practice had also become fun and not just a matter of piety. Much of the fun and entertainment aspects of pilgrimages manifested in the midst of travel itself, between sites, while more pious or at least seemingly pious behaviour manifested once a group had actually reached a specific site.

This transformed idea of religious pilgrimage is one form within which warzone travel also evolved at one level. In both phases of tourism that I have discussed in previous chapters, Buddhist travellers in particular, always noted their intention in visiting religious sites such as Naga Vihara in Jaffna town, Naga Dipa Viharaya off the western coast of the Jaffna peninsula, the Kandarodai or Kandurugoa monument complex in Chunakkam, Dambakola Patuna Sagamitta Viharaya, Madagal as well as the main Hindu shrine of the Jaffna peninsula, the Kandasamy Temple in Nallur, among their main objectives. However, it is also quite clear that some travellers spent considerable time among ruins of war, while they lasted, and the new post-war victory monuments set up by the government despite these claims of religiosity. In their conversations at least, the idea of pilgrimage was very much evident irrespective of the seriousness of religiosity or piety in the actual travels. On the other hand, with regard to older travellers, particularly those who had visited these religious sites in the pre-war period, the idea of pilgrimage in the more conventional sense was paramount in their minds even though many of them also visited war-related sites as well. Yet, from the very outset, the general personality and structure of many such travels into the warzone were not somber processes. Instead, they were considered as times for relaxation and leisure, times of vacation away from work and school and times of song and food. As such, though the idea of pilgrimage was one aspect that gave meaning and structural reference to the newly emergent warzone travel, it was clearly not structured solely on the basis of the more somber ancient idea of pilgrimage, which nevertheless everyone held on to as the ideal model. More realistically, contemporary warzone travel was organized on the basis of the more contemporary form of pilgrimage to which practices of fun and relaxation had seeped in, which many people practiced as matter of habit.

On the other hand, there is a more specific form of ritualized pilgrim practice within which contemporary warzone travel also finds at least partial meaning. Among Sinhala Buddhists, there are two important practices of worship known as *atamasthana wandanawa* and *solosmasthana wandanawa*, which can be literally translated as the 'worship of eight great places' and the 'worship of sixteen great places'.[4] All these sites are existing places of Buddhist worship or holy places reputed to have existed in ancient times as put down in the country's Pali language historical chronicles and in popular belief. The significance of the two processes of worship is that they establish the existence of a somewhat ancient and well entrenched tradition of worshiping specific sites in relatively quick succession as allowed by the forms of travel available at different historical periods, but often as part of a single pilgrimage. In this context, collectively, these pilgrimages are known as *wata wandanawa*, which literally means 'round pilgrimage' or 'circular pilgrimage' because they take a pilgrim from his home to the sites in the pilgrim cycle, one after another and hopefully back home. This is not very different in structural terms from pilgrim practices in ancient India that Eck has described. When Hindu pilgrims travelled to their sacred places, they navigated across a 'sacred geography' within which everything happened to be 'part of a living, storied, and intricately connected landscape' (Eck 2012: 2). In their travels, these pilgrims dealt with a 'polycentric' landscape where each site had its own significance (Eck 2012). The wanderings of these pilgrims painted on the ground a much more different and nuanced map which was experientially rooted than the formal cartographic representations of these areas. In other words, these were emotional, sacred, experiential and imagined maps that made more sense in the lives and imagination of people.

On the other hand, despite the longevity of the idea of pilgrimage and its practice in Sri Lanka, most scholars agree that *solosmasthana wandanawa* as a specific prescription for pilgrimage does not extend prior to the Kandyan period or specifically before the 1760s (Weerasinghe 2002: 2). The wider popularization of the worship of the sixteen great places as a 'tour' seem to have occurred even later, in the latter part of the 19th century with the emergence of a class of commercially successful Buddhist bourgeoisie representing different caste groups within the Sinhala caste system through their sponsorship of this activity (Weerasinghe 2002: 2) as well as introducing new practices which Obeyesekere has collectively called 'Protestant Buddhism'.

In this historical context, the eight great places are located within the boundaries of the ancient Anuradhapura Kingdom while the 16 great places are located all over the country including the present-day northeast. In the case of the former, the location of the holy sites affectively marked the cultural and political influence as well as the boundaries of the Anuradhapura Kingdom, while in the case of the latter, the sites demarcated the boundaries of the island as a geographic, cultural and political entity. Stated differently, the latter also marked religiously significant locations within *Tun Sinhala*, the constellation of the three major regions of the country known separately as Ruhuna, Maya and Pihiti. During most periods of the island's recorded history, these areas consisted of separate and relatively independent kingdoms as well as smaller political units within them. Nevertheless, the aspiration of more powerful rulers was always to annex all these entities into a single unit and the entire island to be ruled by a single king. In fact, powerful kings such as Dutta Gamini Abhaya (205 BC), Vijayabahu the First (AD 1055–1110), Parakrama Bahu the First (AD 1123–1186) and others achieved this ideal. This idealized process of amalgamation was called *ek-sesath*, which literally means 'bringing under the purview of a single banner'.[5]

As such, worship in the wider sense, at shrines located in different parts of the island as in the case of undertaking a pilgrimage to the sixteen great places, was possible only if the country was under a single ruler or if political relations among kingdoms were cordial. In this context, particularly the worship of the sixteen great places, in addition to a matter of piety, was also a political act of travelling across the political dimensions of the island. This act therefore also marks the political reach of institutional Sinhala Buddhism. Weerasinghe notes that pilgrimages to the sixteen great places would 'take a pilgrim around the country, through the four cardinal directions of the island, to the north central province, to the eastern province, to the central mountains and to the southern coastal regions' which 'also becomes a survey of the territory of Sri Lanka thus converting it to a spiritual landscape of Buddhism and also to a landscape of the history of Buddhism in Sri Lanka as narrated in the 6th century Chronicle "Mahavamsa"' (Weerasinghe 2002: 1). Pilgrimage in this sense is not merely a spiritual act, but also a political act linked to emotional ideals of territory. In a comparable context, Indian scholars have argued for the significance of pilgrimage networks in constructing a tangible sense of Indian 'nationhood' 'not as a nation-state' in the contemporary understanding of the term, but as a shared, living landscape embedded with a significant degree of cultural complexity (Eck 2012: 15).

All the shrines in the two circuits are closely associated with the Gautama Buddha or previous Buddhas in terms of history or myth. The sites which constitute the sixteen great places are all supposed to be places that Gautama Buddha had visited during his three reputed visits to the island as narrated in the *Mahwamasa* while, according to the same text, the eight great places have also been visited by previous Buddhas. The historical validity of these beliefs is of no specific value in creating the overall sanctity of these places as well as the structure of worship. What is important is the fact that travel to each location marked the extent of the kingdom and the island as well as their political integrity and influence beyond mere religious considerations. This genre of worship was possible for long periods of time despite intermittent disruptions due to wars and natural calamities in ancient times.

However, *solosmasthana wandanawa* was clearly not possible in the civil war period with regard to the shrines in the north-east. Structurally, the two phases of warzone tourism are very similar to the ancient practices I have briefly outlined, though the religious aspect of warzone tourism manifests as an important but secondary consideration to the pleasure dynamics and spatial politics of these travels. Like the ancient practice, travellers went from place to place as part of a single tour or 'pilgrimage' casting their gaze upon each site, which varied from religious sites to war remnants to post-war sites of memory. In the older practice, pilgrims recited Pali stanzas commemorating the places they visited and worshiped while in the contemporary practice the repetition of the stanza is literally replaced by the more contemporary practice of clicking the camera and recording the visit to specific sites. The stanzas still have their utility when an individual actually visits a site from the ancient itinerary such as Naga Dipa. As in the ancient practice, the present practice reiterated the political and spatial integrity of the country which was once ruptured as the result of the LTTE's war of separatism while the earlier phase during the ceasefire established the reality of that rupture, given its restricted reach.

There is another constellation of meaning within which warzone travels draw contextual sense, which does not relate to the idea of pilgrimage as outlined above. As travel conditions improved, and television made inroads into people's living rooms and their decision-making practices with regard to leisure since the 1980s, a number of programmes emerged that introduced people to places of 'beauty', 'romance' and 'scenic value' that were not readily available in the travel discourse of the time. These included far away and inaccessible villages nestled among hills, where life was supposed to be simple and 'closer to what it once was everywhere'; archeological sites not too well-known; lesser known as well as better known temples; tea estates high on top of mountains seemingly hugging the clouds and so on. These programmes not only introduced people to places of interest but also informed them on how to get to these places, where to stay, what to eat and so on. These were essentially ideas for travel presented along with the pictorial testimony of the presenter who had already travelled to the places concerned and had essentially 'tested' them. The programme aired on television was in fact his recommendation. In addition to these, television also introduced people to seemingly exotic places as backdrops for musical programmes, current affairs programmes and the like which were shot, at least in part, in these locations. At the same time, print versions of this genre of reporting was also presented through Sinhala and English language newspapers, though much less affectively compared to television, which nevertheless offered clues for travel.

Through these genres of programmes, particularly those on television which became very popular among Sinhala language audiences, people were made familiar with unfamiliar but perceivably 'interesting' places. They were extremely popular, to the extent of compelling many families to undertake low budget trips to some of the destinations featured this way. The north in the ceasefire period and more clearly the extended areas of the north-east in the post-war period were quickly featured in these programmes. Before this, many of the sites such as the LTTE leader's famed bunker in Mullaitivu, captured LTTE weaponry, the remnants of the Farah 3 ship and so on were repeatedly featured in many news programmes of the evolving end of the war itself, situating these sites and objects within a sensibility of curiosity in the minds of many people in the south. These new sites essentially became 'must see' objects in this discourse of adventure tourism, which at the beginning were places 'not too many people had seen or been before' just the same way initial 'off the beaten track' travel destinations popularized by television were. Soon after the A9 road was opened in both phases however, all these sites became over-consumed by the relentless sight of thousands.

Within the structure of these pre-existing religious practices as well as television-induced holiday-making, warzone tourism of the two phases manifested fundamentally as a secular practice which nevertheless had 'religious' stops as well. For Sinhala tourists, the entire first phase of warzone tourism was a matter of discovery and curiosity. Discovery, in the sense that many of them had not travelled north of Anuradhapura or Vauniya in nearly 25 years and they were eager to explore and discover its 'innocent' mysteries they had heard from stories narrated by elder kin and family friends who might have visited the areas in pre-war times. Like all tourists everywhere, they too wanted to eat the local food, palmyra jaggery and purchase the much famed local wine. On the other hand, they were curious to meet, at least in a cursory manner, members of the LTTE and see what they were all about, given the fact that the organization ruled much of the north at the time and were a major military threat to the government. At the time, the LTTE also had an aura of invincibility. But none of these touristy considerations born out of a sense of curiosity and spirit of adventure offered space for any sense of sensitivity or piety. The entire first phase of tourism was carried out within this frame of mind irrespective of the fact whether people visited LTTE cemeteries, monuments or remnants of war that still remained in abundance at the time. In other words, this constituted the overall structure of the most consistent and dominant narrative that emerged from the darker places in paradise. It was a narrative of curiosity and relative innocence which was also delinked from the actual experiences of war and its calamities as witnessed and experienced by local people.

But the second phase of tourism did not emerge within the same frame of reference marked by a sense of innocent curiosity. Though curiosity was still an important drive for undertaking travels in the warzone in the second phase, it had lost its former innocence. Instead, it was preceded and motivated by a sense of triumphalist Sinhala nationalism sponsored by the state and popularized by both the electronic and print media, which also had quick reception among many Sinhalas. The very first buses that went north even carried fluttering national flags while some had painted images of Sinhala war heroes on the back windshields or on other parts of the vehicles' bodies. I noted at the very outset of this book that if the residues of a warzone is to be successfully transformed into a tourist attraction, that transformation needs to take into account and manage the 'sharp juxtapositions between tourist pleasure and pilgrim piety' which might often be within a single site (Figal 2008: 84). The failure in this attempt was self-evident in the first phase, as I had outlined earlier in this book. That failure continued well into the second phase as well, even as the government had removed all LTTE cemeteries, monuments and other structures of potential memory and piety by 2010, and the bunker of its leader as late as October 2013.

With these removals, the government also introduced a series of victory monuments, which were expected to be shrines for the heroism of the Sinhala sense of bravery, erasing the entire monumental landscape of LTTE memory. In effect, this was a matter of re-arranging geographies and space in the context of which many histories were rewritten while some histories have been completely erased. In his recent book, *Sacred Modernity*, Jazeel refers to 'the implication of Sri Lanka's environment and natural history within productions of ethnicized identity and difference that have fuelled the violently contested politics of postcolonial Sri Lankan nationhood' (2013: 2). In a related context, the LTTE structures embedded in the natural landscape and environment of the north was a specific text of the history of an era in which it dominated all aspects of the social and political life in the landscape it controlled. In the first phase of tourism, it was possible for Sinhala tourists to 'read' this history as they travelled across the northern lands even if they might have lost some of their more subtle nuances. As the second phase progressed, however, this text embossed on nature was deliberately erased by the state and a new text inscribed in its place. It narrated a new hegemonic history. This rearrangement of space by reordering and transforming built-space and differentially emphasizing the natural environment from a radically different ethno-political and cultural perspective is not very different from the 'powerful ways that archaeological practice and its scientific truth claims effectively construct taken-for-granted narrativizations of the past, authorizing particular, often state-sanctioned, historical accounts of place and people' as pointed out by Jazeel (2013: 49). Of course, what has happened in this context in recent times in northern Sri Lanka is not a matter of practicing archaeology as such. Post-war state practices and politics nevertheless have rearranged spatial history on the ground so that a state sanctioned and edited narrative of place, people and victory has emerged, drowning all pre-existing histories. In that process, through a concerted act of erasure and a consistent act of rebuilding, the state has also established the archaeology for the future as a singular hegemonic narrative. As such, residues of LTTE memory in particular and Tamil memory more generally have rapidly moved from public space to the domains of the private, from realms of visibility to domains of invisibility and from overt vocality to relative inaudibility.

This brings us back to the ideas of Urry which I mentioned at the beginning of this book where he notes that a tourist's 'gaze in any historical period is constructed in relationship to its opposite, to non-tourist forms of social experience and consciousness' (Urry 2002: 1). A tourist's gaze is not simply predicated upon what a brochure, a map or descriptions in mass media might narrate about a specific place or a tour though such discursive practices certainly play a part in formulating a tourist's overall gaze. But at the same time, that gaze also has to negotiate with how the people in a particular locality might interpret a specific place. That is, this has to do with how a 'place' is understood. No place is a simple and fixed geographic location or a 'preexisting empty stage that can simply be filled with activity' (Khan 1996: 188). They become meaningful through the interactions of people who live in these places, who visit them as well as those who might have been expelled from them and would see them only from a distance.

In the two phases of tourism I have described in this book, some of the crucial but almost exclusively independent discursive practices never interacted equally within the realms of their circulation. So the innocent, happy and triumphalist discourses of the travellers from the south and the discourse of pain, anxiety, loss and defeat which bound the moral communities of the people of the localities they visited almost never flowed into a single arena which would have allowed their different manifestations to blossom. If it had happened, a more nuanced and more complete history of war, pain, defeat, victory and nationhood might have emerged. So the stories from the darker places in paradise narrated by southern tourists at best remained partial truths, with numerous and significant gaps which could not be reconciled as these stories ventured beyond the limiting circumstances of the tourist trail. In other words, these two kinds of tales of the darker places in paradise were narrated in entirely different registers and in entirely different places for very different audiences. The more dominant of these has drowned the other, which ensured that the ghostly darker shadows of paradise remained in place and grew longer over time.

In this context, as the LTTE's presence and the contextual histories of local places are made to disappear within the emergent dominant narrative, if some tourists might pause to wonder how all this came about however sanitized it might be, within that pause, shadows of an erased past and muted voices might materialize as a liminal presence. At present however, in real terms, darker places of paradise can only have one sensible meaning. And that is the story of paradise that was lost. But most tourists who venture northwards will not hear that story. It is in such a context that Steves' idealized notion of the 'positive' attributes of travel with which I began this book tends to get unravelled. That is, he noted, 'ideally, travel broadens our perspectives personally, culturally, and politically'. That expectation however remains unfulfilled in the manner warzone travels took root and expanded in Sri Lanka.

Notes

1. A cursory search for the words 'Sri Lanka paradise' on the internet would offer thousands of hits giving a reasonable indication of its general use. For example, on 1 November 2015, about 4,01,00,000 results were generated in such a search within 0.75 seconds.

2. The *wamsas* include the *Deepawamsa* (3rd to 4th centuries), the *Mahawmasa* (5th or 6th century) and the *Chulawamsa* (4th to 16th century).

3. For such pilgrimages which require the crossing of international borders, travel services have been offered by the private-sector for a very long time while the Sri Lankan government has maintained a rest place for such pilgrims in Delhi since the 1950s.

4. Both terms derives from the Sinhala words *ata maha sthana* (eight great places) and *solos maha sthana* (16 great places), which have become *atamasthana* and *solosmsthana* in popular usage based upon easier pronunciation. Atamasthana includes the following shrines: (a) Sri Maha Bodhiya (Anuradhapura District); (b) Ruwanwelisaya (Anuradhapura District); (c) Thuparamaya (Anuradhapura District); (d) Lovamahapaya (Anuradhapura District); (e) Abhayagiriya (Anuradhapura District); (f) Jetavanaramaya (Anuradhapura District); (g) Mirisavetiya (Anuradhapura District); and (h) Lankaramaya (Anuradhapura District). Solosmasthana includes the following shrines: (a) Mahiyangana Raja Maha Viharaya (Badulla District); (b) Naga Dipa Raja Maha Viharaya, Nainativu (Jaffna District); (c) Kelaniya Raja Maha Vihara, Kelaniya (Gampaha District); (d) Sri Pada (Ratnapura District); (e) Diva Guhava (Ratnapura District); (f) Dighavapi Raja Maha Vihara, Dighavapiya (Ampara District); (g) Muthiyangana Raja Maha Viharaya, Muthiyanganaya (Badulla District); (h) Tissamaharama Raja Maha Viharaya, Tissamaharama (Hambantota District); (i) Sri Maha Bodhiya (Anuradhapura District); (j) Mirisawetiya (Anuradhapura District); (k) Ruwanvelisaya (Anuradhapura District); (l) Thuparamaya (Anuradhapura District); (m) Abhayagiriya (Anuradhapura District); (n) Jetavanaramaya (Anuradhapura District); (o) Sela Cetiya, Mihintale Raja Maha Vihara, Mihintale (Anuradhapura District); (p) Kiri Vehera, Kataragama (Moneragala District).

5. In fact, soon after the war ended, it was not an accident that President Mahinda Rajapakasa was depicted in government propaganda including in billboards and posters as the latest ruler to bring the entire country under a single ruler as had been done by some of these ancient kings. In these images, he was depicted standing in the foreground striding forward while the images of some of the kings were in the background.

6. Excerpt from interview conducted in Jaffna 2012.

Epilogue:
Decoding Sri Lankan-space

In order to complete the exact map of the world, I must learn to look at the problem from another perspective.... Each of us has the right to speak of his [her] coastline, his [her] mountains, his [her] deserts, none of which conforms to those of another. Individually, we are obliged to make a map of our homeland, our own field or meadow. We carry engraved in our hearts the map of the world as we know it.

—James Cowen (1996: 31)

The imaginative geographies of 'tourist trails' in a particular warzone cannot, and should not, be divorced from the imagined, lived-in geographies of the trials and tribulations of those who have been harmed—physically and mentally—by war. It is useful to note that a 'warzone' in the era of globalization, including globalization of war itself, is not easy to discern and define neatly. The embedded places of warzones are at the same time intimately connected to, and implicated in, the flows of international geopolitical economy. The gaze of a tourist travelling in a warzone could therefore be the gaze of someone who has suffered, or escaped or watched from a safe distance the vagaries and violence of that war, depending upon his or her physical and ideological location. Certain commonalities among various warzones on the face of the globe notwithstanding, seeking generalizations runs the risk of losing (in)sight of specificities, especially those related to *civil warzones* such as Sri Lanka.

Warzone tourism has been variously described as a form of 'dark tourism', a 'new trend' and the 'new frontier of adventure tourism'. A complex mix of motives, interests, agendas and linguistic tropes constitutes the sites and sights of warzone tourism. Large-scale politicization, securitization and even militarization of the apparently 'innocent' pursuit of adventure and pleasure by competing territorial nationalisms, warring factions in civil wars, state security agencies and even the tourism industry seem to characterize warzone tourism. The manner in which the website of 'Warzone Tours' describes the 'ultimate in adventure travel' and 'extreme travel' by citing Paulo Coelho, the well-known Brazilian lyricist and author, is quite revealing: 'You have to take risks. We will only understand the miracle of life fully when we allow the unexpected to happen'.[1] The potential 'daredevil' clients are promised 'safety' as they see 'what is really going on in places you had just previously seen in the televised news and print media etc'.[2] Invoking highly imaginative geographies about one of its major locations, the website of this tour operator would describe Iraq as a 'beautiful but potentially dangerous place'.[3] This is one example of how 'maps of meaning' imposed from above camouflage a highly diverse and dynamic universe of everyday struggles in the warzones over 'meaning of maps'. Maps as visual forms as well as representations of geopolitics continue to invite resistance against both what they *reveal* and *conceal*.

As passionately argued and persuasively illustrated by Sasanka Perera in this path-breaking study, 'warzone tourism' in Sri Lanka has a far more complex geography and history to it than often acknowledged. It has evolved in the context of post-colonial nation-building marred by the socio-spatial legacies of a protracted civil war. These legacies have also manifested themselves through highly convoluted and contested discursive battlefields of competing, often colliding, ethnographies, cartographies and iconographies. Mental borders as social constructions have proved to be far more stubborn than the walls, fences, barriers and check posts built during the civil war.

Perera's ethnographic critique of the 'tourist gaze' cast by the Sinhala citizens on diverse scenes, landscapes, sacred sites of pilgrimage, museums, memorials and monuments while travelling to northern Sri Lanka, during the two distinct phases, reveals both commonalities and differences between them. A sense of curiosity, coupled with the excitement associated with discovery and adventure, was the hallmark of the first phase of warzone tourism (2002–2005) that witnessed south-to-north travels by Sinhala citizens of Sri Lanka when the ceasefire was in operation. The discourse and practices of warzone tourism in Sri Lanka were dictated and driven by complex encounters between landscapes, bodyscapes and mindscapes. The tourists, carrying a heavy backpack of past prejudices, fears and anxieties, simultaneously *produced* the places they *visited*.

Whereas the second phase, which started after the war ended in 2009 and the main road was opened, saw a large scale state-facilitated warzone tourism being deployed at the service of post-war geopolitical and geo-economic reordering of Sri Lankan-space, spatiality and spatial imagination. The official tourist gaze was strategically deployed at carefully chosen sites to reclaim, recover and repair the organic unity and territorial integrity of the 'geobody' of the Sri Lankan nation. Erased and silenced in the process were the Tamil voices, war experiences and memories. The entire edifice of Tamil iconography and the monumental landscape of LTTE memory was dismantled and replaced by 'victory monuments' enacted by the government.

Seen together, the analysis by Perera of the two phases of warzone tourism in Sri Lanka reveals complex assemblages of practices, including state sponsored practices, and insightfully unravels several entangled logics and emotions. Against the backdrop of deep-rooted mistrust, large-scale destruction and displacement, they have left behind both intended and non-intended imprints on the mindscapes of both the visitors and the visited. The manner in which profane and sacred geographies have intersected in time and space defies a simple and straightforward answer as to why different generations of 'Sinhala tourists' think and behave the way they do while touring 'Tamil sites'. The choices made—or made available—in favour of a particular trail, route and site by the Sinhala tourists feed into, and in return are fed by, the prevailing hegemonic and homogenizing ethno-national sense of place. But this does not take place without inviting some resistance. Equally intriguing is the manner in which the memories, memorials and monuments of 'tourist interest' are constructed in the warzone to encourage some forms of practice and discourage others. In the cacophony of sights and sounds of warzone tourism in Sri Lanka, it is the emotions, experiences, memories and voices of the 'winning' Sinhala side that have so far prevailed over those of the 'losing' Tamil side.

One key message, or rather a note of caution, that comes out loud and clear from this book is that a lot more ethnographic research is needed to ascertain how warzone tourists from diverse locations site, sight and cite the monuments and the memories they visit. Through grounded ethnographic research, Perera provokes South Asians to collectively and critically think through the question of how various discourses and practices of 'warzone tourism', emanating from and feeding into what Doreen Massey (1997) has described as an exclusivist 'reactionary' sense of place, be reversed, subverted and replaced by a 'progressive' sense of place that is more inclusive, eclectic and tolerant. After all, the history of mobility—of both ideas and humans—in South Asia is much older than the history of borders and boundaries.

There is a powerful normative appeal made by Perera in favour of broadening and deepening the ethnographic research agenda on warzone tourism in Sri Lanka. First and foremost is the need to make the Tamil experiences, memories, versions and voices more audible and visible. Perera ensures that major silences in his ethnographic study focusing on Sinhala tourists in the warzone speak loud enough to provoke more research on the experiences and emotions of not only the Tamil citizens of Sri Lanka residing in southern parts of the country, but also the diaspora communities living overseas.

In order to make the dominant but partial and incomplete map of meanings more inclusive and representative of various perspectives, the 'Tamil' and the 'Sinhala' memories and memorials (and those of others) should co-exist, not in isolation but in conversation. And for this to happen, a large-scale campaign *from below* would be needed to pluralize the dominant state-centric ethno-national spatial imaginations of place and scale by taking it beyond the nationalizing version of the 'paradise' lost and regained. The discourse and practices of tourism can be re-thought, re-imagined and re-deployed to facilitate the transformation of warzones into peace zones. As increasing numbers of tourists from South Asia and beyond travel to Sri Lanka, a rejuvenated humane focus on ethno-cultural geographies will be needed. A new cognitive mapping of Sri Lankan 'warzone' as homelands of ordinary people is likely to reveal the brighter side—even though liminal at present—of a 'paradise' with a progressive sense of place that has not been completely lost to geopolitics of fear.

In *hope* lies the key to a new mapping and map of Sri Lanka; a 'not to scale' map that remains highly resistant to its manipulation by a cartography serving the logic of dominant spatiality and remains open to new interpretations. The guiding future icon on the new map of Sri Lanka could be that of a *unicorn's horn*. I would like to conclude the inconclusive by adding a few more insights to the epigraph with which I began, and from the same source.

Surely this is exactly what makes a unicorn's horn, so mysterious. While its origins might lie in a whale's tooth, its significance depends upon another consideration altogether, namely that of interpretation. The map [new map of Sri Lanka] represents none other than the transformation of a whale's tooth into a unicorn's horn. It is not the origin that counts but what it inspires. The craftman's task is to extract a form from what has been given to him, and to make of it something that appeals to the heart as well as the mind. (Cowen 1996: 111)

Sanjay Chaturvedi
Centre for the Study of Geopolitics
Department of Political Science
Panjab University
Chandigarh

Notes

1. http://www.warzonetours.com/ (accessed on 25 January 2016).
2. http://www.warzonetours.com/ (accessed on 25 January 2016).
3. http://www.warzonetours.com/ (accessed on 25 January 2016).

References

Basso, Keith. 1996. 'Wisdom Sits In Places'. In *Senses of Place,* edited by Steven Feld and Keith H. Basso, 53–90. Santa Fe, NM: School of American Research Press.

Barthes, Roland. 1981. *Camera Lucinda: Reflections on Photography.* New York: Hill and Wang.

Balachandran, P.K. 2009. 'Lankan War Memorial at Prabhakaran's Death Site', 10 December, *The New Indian Express.* Available at http://newindianexpress.com/world/article81131.ece?service=print (accessed on 26 October 2013).

Baudrilard, Jean. 1994. *Simulacra and Simulation.* Translated by Sheila Glasser. Ann Arbor, MI: University of Michigan Press.

———. 1995. *The Gulf War Did Not Take Place.* Bloomington, IN: Indian University Press.

Bourdieu, Pierre. 1995. 'Metamorphosis of Taste'. In *Sociology in Question,* 108–16. London: SAGE.

Butler, J. 2005. 'Photography, War, Outrage'. *PMLA,* 120(3): 822–27.

Cheran, R. 2011. *You Cannot Turn Away: Poems in Tamil.* Edited and translated by Chelva Kanaganayagam. Toronto: TSAR Publications.

———. 2013. *In a Time of Burning.* Translated by Lakshmi Holmstrom. Todmorden: Arc Publications.

Collier, J. and M. Collier. 1986. *Visual Anthropology: Photography as a Research Method.* Albuquerque, NM: University of New Mexico Press.

Crick, Malcolm. 1994. *Resplendent Sites, Discordant Voices: Sri Lankans and International Tourism.* Zur: Harwood Academic Publishers.

Daily Mirror. 2010. 'Lanka to Clear LTTE Legacy'. *Daily Mirror,* 18 March. Available at http://www.dailymirror.lk/news/2454-govt-to-clear-tiger-legacy.html (accessed on 13 September 2013).

Eagleton, Terry. 1997, 24 October. 'Edible Ecriture'. *Times Higher Education.* Available at http://www.timeshighereducation.co.uk/features/edible-ecriture/104281.article (accessed on 5 April 2014).

Eck, Diana L. 2012. *India: A Sacred Landscape.* New York: Harmony Books.

Eelam View. 2012, 23 September. 'Remembering Lt Col. Thileepan'. Available at: http://www.eelamview.com/2012/09/23/remembering-lt-col-thileepan/ (accessed on 25 September 2013).

Enders, Walter, Todd Sandler and Gerald F. Parise. 1992. 'An Econometric Analysis of the Impact of Terrorism on Tourism'. *Kyklos*, 45(4): 531–54.

Ferreira, Sanette and Alet Harmse. 2000. 'Crime and Tourism in South Africa: International Tourists' Perception and Risk'. *South African Geographical Journal*, 82(2): 80–85.

Figal, Gerald. 2008. 'Between War and Tropics: Heritage Tourism in Postwar Okinawa'. *The Public Historian*, 30(2): 83–107.

Hall, C. Michael and Vanessa O'Sullivan. 1996. 'Tourism, Political Instability and Violence'. In *Tourism, Crime and International Security Issues*, edited by Abraham Pizam and Yoel Mansfield, 105–21. New York: John Wiley.

Harrison, Margaret. 2012, 26 December. 'Sri Lanka's Killing Fields Tourism'. *Huffington Post*. Available at http://www.huffingtonpost.co.uk/frances-harrison/sri-lankas-killing-fields-tourism_b_2356247.html (accessed on 13 April 2014).

Jayasuriya, Ranga. 2005, 14 August. 'People Suffer, NGO Wallahs Enjoy'. *Sunday Observer*. Available at http://www.sundayobserver.lk/2005/08/14/fea04.html (accessed on 18 October 2013).

Jayatilake, Malith. 2008. *Alimankada Parajayen Pasu Sri Lankawa Saha Indiyawa*. Mulleriyawa: Wijesuriya Granta Kendraya.

Jazeel, Tariq. 2013. *Sacred Modernity: Nature, Environment, and the Postcolonial Geographies of Sri Lankan Nationhood*. Liverpool: Liverpool University Press.

Kanaganayakam, Chelva, ed. 2009. *Wilting Laughter: Three Tamils Poets: R. Cheran, V.I.S. Jayapalan, Puthuvai Ratnathurai*. Toronto: TSAR Publications.

Kanagasabapathipillai, Dushiyanthini. 2014. 'Burnt, Rebuilt: Jaffna Library Reminds of Sri Lanka Conflict'. Available at http://www.aa.com.tr/en/world/burnt-rebuilt-jaffna-library-reminds-of-sri-lanka-conflict/153795 (accessed on 31 October 2015).

Lacoste, Yves. 1973. 'An Illustration of Geographical Warfare: Bombing the Dikes on the Red River, North Vietnam'. *Antipode*, 5(2): 1–13.

MacDougal, David. 1999. 'The Visual in Anthropology'. In *Rethinking Visual Anthropology*, edited by Marcus Banks and Howard Morphy, 276–95. New Haven, CT: Yale University Press.

Mihalic, Tanja. 1996. 'Tourism and Warfare: The Case of Slovenia'. In *Tourism, Crime and International Security Issues*, edited by Abraham Pizam and Yoel Mansfield, 231–46. New York: John Wiley.

Murray, J.K. 1995. 'Buddhism and Early Narrative Illustration in China'. *Archives of Asian Art*, 48: 17–31.

Ness, Sally Ann. 2005. 'Tourism-terrorism: The Landscaping of Consumption and the Darker Side of Place'. *American Ethnologist*, 32(1): 118–40.

Newman, David. 2003. 'On borders and power: A theoretical framework'. *Journal of Borderlands Studies*, 18(8): 13–25.

Newman, David. 2006. 'The lines that continue to separate us: borders in our "borderless" world'. *Progress in Human Geography*, 30(2): 1–9.

Office of the United Nations High Commissioner for Human Rights. 2013. *Report of the Office of the United Nations High Commissioner for Human Rights on Advice and Technical Assistance for the Government of Sri Lanka on Promoting Reconciliation and Accountability in Sri Lanka*. New York: United Nations General Assembly.

Pali Text Society. 2012. *Mahawamsa or the Great Chronicle of Ceylon*. Translated by W. Geiger. London: Pali Text Society and Oxford University Press.

Perera, Sasanka. 2002, 4 September. 'The Jaffna Photo Album'. *The Island* (Colombo). Available at http://www.island.lk/2002/09/04/midwee01.html (accessed on 15 January 2016).

———. 2005. *Alternate Space: Trivial Writings of an Academic*. Colombo: Yellow House Publications in association with Colombo Institute for the Advanced Study of Society and Culture.

———. 2011. *Artists Remember; Artists Narrate: Memory and Representation in Contemporary Sri Lankan Visual Arts*. Colombo: Colombo Institute for the Advanced Study of Society and Culture Theertha International Artists' Collective.

———. 2015 *Violence and the Burden of Memory: Remembrance and Erasure in Sinhala Consciousness*, New Delhi: Orient BlackSwan, 274–77.

Pimenta, S. and R. Pooviah. 2010. 'On Defining Visual Narratives'. *Design Thoughts*, 25–46. Available at http://www.idc.iitb.ac.in/resources/design-thoughts.html (accessed on 3 June 2014).

Pinney, Christopher. 1997. 'The Nation (Un)pictured: Chromolithography and Popular Politics in India'. *Critical Inquiry*, 23(3): 834–67.

———. 2011. *Photography and Anthropology*. New Delhi: Oxford University Press.

Pizam, Abraham. 1999. 'A Comprehensive Approach to Classifying Acts of Crime and Violence at Tourism Destinations'. *Journal of Travel Research*, 38: 5–12.

Pratt, A. 2005. *Securing Borders: Detention and Deportation in Canada*. Vancouver: UBC Press.

Ratnatunga, Kavan. 2012, 1 April. 'First Stop Prabhakaran's Bunker'. *Sunday Times*, Available at: http://sundaytimes.lk/120401/Plus/plus_01.html (accessed on 2 March 2014).

Rogerson, Christian M. 2004. 'Adventure Tourism in Africa: The Case of Livingstone, Zambia'. *Geography*, 89(2): 183–88.

Rodman, Margaret. 1992. 'Empowering Place: Multilocality and Multivocality'. *American Anthropologist*, 94(3): 640–56.

Rushdie, Salman. 2009. *Enchantress of Florence*. New York: Random House.

Rutnam, Easwaran. 2005, 26 June. '1-9 Lodge; A Paradise in War Zone'. *The Sunday Leader*. Available at http://www.thesundayleader.lk/archive/20050626/review.htm (accessed on 20 October 2013).

Said, Edward. 1979. *Orientalism*. New York: Vintage Books.

Scott, James C. 1998. *Seeing Like a State: How Certain Schemes to Improve the Human Condition Have Failed*. New Haven, CT: Yale University Press.

Shashikumar, V.K. 2005, 16 April. 'Tiger Rising: Has the Long Wait for Eelam Ended?' *Tehelka*. Available at http://archive.tehelka.com/story_main11. asp?filename=Ne041605tiger_rising.asp (accessed on 20 October 2013).

Shell, Hanna Rose. 2012. *Hide and Seek: Camouflage, Photography and the Media of Reconnaissance*. New York: Zone Books.

Sontag, Susan. 2002, 9 December. 'Looking at War: Photography's View of Devastation and Death.' *The New Yorker*. Available at http://www.newyorker. com/archive/2002/12/09/021209crat_atlarge?currentPage=all (accessed on 5 June 2014).

Steele, Jonathan. 2002, 23 February. 'Sri Lanka Ceasefire brings Hope of Final Settlement', *The Guardian*. Available at http://www.theguardian.com/ world/2002/feb/23/srilanka (accessed on 8 November 2013).

Stewart, James. 2013. 'War Tourism in the North of Sri Lanka.' *Overland: Progressive Culture since 1954*. Available at http://overland.org.au/2013/06/ war-tourism-in-the-north-of-sri-lanka/ (accessed on 20 October 2013).

Tagore, Rabindranath. 2011. *The Home and the World*. New York: Digireads.com Publishing.

Tamil Guardian. 2010, 24 March. 'Sri Lanka demolishes Heroes' Resting Homes in the name of removing Tiger legacy', *Tamil Guardian*. Available at http://www.tamilguardian.com/print.asp?articleid=2721 (accessed on 13 September 2013).

Tamil Net. 2005, 17 January. 'Colonel Kittu remembered in Jaffna, Trincomalee'. Available at http://www.tamilnet.com/art.html?catid=13&artid=14010 (accessed on 27 September 2013).

———. 2010, 23 March. 'Sinhalese soldiers, hooligans destroy Thileepan memorial in Jaffna.' *Tamil Net*. Available at http://www.tamilnet.com/art. html?catid=13&artid=31414 (accessed on 15 March 2014).

The Guardian. 2002, 23 February. 'Sri Lanka Ceasefire Brings Hope of Final Settlement'. Available at http://www.theguardian.com/world/2002/feb/23/ srilanka (accessed on 8 November 2013).

Thurairajah, V.S. 2002, 12 December. 'Jaffna Library Rises From Its Ruins'. *Daily News*. Available at http://archives.dailynews.lk/2002/12/12/fea01.html (accessed on 28 February 2014).

Urry, John. 2002. *The Tourist Gaze*. 2nd ed. London: SAGE.

Weaver, Matthew and Chamberlain, Gethin. 2009, 19 May. 'Sri Lanka declares end to war with Tamil Tigers', *Guardian*. Available at http://www.theguardian.com/world/2009/may/18/tamil-tigers-killed-sri-lanka (accessed on 5 March 2014).

Weerasinghe, Jagath. 2002. 'Round Pilgrimages and the Religious Landscape'. Paper presented at the South Asian Landscape Conference, Institute of Archaeology, University of London, 15–16 February 2002.

Wolbert, Barbara. 2000. 'The Anthropologist as Photographer: The Visual Construction of Ethnographic Authority'. *Visual Anthropology*, 13: 231–343.

Wonders, N. A. 2006. 'Global Flows, Semi-permeable Borders and New Channels of Inequality.' In *Borders, Mobility and Technologies of Control*, edited by S. Pickering and L. Weber, 63–86. Amsterdam: Springer.

Zurick, David N. 1992. 'Adventure Travel and Sustainable Tourism in the Peripheral Economy of Nepal'. *Annals of the Association of American Geographers*, 82(4): 608–28.

Index

About the Author

Having been trained as a cultural anthropologist, **Sasanka Perera** has been with the Department of Sociology, South Asian University, New Delhi since 2011 where he is the founding professor and was its chairman until 2014, and is the Dean of the Faculty of Social Sciences from 2011 to the present as well as the Vice President of South Asian University since February 2016. Prior to that, he was with the Department of Sociology at the University of Colombo for 20 years until his resignation in 2011 as its Chairman. His research interests are located in the intersections of contemporary social theory and culture and its politics. More specifically, he focuses on spatial politics and dynamics of the urban experience in South Asia/Sri Lanka; issues of education; political violence and nationalism in Sri Lanka; transformation and politicization of religion in Sri Lanka and Nepal; the politics of memory; and the interpretation of culture and the politics of visual arts. His research and professional interests have enabled him to work in Sri Lanka, USA, Cambodia, Pakistan, Nepal, Japan and India. He has written and published extensively in the English and Sinhala languages while some of his works have also been published in Tamil and Japanese. He was the founding editor of *South Asia Journal for Culture* published by the Colombo Institute for the Advanced Study of Society and Culture, from 2007 to 2012. At present, he edits *Society and Culture in South Asia*, co-published by South Asian University and SAGE India. His book, *Violence and the Burden of Memory: Remembrance and Erasure in Sinhala Consciousness* was published by Orient BlackSwan in 2015. In his spare time, he writes poetry and engages in blogging, photography and print-journalism.